THE WAY *of* *the* WILD HEART MANUAL

CRAIG McCONNELL
and
JOHN ELDREDGE

NELSON IMPACT
A Division of Thomas Nelson Publishers
Since 1798

www.thomasnelson.com

Published by Nelson Impact, a Division of Thomas Nelson, Inc., P.O. Box 141000, Nashville, Tennessee 37214.

Published in association with Yates & Yates, LLC, Literary Agent, Orange, California.

ISBN 10: 1-4185-1413-6
ISBN 13: 978-1-4185-1413-6

Printed in the United States of America
06 07 08 09 VIC 6 5 4 3 2 1

Contents

Introduction

About nine years ago I wanted to learn how to hunt elk, so I began to join a group of guys each fall on their annual trip. Now, you need to understand—I was raised in the suburbs. Knew nothing about guns or elk or any of that. These guys had been hunting for years together. I felt like the geek, the hunting idiot. A boy scout among men. But I wanted to learn and I figured if I hung in there with these guys, in a few years I wouldn't be the "new guy" anymore.

This summer, I needed to figure out how to work on my car. (I didn't learn any of this stuff from my father.) But I don't know anyone who is good at car repair (all my friends just take theirs to the shop), so I bought a car repair manual and I'm working my way through it. When my computer breaks down, I ask a buddy who's one of those computer geniuses to give me a hand sorting things out. It's just the way it goes—we all need some help when entering into new territory, someone to show us the way. It makes sense, doesn't it? When you're faced with a frontier, get some help from somebody who's been there.

That is the spirit of the manual you are holding.

This is a companion piece to the book *The Way of the Wild Heart*. It's like the instruction manual you get with a new power tool, or car, or computer. Or better, it's like a set of directions to a secret fishing hole given to you by your uncle, or the old-timer down the street who knows those hills like the back of his hand. We wrote this because we want to help you find your way, to figure things out, and to get the most out of the book, which itself is a map to the masculine journey. A journey worth taking. A journey with many challenges. And many rewards. The essence of *The Way of the Wild Heart* is that every man needs someone to guide him through the process of masculine initiation, but there are few men who have anyone around to do that for him. So God steps in to take the role of a

Father in our lives, and show us the way. This tool is designed to help you walk with your Father through your own journey.

Now, most guys are just going to blow through the book in one reading and assume that's that. But that would be the equivalent of just driving a Ferrari around the parking lot, or of showing up at the fishing hole for one hour in the heat of the day. Not much is going to happen. But you—you are not that man. If you're reading this, you must be taking your life a bit more seriously. Way to go, my brother. You will be very glad you did. This is not a book to rush through. It's a map for the most important mission of your life, your initiation as a man. Using this manual will help you a lot.

I asked my friend and colleague Craig McConnell to work on the manual as I was working on the book itself, and I think he's done a great job. He's walked with a lot of men over the years, and I think you'll find the way he laid this manual out to be a good fit for the book and for the heart of a man. It's almost as if we are both by your side, talking with you about the book and about your life as you read along.

If I could add a couple pieces of counsel, they would be as follows:

Don't Rush. Take your time. There's a good bit to chew on here, and lots of hidden treasures. Enjoy the journey. Read the chapter in the book first. Then, make your way through the corresponding chapter in this manual. There are no "right" answers, by the way. This is not a test.

Find a place that works for you. I wrote the book in my garage, sometimes in the barn on my ranch, and, as a last resort, my office at home where at least I can shut the door. I just couldn't write a book like this at the mall. There's a place where your heart settles down, a place where you are going to be more present to this. Find this place. Maybe it's an old favorite chair and a cup of coffee at 5 AM. Maybe it's the back porch in the evening. Or a cabin in the woods. Your car during lunch time. Find a spot that works for you, a spot you can return to as your private refuge in which to take this journey.

Be honest. Most men fake their way through most of their life. Fake an intimacy with their wife they don't have. Fake bravado or courage when they're really afraid. Fake Christianity. That never helps. There's a life of true masculinity available to you, there really is. Be honest with your work here, and you'll find your way.

Hang in there. I can't begin to name the number of guys that get taken out simply through busyness and distraction. But of course—the enemy doesn't want men entering into this. They will be dangerous men. So head's up, I'm warning you—there will be a dozen reasons to bail on this every single week. You know that. Fight for it. You matter. Your journey matters. Everything else in your life depends on it.

Don't walk alone. Maybe in your first pass through this, you'll want to do so privately.

But I'd really urge you to share this process with a few other guys, at least the second time around. That's how Craig and I did it, and it really helps to have someone to bounce your thoughts off of, press into the hard questions with, and to just be an encouragement along the way. Get a few guys together and do the book and manual as a band of brothers.

Pass it on. As you get into this journey, you are going to realize how many men (and boys) there are around who just don't have a clue what it means to be a man, nor anyone to show them the way. Maybe after you get through the book and manual, you'll want to lead some other guys through it, to be a mentor of sorts. It might be one of the most rewarding things you ever do.

Okay. Enough of that. You are poised for an incredible experience, something most men have been waiting for their whole life. Go for it. Jump in.

JOHN ELDREDGE

I

The Masculine Journey

Stand at the crossroads and look;
ask for the ancient paths,
ask where the good way is, and walk in it,
and you will find rest for your souls.
—Jeremiah 6:16 niv

BEFORE STARTING

And so, you have either read or are reading *The Way of the Wild Heart*, and while we all may acknowledge that "yes, I'm on a journey," most of us have some real questions of where this will all end. Will anything change—will life get better, easier? Will I ever be able to deal well with sprinklers, teenage children, a changing career landscape? Will life be more fulfilling? Will I just live my "three score and ten" years and die with an ache that I could have done so much more, been so much more? Or can things change and I will find this "journey" taking me more and more into the man I long to be, dream of being, and that God has designed me to be?

We believe you can.

You're beginning a journey by going through this *The Way of the Wild Heart Manual.* A journey in which you hope to encounter God in a life-changing way. The design of the manual is to, in every way we can, facilitate your meeting him in ways and places that you haven't yet experienced. The beginning of this journey will determine much about the journey itself. A couple of thoughts:

- Start with a surrender of yourself to God and his purposes for you in this manual. We'd suggest you yield your mind, volition, heart, spirit, soul, and masculinity to God and simply invite him to do whatever he'd like.
- Commit yourself to the pace God would have you go through the material, determine to be responsive to his prodding you to take a little more time on a

particular section or question, or to take a walk or break and allow in a more natural context for him to speak. A simple way of putting all this is, *walk with God.*

- Another thought on the pace of this journey: it would be cruel to your heart to set a deadline on finishing this manual if the deadline in *any* way keeps you from times of reflection, prayer, movie viewing, and various other exercises. You'll find yourself limiting God and quickly moving into the "just get through the material" stride that will profit your heart little.

Christ, I come thirsty and hungry for more of you. I yield myself completely and totally to you. I give you my expectations for this study. I surrender my heart, mind, spirit, and soul to you, inviting you to touch, deliver, speak, heal, counsel, teach, and train me in whatever areas and ways you choose. Protect me from the ploys of the evil one, and I stand in your authority against all distraction, impatience, diminishment, self-contempt, against every lie, deception, and temptation to turn to any other god for comfort. Fill me with your life that I might more fully live in your Larger Story and with you rescue the hearts and souls of many.

FIRST REACTIONS

Reread/read chapter 1, "The Masculine Journey," before you go any further in this exercise. Don't filter your thoughts here but simply write out what first comes to mind.

What struck you? What stirred you, got your blood pumping? New thoughts? Frustrations?

As you were reading the chapter, what did you want to do?

Do you find yourself anticipating God showing up for you in some profound ways?

Are you a bit anxious of where this all may go and what it may require of you?

Or, do you find yourself a little noncommittal, keeping yourself a little protected and even skeptical . . . kind of a "wait and see" posture?

KEY POINTS OF THE CHAPTER

We would highlight these points/ideas as being key to this chapter (you may find yourself adding another point or two.)

- A boy has a lot to learn in his journey to become a man, and he becomes a man only through the active intervention of his father and the fellowship of men. It cannot happen any other way.
- This we must understand: Masculinity is *bestowed*. A boy learns who he is and what he's made of from a man (or a company of men). This can't be learned in any other place. It can't be learned from other boys, and it can't be learned from the world of women.
- Masculine initiation is a journey, a *process*, a quest really, a story that unfolds over time. It can be a very beautiful and powerful event to experience a blessing or a ritual, to hear words spoken to us in a ceremony of some sort. Those moments can be turning points in our lives. But they are only moments, and moments, as you well know, pass quickly and are swallowed in the river of time. We need more than a moment, an event. We need a process, a journey, an epic story of many experiences woven together, building upon one another in a progression. We need *initiation*. And, we need a Guide.
- We aren't meant to figure life out on our own. God wants to father us.
- A man's life is a process of initiation into true masculinity. It is a series of stages we soak in and progress through. And as for God, I believe that what he is *primarily* up to at any point in a boy's or a man's life is initiating him. So much of what we misinterpret as hassles or trials or screw-ups on our part is in fact God fathering us, taking us through something in order to strengthen us, or heal us, or dismantle some unholy thing in us. In other words, to initiate us—a distinctly masculine venture.
- The result of having abandoned masculine initiation is a world of unfinished, uninitiated men. But it doesn't have to be this way. We needn't wander in a fog. We don't have to live alone, striving, sulking, uncertain, angry. We don't have to figure life out for ourselves. There is another way. Wherever we are in the journey, our initiation can begin in earnest.

ALL I WAS TRYING TO DO WAS FIX THE SPRINKLERS . . .

Sure enough, I couldn't do it, couldn't get the solder to melt into the joint as needed to prevent leaks.

Suddenly, I was angry. I'm trying to play the man and fix my own sprinklers but I can't and there's no man here to show me how and so I'm watching a cute little video for the mechanically challenged and feeling like about ten years old. A cartoon for a man who is really a boy. Armed with information and wobbling confidence, I go back out, give it another try. Another miss.

At the end of the first round I merely felt like an idiot. Now I feel like an idiot doomed to failure. And I'm seething.

Sound familiar? In what situations have you felt like an idiot? (Working on a car or computer, putting together a swing set, fixing an appliance, filling out tax forms, etc.)

The short list: most problems with my cars, learning to fly fish, parenting teenagers, buying our first home, the changes that age is bringing to my sexual relationship with my wife, pulling the third seat out of my Surburban. (Craig)

REFLECTING ON HIS REACTION, JOHN ASKS HIMSELF, *Wow, that part of me says. Have a look at this. What are you so hacked-off about?* And realizes, *There's no one there to show me how to do this. Why do I always have to figure this stuff out on my own? And I'm also hacked because I can't do it myself, mad that I need help. Now, I do know this—I know that I am not alone in feeling alone. Most of the guys I've ever met feel like this at some point.*

Why do you get hacked off?

Who do you have in your life to show you how to deal with imposing circumstances, such as a relational, emotional, or spiritual issue? If you have no one, are you aware of a desire to have someone you can turn to?

John concludes,

THIS IS PERHAPS THE DEFINING VOW OR COMPELLING FORCE OF MY ADULT life: You are alone in this world and you'd better watch it 'cause there isn't any room for error, so Get It Right. The detached observer in me says, *Wow—this is huge. You just hit the mother lode. I mean, jeez—this has defined your entire life and you've never even put it into words. And now here it is and you know what this is tied to, don't you?* Lying there in the dark of my bedroom, the broken sprinkler system lying in misery just outside the window by my head, I know what this is about.

It's about fatherlessness.

Has it occurred to you that maybe all this anger, drivenness, the avoiding of difficult situations, perhaps the paralysis and the fear, is about "fatherlessness"?

Are you free to even call it that? Or does doing so feel like a slam against or betrayal of your father (if you have one)?

UNFINISHED MEN

A BOY HAS A LOT TO LEARN IN HIS JOURNEY TO BECOME A MAN, AND HE becomes a man only through the active intervention of his father and the fellowship of men. It cannot happen any other way. To become a man—and to know that he has become a man—a boy must have a guide, a father who will show him how to fix a bike and cast a fishing rod and call a girl and land the job and all the many things a boy will encounter in his journey to become a man.

This we must understand: Masculinity is *bestowed*. A boy learns who he is and what he's made of from a man (or a company of men). This can't be learned in any other place. It can't be learned from other boys, and it can't be learned from the world of women.

A boy becomes a man *only through the active intervention of his father and the fellowship of men. It cannot happen any other way.* Put words to your reaction to this thought.

What does this statement stir up in you? Is it:

Hopelessness: *"I never had that . . . I'll never be the man I want to be,"* or, *"There's no one who can guide me."*

Pride/Arrogance: *"I'm a self-made man who made it* **because** *I didn't need anyone else."*

Impatience: *"Journey? Process? Not interested. I'm looking for something quicker."*

Yes!!!: *"A map and a compass. Thank God!"*

If you didn't have masculine guides to bestow masculinity, where did you turn instead?

As a young boy/man, who were your models? Who are they now?

Where did you look for your definition/understanding of masculinity? How about now?

WHEN I WAS YOUNG, MY FATHER WOULD TAKE ME FISHING EARLY ON A Saturday morning. We'd spend hours together out there, on a lake or a river, trying to catch fish. But the fish were never really the issue. What I longed for was his presence, his attention, and his delight in me. I longed for him to teach me how, show me the way. This is where to drop that line. This is how you set the hook. If you can get a group of men talking about their fathers, you'll hear this core longing of a man's heart. Whatever the details might be, when a man speaks of the greatest gift his father gave him—if his father gave him anything at all worth remembering—it is always the passing on of masculinity.

What memories does John's story of his father stir up in your heart?

They're too brief, too sparse to be memories; they seem more like moments that passed so quickly. They could have had an impact but for their brevity or they were diminished by the conflicting messages that quickly and more definitively followed. A moment of my step-dad helping me fish (followed with a complaint that I can't do anything myself). He and I pitching a pup tent together (followed by "here, let me do it right"). I wish I had memories, but my moments for the most part were disappointing to say the least. As an older man, I see the result of not having a father. (Craig)

What were the greatest gifts your father gave you?

LIFE WILL TEST YOU. LIKE A SHIP AT SEA, YOU *WILL* BE TESTED, AND THE STORMS will reveal the weak places in you as a man. They already have. How else do you account for the anger you feel, the fear, the vulnerability to certain temptations? Why can't you marry the girl? Having married, why can't you handle her emotions? Why haven't you found your life's mission? Why do financial crises send you into a rage or depression? You know what I speak of. And so our basic approach to life comes down to this: We stay in what we can handle, and steer clear of everything else. We engage where we feel we can or we must—as at work—and we hold back where we feel sure to fail, as in the deep waters of relating to our wife or our children, and in our spirituality.

Think through the seasons and stages of your whole life. What have been the tests/storms you've faced?

What question about your life or your masculinity haunts you?

Whatever the question, you simply must not rush through it . . . give it time.
What were the weak places in you as a man that were revealed?

Where and how have you "stayed" in what you can handle and "steered clear" of everything else?

WHAT WE HAVE NOW IS A WORLD OF UNINITIATED MEN. PARTIAL MEN. Boys, mostly, walking around in men's bodies, with men's jobs and families, finances, and responsibilities. The passing on of masculinity was never completed, if it was begun at all. The boy was never taken through the process of masculine initiation. That's why most of us are Unfinished Men. And therefore unable to truly live *as* men in whatever life throws at us. And unable to pass on to our sons and daughters what *they* need to become whole and holy men and women themselves.

It takes some guts to admit that you fit the descriptor "*partial men, boys, mostly, walking around in men's bodies.*" And yet, if we were honest about how we often feel and view ourselves, it's true, isn't it? What are your thoughts here?

It is hard to admit this! God has done so very much in my life and with that being true, I am so aware of how much more he has to do. This phrase, "partial men, boys, mostly, walking around in men's bodies," is a haunting phrase. I want God to show me where this is true. I realize I am not yet the man I want to be, the man God longs for me to be . . . and in my unfinished places I live, relate, and act too often as a boy in a man's body. I long for the maturity God has for me. (Craig)

Older men, it's hard and humbling to admit that you are an unfinished man (without giving up), that your journey missed some essential components to your masculinity. Can you acknowledge this?

At 53 years old, so much of me wants to avoid these questions. There's a sense that I ought to be further along than this. There has to be redemption in the honesty and desire that facing these questions produces. (Craig)

THERE ARE BOYS AND YOUNG MEN AND MEN OUR OWN AGE AROUND US WHO are all very much in need—desperate need—of someone to show them the way. What does it mean to be a man? *Am* I a man? What should I do in this or that situation? These boys are growing up into uncertain men because the core questions of their souls have gone unanswered, or answered badly. They grow into men who act, but their actions are not rooted in a genuine strength, wisdom, and kindness. There is no one there to show them the way.

What are the questions about your masculinity you'd love to have answered?

In your life, what are/have been the results of not really knowing whether or not you are a man?

AND SO THE MASCULINE INITIATION IS A JOURNEY, A *PROCESS*, A QUEST really, a story that unfolds over time. It can be a very beautiful and powerful event to experience a blessing or a ritual, to hear words spoken to us in a ceremony of some sort. Those moments can be turning points in our lives. But they are only moments, and moments, as you well know, pass quickly and are swallowed in the river of time. We need more than a moment, an event. We need a process, a journey, an epic story of many experiences woven together, building upon one another in a progression. We need *initiation*. And, we need a Guide.

React to the paragraph above. What all does it provoke in you?

Yes! Living under the pressure of immediate and quick maturity produces legalistic externalists. I want the godliness, the masculinity, the maturity that takes time. Yes, I wish it were faster! (Craig)

Does the reality of masculine initiation being a journey, a process that unfolds over time, encourage or discourage you? Why?

INITIATION

WE AREN'T MEANT TO FIGURE LIFE OUT ON OUR OWN. GOD WANTS TO FATHER us. The truth is, he has been fathering us for a long time—we just haven't had the eyes to see it.

How new is the thought that God wants to father you? What's your internal reaction to that thought?

The idea is not new. For years, I've talked, taught, preached about God wanting a personal intimate relationship with us. But internalizing this has never been deeply done till recently. My internal reaction is that I would love to know God as my Father, but I'm not sure fully how to "get there." (Craig)

HE WANTS TO FATHER US MUCH MORE INTIMATELY, BUT WE HAVE TO BE IN A posture to receive it. What that involves is a new way of seeing, a fundamental reorientation of how we look at life, and our situation in it.

First, we allow that we are unfinished men, partial men, mostly boy inside, and we need *initiation*. In many, many ways.

Be still and quiet, then reread the paragraph above. Can you allow God to father you?

Father, it is you that lures me, it is you that has revealed a greater and deeper need for you, it is you that makes me hunger and thirst for more. I come to you, Father, as an unfinished man. I come needy, I come asking you to make me a whole man, a strong man, an initiated man. I invite you to disrupt, heal, encourage, deliver, convict, and counsel me as you desire. I surrender myself entirely to your fathering of me.

SECOND, WE TURN FROM OUR INDEPENDENCE AND ALL THE WAYS WE EITHER charge at life or shrink from it; this may be one of the most basic and the most crucial ways a man repents. I say "repent" because our approach to life is based on the conviction that God, for the most part, doesn't show up much. We must be willing to take an enormous risk, and open our hearts to the possibility that God *is* initiating us as men—maybe even in the very things in which we thought he'd abandoned us. We open ourselves up to being fathered.

Ask him to speak to you here. Linger and listen. What must you repent of?

WHAT I AM SUGGESTING IS THAT WE REFRAME THE WAY WE LOOK AT OUR lives as men. And the way we look at our relationships with God. I also want to help you reframe the way you relate to other men, especially you fathers who are wondering how to raise boys. The reframing begins when we see that a man's life is a process of initiation into true masculinity. It is a series of stages we soak in and progress through. And as for God, I believe that what he is *primarily* up to at any point in a boy's or a man's life is initiating him. So much of what we misinterpret as hassles or trials or screw-ups on our part is in fact God fathering us, taking us through something in order to strengthen us, or heal us, or dismantle some unholy thing in us. In other words, initiate us—a distinctly masculine venture.

John is suggesting that we reframe the way we view our lives and all that unfolds before us. React. What strikes you the most in the paragraph above? What's a new thought, or an idea that needs a little more reflection?

A MAN'S LIFE IS A PROCESS OF INITIATION INTO TRUE MASCULINITY. IT IS A series of stages we soak in and progress through.

Have you seen God as intimately and sovereignly involved, from day one, in taking you on a journey or process that culminates in your true masculinity?

WHAT GOD IS PRIMARILY UP TO AT ANY POINT IN A BOY'S OR A MAN'S LIFE is initiating him.

Do you agree or disagree that at any point, in any circumstances, and at all times, God is primarily concerned with initiating you?

Whoa, what a reorientation. This presents God as much more engaged and sovereign in my life than I have traditionally thought (and theologically, I've always held a pretty high view of God's sovereignty). Frankly, I've always thought that what God was primarily up to involved other people, cultures, and places. This is far more personal and even intimate than I've thought. (Craig)

SO MUCH OF WHAT WE MISINTERPRET AS HASSLES OR TRIALS OR SCREW-UPS on our part are in fact God fathering us, taking us through something in order to strengthen us, or heal us, or dismantle some unholy thing in us. In other words, initiate us—a distinctly masculine venture.

THE STAGES

Looking back on John's introduction to the Stages on pages 10–15 in *The Way of the Wild Heart* book again, allow yourself the space to let your memory wander and your heart's desires to rise up. Sometimes the painful or empty memories we quickly stuff or pass over will point most clearly to deepest desires of our heart. The isolation and feelings of being an orphan who has no father point to a crucial desire to be fathered. One cannot pin an exact age to each stage. They overlap, and there are aspects of each stage in every other. Why is that important to know prior to going through the stages?

NO, THERE IS A PATH THAT MUST BE TAKEN. THERE IS A WAY. NOT A FORMULA. A Way. Each stage has its lessons to be learned, and each stage can be wounded, cut short, leaving the growing man with an undeveloped soul. Then we wonder why he folds suddenly when he is forty-five, like a tree we find toppled in the yard after a night of strong winds. We go over to have a look and find that its roots hadn't sunk down deep into the earth, or perhaps that it was rotten on the inside, weakened by disease or drought. Such are the insides of Unfinished Men.

There is a Way. Not a formula. A Way. What do you like and what do you chaff at regarding this reality of our walking with God in this masculine journey?

There's something restful, hopeful about life being a way not a formula. This is from a guy who very much wants to know the steps, directions, and dos and don'ts that will insure my success with God. (Craig)

YOU'LL FIND THE STAGES EVERYWHERE

Now that you have an outline for the Stages of the masculine journey, you will begin to see them throughout all the great stories. John gives a number of biblical stories and contemporary movies in the book that make and support this point, such as the story of the life of David as told in the book of 1 Samuel, the stages in the life of Jesus as recorded in the Gospels, and in films such as *The Prince of Egypt* and Tolkien's trilogy, *The Lord of the Rings.*

Reread this section in the book and think about the lives of the biblical characters referenced.

What struck you from these examples?

Do you see the stages of masculine journey in David's and Jesus' lives? What other biblical characters does your mind go to as examples?

Name your favorite movies. What "stage" is the hero in? Is he in some sort of initiation, trial, or testing as a man?

A PAUSE IN THE JOURNEY

an opportunity to rest/reflect on the ground you've just covered

Some evening soon you may want to re-watch one of your favorite movies through the lens of how the hero or main character is being initiated through the adventures and struggles of the story line. If you need a couple of movie ideas, we suggest:

The Prince of Egypt
J. R. R. Tolkien's trilogy, *The Lord of the Rings*
The Lion King

TAKING UP THE QUEST

NOW, WE DON'T KNOW MUCH ABOUT STAGES OF DEVELOPMENT IN OUR instant culture. We don't need to wait for our leather jackets or our jeans or caps to age to get that rugged look—they come that way now, prefaded, tattered. Character that can be bought and worn immediately.

But God is a God of *process*. If you want an oak tree, he has you start with an acorn. If you want a Bible, well, he delivers that over the course of more than a thousand years. If you want a man, you must begin with the boy. God ordained the stages of masculine development. They are woven into the fabric of our being, just as the laws of nature are woven into the fabric of the earth. The result of having abandoned masculine initiation is a world of unfinished, uninitiated men.

But it doesn't have to be this way. We needn't wander in a fog. We don't have to live alone, striving, sulking, uncertain, angry. We don't have to figure life out for ourselves. There is another way. Wherever we are in the journey, our initiation can begin in earnest. Far better for us—and for those who have to live with us, who look to us—to rediscover the stages and honor them, live within them, raise our sons through them. Which brings us back to our predicament: Who is going to do this for us?

Do you want to be an oak tree? Are you "up" for the time the process will take?

So, forgetting age as a determining factor and some self-imposed pressure or expectation of where you "ought" to be, what stage do you think you're primarily in now? Did any of the prior stages get cut short?

Father, do this for me. Initiate me. I invite you, I give you permission to do whatever you desire that my journey would culminate in my living the full life you have for me as a man. Open my eyes to all you have for me in each of the stages. Come for me, Father, come for me.

2

True Son of a True Father

I will be a Father to you,
and you will be my sons . . .
—2 Corinthians 6:18 NIV

BEFORE STARTING

Before you begin this chapter, we'd suggest that you look back over the chapter you recently completed, skim over your notes, responses, and thoughts one more time . . . What were those things God seemed to highlight for you personally? Is there a bit more time or prayer to be spent on any of those "key" points?

A number of times throughout the book John refers to the film *The Kingdom of Heaven. The Kingdom of Heaven* is a picture of the masculine journey. As Norman Maclean wrote, "The nearest anyone can come to finding himself at any given age is to find a story that somehow tells him about himself." This is a good story to begin with. While there may be some scenes and themes you might not agree with overall, this is a film worth watching in its entirety. You'll better understand the message of this book through the movie's powerful visuals. We suggest that you view the film *prior* to your working on this chapter. Again, remember, your goal isn't to get through this manual in a set number of weeks, but to have an encounter with God that furthers your journey as a man. There are some helpful observations in the Appendix to use regarding *The Kingdom of Heaven* as you watch it.

KEY POINTS OF THE CHAPTER

- Most of us feel fundamentally fatherless.
- Our core assumptions about the world boil down to this: We are on our own to make life work. We are not watched over. We are not cared for.
- "The hardest, gladdest thing in the world is to cry *Father!* from a full heart . . . the refusal to look up to God as our father is the one central wrong in the whole human affair; the inability, the one central misery." (George MacDonald)
- You have a good Father. He is better than you thought. He cares. He really does. He's kind and generous. He's out for your best. You *are* the son of a kind, strong, and engaged Father, a Father wise enough to guide you in the Way, generous enough to provide for your journey.
- Coming home to our heavenly Father is the goal of human existence.
- We are Unfinished Men. And in truth, the Father has been fathering us for a long time now or, at least, trying to. What I'm suggesting is a new way of looking at your life as a man. To see your life as a process of initiation into masculine maturity, and your Father doing the initiating.

BALIAN, SON OF GODFREY, BARON OF IBELIN

THE TIME IS THE MIDDLE AGES, 1184 AD, THE YEAR OF OUR LORD. THE TIME between the Second and Third Crusades. A young man, a blacksmith called Balian, has lost both his wife and son. And with them, because of their tragic deaths, he has also lost his faith. He is certainly losing heart. As he hammers away in his little smithy, a mysterious figure rides up on horseback, apparently a lord of some sort, armed, asking for shoes for his horses. The captain of a company, he studies the silent, angry young man, watches him at work. He then announces to Balian that he is his true father—Godfrey, Baron of Ibelin, a great warrior returning to Jerusalem with a company of men. He invites Balian to come with him.

At first the young man refuses. Why? Perhaps he has lost the capacity to hope. Perhaps the years of fatherlessness have caused him to mistrust this alleged father. You might answer for him, for his story is also ours in many ways. A fatherless man labors alone under the sorrows of his life. His true father comes to him, a vague and somewhat imposing figure, and calls him on a journey. The man hesitates, as we hesitate, unsure of the father and his intentions.

After Godfrey rides away, Balian changes his mind, catches up with the men in the forest, hoping to find in Jerusalem—for he has heard it to be so—the forgiveness of his sins. A step in the right direction. Balian follows his father, if only to find forgiveness, as so many good men in the church believe in God, if only for forgiveness. But the father intends much more. Godfrey embraces Balian as his Beloved Son, heir to his domain (Rom. 8:17). He gives men in exchange for his life (Isa. 43:4). They take to the road together—for Balian, it is the time of the Cowboy. His father trains him to be a Warrior, and initiates him into the knighthood. He fathers Balian into the great mission of his life, to serve the true King of Jerusalem.

How was *The Kingdom of Heaven*?

What stands out about Balian? How would you describe him at the beginning of this story?

Answer for Balian, why does he refuse his father's invitation?

What similarities, if any, are there between your story and this brief introduction to Balian?

FATHERLESS

Most of us feel fundamentally fatherless. Do *you* feel fatherless? If so, why? And for how long have you felt that way?

Yes. It seems more like a fact than a feeling. I certainly feel fatherless. My father was killed in combat during the Korean War when I was 3 months old. His death, my fatherlessness, has been the most defining and assaulted wound of my life. And so on that level I've certainly felt *profoundly alone and orphaned. In my spiritual life, until recently God the Father has always felt more like Uncle Earl—we're related but there's some distance between us. (Craig)*

John states that,

YOU *ARE* THE SON OF A KIND, STRONG, AND ENGAGED FATHER, A FATHER wise enough to guide you in the Way, generous enough to provide for your journey, offering to walk with you every step.

Was this descriptive of your earthly father?

Do you *long* for such a father?

How would your life have been different if you'd had such a Father?

John states that,

THIS IS PERHAPS *THE* HARDEST THING FOR US TO BELIEVE—REALLY BELIEVE, down deep in our hearts, so that it changes us forever, changes the way we approach each day. I believe this is *the* core issue of our shared dilemma as men. We just don't believe it.

Do you believe it?

OUR CORE ASSUMPTIONS ABOUT THE WORLD BOIL DOWN TO THIS: WE ARE on our own to make life work. We are not watched over. We are not cared for. When we are hit with a problem, we have to figure it out ourselves, or just take the hit. If anything good is going to come our way, we're the ones who are going to have to arrange for it. Many of us have called upon God as Father, but, frankly, he doesn't seem to have heard. We're not sure why. Maybe we didn't do it right. Maybe he's about more important matters. Whatever the reason, our experience of this world has framed our approach to life. We believe we are fatherless.

So, which of these assumptions have you felt at times about life? About yourself? About God? If you can, be specific about the seasons of life, events, or circumstances that attach themselves to these assumptions.

You are on your own to make life work. You are not watched over. You are not cared for. You have to figure out problems yourself, or just take the hit. If anything good is going to come your way, you'll have to arrange for it. God as Father, doesn't seem to have heard your needs or cry. You're to blame for God's apparent uninvolvement in your life. You are fatherless. (Craig)

MY FRIEND SAM ONCE SAID TO ME, "I GUESS I FIND IT HARD TO BELIEVE THAT God wants anything good for me."

Such a simple statement, but one I've heard repeated hundreds, perhaps thousands, of times before, in one form or another, from different men at different stages, touching on the same basic doubt in our hearts. Whatever life has taught us, and though we may not have put it into these exact words, we feel that we are alone. Simply look at the way men live. If I were to give an honest assessment of my life for the past thirty years, I'd have to confess the bulk of it as Striving and Indulging. Pushing myself hard to excel, taking on the battles that come to me with determination but also with a fear-based drivenness, believing deep down inside that there is no one I can trust to come through for me. Striving. And then, arranging for little pleasures along the way to help ease the pain of the drivenness and loneliness. Dinners out, adventure gear. Indulging. A fatherless way to live.

A fatherless man, a man who feels alone in life, is marked by several characteristics. Look at the way you live. If you were to give an honest assessment of your life, does it reflect the characteristics of a man who believes he is alone in this world, that he is fatherless? Which of these characteristics would you, or those who know you, use to describe you?

Striving
Cynical
Indulgent
Pushing hard to excel
Taking on life and its battles with a fear-based drivenness
Deep-down belief that there is no one you can trust to come through
Disengaged
Checked out
Arranging for little pleasures to help ease the pain
Angry
Running
Resigned
Excessive dinners out
Excessive adventures and gear
Impulsive
Indulgent

Can you see how the core belief that you are alone is what lies beneath so much of your striving or resignation, and indulging?

Best I've been able to understand, my addictions (my indulgences) seem to be motivated to lessen the pain of being absolutely alone and to provide a little bit of euphoria, a bit of heaven, in the here-and-now. (Craig)

With all we profess and believe about God being loving, good, kind, and "for us," why do we find it hard to turn to him as our Father?

The truth is that I've never honestly reflected upon him really being a father to me. I've conveniently put the picture of God as a father in a long list of metaphors regarding him that I've never mulled over much—the potter, the vine, the shepherd, the lily of the valley . . . (Craig)

GEORGE MACDONALD WAS SO RIGHT WHEN HE SAID, "THE HARDEST, GLADDEST thing in the world is to cry *Father!* from a full heart . . . the refusal to look up to God as our father is the one central wrong in the whole human affair; the inability, the one central misery." The one central misery. That's worth thinking about. I didn't used to believe it, really. You see, this fatherlessness has become so normal—our normal—we don't even think about it much.

Think about it. Have you found that "*the hardest, gladdest thing in the world is to cry Father! from a full heart*"?

Has your fatherlessness, and all its characteristics, become your "normal" to the point you don't even think about it much?

That's been the case for many, many years. (Craig)

TRUE SONS OF A TRUE FATHER

JESUS KEPT COMING BACK TO THIS CENTRAL ISSUE, OVER AND OVER, DRIVING at it in his teachings, his parables, his penetrating questions. If you look again, through the lens that most of us feel fundamentally fatherless, I think you'll find it very close indeed to the center of Jesus' mission.

> Which of you, if his son asks for bread, will give him a stone? Or if he asks for a fish, will give him a snake? (Matt. 7:9–10 NIV)

> If you, then, though you are evil, know how to give good gifts to your children, how much more will your Father in heaven give good gifts to those who ask him! (v. 11 NIV)
>
> Look at the birds of the air. Consider the lilies in the field. Are you not much more valuable to your true Father than they? (Matt. 6:26, 28 NIV)
>
> What do you think? If a man owns a hundred sheep, and one of them wanders away, will he not leave the ninety-nine on the hills and go to look for the one that wandered off? (Matt. 18:12 NIV)

Let's take the questions personally. Jesus is asking *you* a real question and he wants a real answer. How would you answer the four questions above?

REFERRING TO THE ONE LOST SHEEP, THE PASSAGE CONTINUES, "AND IF HE finds it, I tell you the truth, he is happier about that one sheep than about the ninety-nine that did not wander off. In the same way your Father in heaven is not willing that any of these little ones should be lost" (Matt 18:13–14 NIV).

What is Jesus disclosing about God's heart as a father?

What is God's heart for you?

WHETHER YOU ARE ABLE TO BELIEVE IT AT THIS MOMENT IN YOUR LIFE, AT least can you see what Jesus is driving at: You have a good Father. He is better than you thought. He cares. He really does. He's kind and generous. He's out for your best.

This is absolutely central to the teaching of Jesus, though I have to admit, it never really struck a chord in me until I began to think through the need for masculine initiation, and came straight up against the question *But who will do the initiating?* Most of our fathers are gone, or checked out, or uninitiated men themselves. There are a few men, a very few, who have fathers initiating them in substantive ways. Would that we all were so lucky. And, some guys have found a mentor, but they also are hard to come by. Especially those who understand masculine initiation. So, again, I still find myself wondering, *Where can we find a true father to initiate us?* Where can you turn?

Looking back, who has initiated you? Did you have a true father who initiated you? Or were you left alone to find your way? Were there good men around you, but they were either checked out or uninitiated themselves?

There's a voice right now saying, "Ah, don't be such a whiner." I don't want to be a whiner but there's nothing compelling me to answer this question and yet I must. No, I didn't have a father to initiate me. There were men, family members around, but I can't recall any of them taking the initiative to mentor, guide, or father me. I think they were all busy in their own stories and had little more to offer than a greeting at family gatherings, maybe a pat on the back, and what felt like an in genuine question about how I was doing. I say in genuine, because their disinterest and vulnerability to distractions seemed to always cut the conversation short in mid-sentence. (Craig)

Where will you find a true father to continue your initiation? Where can you turn?

BUT WE HAVE FATHERS

IN WILD AT HEART, JOHN GIVES A LOT OF TIME TO THE ISSUE OF HOW A BOY derives his identity, his masculinity, and the answers to his deepest questions about himself from his father. It is a double-edged sword. What was created by God to be a good, powerful, and beautiful thing has become for many men a sort of deathblow. A verdict pronounced over their life. For the deepest wound a man carries is his father wound. Whether through violence, or rejection, or passivity, or abandonment, most men did not receive the love and validation they needed as boys from their fathers. They received something else—a wound. For if your father had the power to validate, then he also had the power to invalidate. And that is the story of most of the men reading this book. Either your father did not bestow on you a deep sense of masculinity, and validation, and just left you with silence, or he invalidated you, emasculated you. Either way, it's a wound that becomes defining for a man.

So let me ask, *Do you have what it takes?* Listen to your own answer. Who told you that? My guess is . . . it was your dad. Was your father silent, emasculating, or invalidating?

What was the verdict pronounced over you?

MOST MEN FEEL SENTENCED BY THEIR FATHERS IN THREE WAYS: BY THE wound, by the fact that there is now no one to lead us on in our need for masculine initiation, and by the legacy of our fathers—their sins, their failures, what they were as men. It feels like the hand you have been dealt. As if you might, with effort, make it a little farther than he, but you will always be his son. After all, there are those sayings, such as, "The apple doesn't fall far from the tree." If the family tree is a source of pride to us, then we can move on with confidence. But if it is not, we must realize that we can come out from under its shadow.

What's the legacy of your father you'd like to continue?

Like him, I'd like to live heroically in a Larger Story. A story worth giving my life to and for. (Craig)

What's the legacy you fear continuing? Do you feel sentenced to the inevitability of living out his legacy?

NOW, IN LIGHT OF THIS, HEAR THE WORDS OF GOD. . . .

A RADICAL SHIFT

FOR YOU DID NOT RECEIVE A SPIRIT THAT MAKES YOU A SLAVE AGAIN to fear, but you received the Spirit of sonship. And by him we cry, "Abba, Father." (Rom. 8:15 NIV)

Because you are sons, God sent the Spirit of his Son into our hearts, the Spirit who calls out, "Abba, Father." So you are no longer a slave, but a son, and since you are a son, God has also made you also an heir. (Gal. 4:6–7 NIV)

But when the time had fully come, God sent his Son, born of a woman, born under law, to redeem those under law, that we might receive the full rights of sons. Because you are sons, God sent the Spirit of his Son into our hearts, the Spirit who calls out, "Abba, Father." So you are no longer a slave, but a son; and since you are a son, God has made you also an heir" (Gal. 4:4–7 NIV)

These are familiar passages you may have heard or read previously. As you read them now, what do you hear God saying to you? About who you are? About his heart for you? About your relationship with him?

MOST OF THE MEN I'VE COUNSELED OVER THE YEARS UNDERSTAND THAT Christianity is an offer of forgiveness, made available to us through the sacrifice of Jesus on the cross. They see God the way Balian sees his father at the start of his journey. What they don't seem to grasp is, there is more. That forgiveness was made available to each of us so *that* we might come home to the Father. Forgiveness is not the goal. Coming home to the Father is the goal.

Do you want to come home? Express your desire to God in prayer.

A MAN WHO MERELY CALLS HIMSELF A CHRISTIAN, ATTENDS CHURCH, AND has some hope of heaven when he dies has *not* received the lion's share of what God intended him to receive through the work of Christ. He will find himself living still very much alone, stuck in his journey, wondering why he cannot become the man he longs to be.

He has not come into sonship.

Where does your heart go as you think about your being a son of God? Does it sound too good to be true? A religious concept that's true, but not *real* practical?

Ahhh . . . when you read it and think about it, it's stunning, incredible, amazing. It's everything I could hope for and want. I, Craig McConnell, am a son of the Most High, a son of God. I know it's true, yet I don't think the reality of it has overwhelmed me, as I think it ought to. Or maybe I haven't embraced it, or believed it fully yet. I'm not sure. I do know I want it to be more than merely a "positional truth" about our identity in Christ. I want to live in the beauty, joy, and intimacy of its reality. (Craig)

TAKE A CLOSER LOOK AT THE STORY OF THE PRODIGAL SON, ONE OF MANY stories Jesus told to try to get it into our hearts where we stand with the Father, and how he feels about us. The story is not primarily about the prodigal. It is about the father's heart. "But while he was still a long way off, his father saw him and was filled with compassion for him; he ran to his son, threw his arms around him and kissed him" (Luke 15:20 NIV). This is the kind of Father you have. This is how he feels about you. *This* is the purpose for which Christ came.

What does the story tell you about your Father's heart?

When and in what ways have you been *"a long way off"*?

How do you think his father's embrace affected the prodigal?

How do you think your experience of God's embrace will affect you?

A CROSSROAD IN YOUR JOURNEY

an important point of decision or action that can/may determine your final destination

We begin to make the one most central, most essential shift in the entire world, the shift Christianity is focused on, by at least beginning with the objective truth. How this plays out in our lives will come later. For now, there are things you must know. You *are* the son of a kind, strong, and engaged Father, a Father wise enough to guide you in the Way, generous enough to provide for your journey. His first act of provision happened before you were even born, when he rescued you through the life, death, and resurrection of our elder brother, Jesus of Nazareth. Then he called you to himself—perhaps is calling you even now—to come home to him through faith in Christ. When a man gives his life to Jesus Christ, when he turns as the prodigal son turned for home and is reconciled to the Father, many remarkable things take place. At the core of them is a coming into true sonship.

Have you come home?

In the course of going over this chapter, where do you find your heart going regarding your actually having the father you were designed to have?

Are the truth and reality of this getting clearer, firmer, a little more deeply rooted? Or does it still seem like religious jargon, too good to be true, "*pie in the sky*"?

If so, we suggest a prayer similar to this:

God, I come to you wanting to know the truth and have the truth set me free. Free from my fatherlessness, free from my loneliness, alive as your son. I long to know you as the Father I believe you are. I ask for your embrace of my heart and the settled confidence of our relationship as father and son.

A NEW FAMILY—AND NEW ALLEGIANCES

NOW FOR A TRUTH THAT IS BOTH DIFFICULT AND DANGEROUS, WONDERFUL and freeing. Because we have come home to our true Father and to true sonship, every other relationship has been fundamentally changed. Forever. Including—no, *especially*—family ties. In order to walk in the freedom and healing, the intimacy with God available to the sons of God, in order to experience the "full rights of sons" and take up our masculine quest, we must know what this shift means regarding the bonds of our earthly fathers and families.

What do you love and/or enjoy about your family? What are the good memories?

The size. There were seven of us and the extended family was huge (it felt like we had 20 aunts and uncles and 100 cousins). Every holiday was like a block party. I loved the different places we lived, each presenting different adventures and challenges for a young boy/man; four generations of family sitting on the deck of the family cabin in Big Bear feeding peanuts to the Jays and squirrels; the early years of flopping on the family room floor watching *77 Sunset Strip*, *Highway Patrol*, and *Combat* as a family. I loved my great-grandparents and grandparents and they loved me. (Craig)

What's particularly hard, perhaps even painful about your family? Does it feel like a violation or being disloyal to even express these?

YOUR LIFE IS SUBORDINATE TO THE FAMILY—ITS NEEDS, EXPECTATIONS, demands. It is a closed and jealous system, and that is why there are stories that will forever "stay in the family," and dark truths, too. This is why sons often go into the family business, even though their dreams lie elsewhere. Why true loves who really ought to be married are separated: "She's not one of us." This is also why stories of emotional, physical, and sexual abuse within families are typically never revealed. Blood runs thicker than water, as the old saying goes.

So, to what degree is your life subordinate to your family? That is, to what extent are your life, career, hobbies, or vacations directed by family expectations and unspoken demands?

Are there areas of your life or desires of your heart you cannot walk in with and/or because of your family? To what extent does your family affect your walk with God?

What words would you chose to describe the effect your family has on you?

Guilt
Pressure
Joy
Expectation
Disappointment
Life
Freedom
Intimacy
Tradition
Lightness
Heaviness
Laughter

THOUGH JESUS GREW UP IN ONE OF THE MOST FAMILY-CENTRIC CULTURES in the world, listen to his take on the supremacy of the family bond:

> Do not suppose that I have come to bring peace to the earth. I did not come to bring peace, but a sword. For I have come to turn
> "a man against his father,
> a daughter against her mother,
> a daughter-in-law against her mother-in-law—
> a man's enemies will be the members of his own household." (Matt. 10:34–36 NIV)

Whoa. What do you do with those strong words? What do Christ's words stir in you?

On the surface it's a tough passage that just doesn't seem to jell with all the categories I think in: God is love; honor your mother and father; love one another; children obey your parents in the Lord. How many times have I heard the order of our priorities should be God first, followed quickly by family? And here Jesus is talking about bringing violence and conflict to the building block of church and society. Hey, I sure don't want to experience this with my daughters, son-in-law, and grandkids! He's gotten my attention . . . so what's he saying to me? (Craig)

OUR DISCOMFORT WITH THE TARGET OF HIS WORDS ONLY REVEALS MY point: the assumed allegiances, and all the false guilt and responsibility that have been assumed the right of family for millennia. Yet, these are the words of Jesus, the One who came to show us the narrow path to life. We won't appreciate the goodness of these words until we remember how family can cripple and bind, how false those allegiances can sometimes be.

How has, or how might, your relationship with God call you into conflict with your family ties?

How would you like to relate differently with your family?

HOW DOES JESUS INTERPRET THE COMMAND TO HONOR OUR FATHER AND mother? While Jesus was still talking to the crowd, his mother and brothers stood outside, wanting to speak to him. Someone told him, "Your mother and brothers are standing outside, wanting to speak to you" (Matt. 12:46–47 NIV). He replied to him, "Who is my mother, and who are my brothers?" Pointing to his disciples, he said, "Here are my mother and my brothers. For whoever does the will of my Father in heaven is my brother and sister and mother" (vv. 48–50 NIV).

Though we know Jesus is love incarnate, how do his words to his parents sound to you?

Christ reframes our understanding of family bonds by saying, "My true family are those who are in the family of God." How will reframing your view of family change things?

Now, I know, I know. People are going to use this as an excuse to do things that seem very unchristian indeed. It is a dangerous teaching—as are all teachings that bring true freedom are in danger of being misused—but that doesn't seem to worry Jesus, who drives at the point again and again: "Anyone who loves his father or mother more than me is not worthy of me" (Matt. 10:37 NIV).

You see, our deepest convictions about ourselves, about life, and about God are handed to us by our families when we are young. When things go wrong in our families, as young children we have no real means of sorting that out. We assume that, somehow, it is our fault. That we could have prevented it. That somehow we could have done more. Something's wrong with us. And this carries on into adulthood. We feel that we are bound to rescue our family members. That somehow, through enough allegiance and good deeds, we will atone for the family sins. It is a false guilt. And Jesus wants to set us free from it, bring us home to our true Father.

> I will not leave you as orphans; I will come to you. (John 14:18 NIV)
>
> My Father will love him, and we will come to him and make our home with him. (John 14:23 NIV)

So, now as an older man, what needs to be sorted out about your family and all it has handed down to you? What impact has it had on your journey?

How is your family's view of you similar or different from God's view of you?

Have you felt bound to rescue your family or felt "false guilt" over what you have or haven't done"?

So, what has all this stirred up in your heart and head regarding family?

How would you like to live and relate differently with your family?

A NOTE ALONG THE WAY

Being a father is a noble undertaking, and a terrifically hard one. A "hazardous conquest," as Gabriel Marcel wrote, "which is achieved step by step over difficult country full of ambushes." (The fathers reading this just said, "Amen.") If our earthly fathers faltered along the way, it may have been that the country they were asked to travel was more difficult than we know. The longer we live, the more I think we will see our fathers' failures with compassion, and—I hope—we will see all that was good in what they were able to offer.

CENTRAL TO JESUS' TEACHING IS THAT OUR LIVES FIND THEIR FULFILLMENT in union with our heavenly Father. Our fathers were meant to teach us truly about our heavenly Father and guide us into that union and teach us to walk with him. Now, if our earthly fathers were good, the transition will be rather seamless. If they were not, we find it a hard transition to make, for we project onto God what we have experienced from our fathers here.

What was/is your relationship with your dad like?

How would you describe him?

What is your relationship with God like?

How would you describe him?

Do you see the connections?

A RADICAL SHIFT HAS TAKEN PLACE FOR THOSE OF US WHO HAVE COME TO faith in Christ. We have been embraced by our Father in heaven. He has taken us into his family. We are his sons. We really are. We have his Spirit in our hearts (Rom. 8:15). We have a new legacy, for we shall be like him (Rom. 8:29).We are free now to love our families here on earth, for we need not live under any of the false guilt, false pressures, false inheritances. Our view of ourselves as men can be healed. Our view of the life before us can be renewed. We are free now to take up our journeys with a Father who cares, who understands, who is committed to see us through. Our initiation can commence.

What reactions has the paragraph above rustled up in you?

As I read this, something is welling up inside of me. It's hard to put into words, but it feels like both longing and insistence. An honesty of a desire saying, I want that! and a clarity of energy and prayer. Oh Dear God, I deeply, truly, really want that! The good news is God wants to give it all to me. (Craig)

To what degree have these truths been deeply embraced in your heart, and to what degree are they merely "positional" truth or religious creed?

Do you long for this to be "truer" than it is, more descriptive of you than it is? Do you find yourself saying, "I don't want to live fatherless anymore!"?

THE FATHER IS INITIATING HIS SONS

YOU SEE, WE NEED FATHERING STILL. ALL OF US. MORE THAN WE KNOW. There are many places in us yet orphaned, many places that need initiation into manhood.

We are Unfinished Men. And in truth, the Father has been fathering us for a long time now or, at least, trying to.

What I'm suggesting is a new way of looking at your life as a man. To see your life as a process of initiation into masculine maturity, and your Father doing the initiating. Invited, like Balian, on a journey by your true Father.

What we need is more than what we have yet experienced. We need fathering. We need initiation.

Are you willing to enter the journey of masculine initiation God is inviting you into . . . of becoming the man he designed and has hopes of you being?

IN ORDER TO GET THERE, WE MUST EMBRACE IN OUR HEART OF HEARTS three truths given to us in Scripture.

First, you have been brought home, through the work of Christ, to your true Father. Given the Spirit of sonship and, with it, the full rights of a son.

Second, you are free from the constraints of your earthly family, free to follow God, free to become the man you were born to be, to surpass your family's legacy.

Third, the premise of this book: Acting as a true Father, and you his true son, God is now raising you up *as* a son.

Can you let this be true for you?

OUR FATHER HAS COME FOR US, AND OUR INITIATION IS UNDER WAY. IT can now proceed with even greater clarity and intimacy. The horizon has opened before us. It is a risky venture, to be sure, this realignment of our view of life as masculine initiation, this turning to God as Father. But I know of few other truths that can bring a man such hope as this.

Father, okay. Okay. I don't know how much of this I believe, but I know this—I need a father. There is so much in me that yet needs fathering. And I don't want to live fatherless anymore. So come to me, and help me make the shift. You have taken me home, through Christ, to be your own son. I accept that. I give my life back to you, to be your true son. Father me. Father me.

For more description and observation on the film *The Kingdom of Heaven*, turn to page 277.

clear that you didn't reap what God designed a boy to grasp in his youth. There are a couple of ways you can react/respond: First, you can view this as God's redemption—to see that he is exposing a void so that he can restore to you that which was missed. He wants to heal, restore, and complete the good work he's begun in you. A second response is to allow the enemy to get a foothold through your woundedness, through the void in your masculine development, to breed anger, shame, self-contempt, and condemnation in your soul. Don't fall for it! God wants to turn your ashes and poverty into glory and the joy of intimacy with him.

Note: Each stage of the Masculine Journey will be covered in two chapters. In the first chapter of each stage we'll focus on reflection, remembering, and self-assessment. In the second—in this case, Raising the Beloved Son—we'll pursue what God is doing to bring us through that stage now.

FIRST REACTIONS

Remembering and reflecting on your boyhood can raise wonderful memories of innocence, exploration, growth, and wonder. It can also surface some of the most painful events of your life. What was the effect of this chapter upon you? Write out your impressions. Are there any new or challenging thoughts or emotions stirring in your heart, or even perhaps some action that you intend to take?

Over the months of talking about the stages of the masculine journey, I have found myself wondering about my journey. I listed all the turning points, the great moments, the most difficult events and circumstances, and I began to ask God, So what kind of journey have I been on? Have I been entirely on my own or have you been more involved than I've known? What have been the good sections, and what have I missed? Am I "off" by a mile or by 20 at this stage? When John gave me a copy of this book it provoked two responses. The first being, Thank you God, this is going to be good. You're going to answer my prayer and address my journey as a man. The second reaction was, Oh crap, I am such damaged goods! This is going to expose the mess I've always known I am. At my age, I'm irreparable. This is going to be miserable.

But a funny, gracious, surprising, and merciful thing happened as I began to read the book. Memories of seasons, people, and events surfaced, and I heard the heart of God whisper, See me in that season/event. I was there. Remember that circumstance, that difficulty? I was initiating you then. I've thought so much of my journey was simply me alone bouncing off the walls of a narrow ally going nowhere. As I've been reading this, God has been revealing his hidden hand in so very much of my life. He was there, he was engaged. I wasn't alone, and he's validating me through the pages of the book. (Craig)

3

BOYHOOD

Keep me as the apple of your eye.
—PSALM 17:8 NIV

BEFORE STARTING

Hopefully the pace you're setting to go through this manual allows all that surfaces in you to be pondered, prayed over, and initiated by God in your heart, mind, and masculine soul. Pausing, ask God if there's a bit more time or prayer to be spent on the previous chapter.

Before you begin to work through this chapter of the manual:

- Without referring back to the book, from your recollection and in your own words, describe the Boyhood Stage.
- While the stages overlap, and there is some aspect of them in every phase of a man's life, this is no exception, and in fact this stage is *the essential* foundation upon which our passing through every other stage well is dependent. Thus the importance for every man, whatever your age or stage, is to move through this section with a teachable, yielded heart.
- Because this stage is meant to be lived early in your life, don't presume you have gleaned all God intended for you. There may be some things for you that were missed, lost, or stolen along the way.

For some of you, remembering your boyhood will raise memories that make it painfully

KEY POINTS OF THE CHAPTER

- So much of the way we now approach life as men was set in motion in our youth—some of it for good, and some not so good. We want to recover what was good, and find healing for all that was not.
- Boyhood is a time of exploration and wonder, and to be a boy is to be an explorer. When God set Adam in the Garden of Eden, he set his son in a world that was, at the very same moment, safe and secure yet full of mystery and adventure. There was no reason whatsoever to be afraid, and every reason to dare. Evil is—for now—held at bay. Such is the world God intended for the boy. And that world is created under the sheltering strength of a father who makes you feel safe.
- This is the time in life when we were meant to come into the knowledge that we are the Beloved Son, the apple of our Father's eye.
- A foundation in the heart of the boy is the lesson that life is not something you have to arrange for. There is someone who cares, someone who wants to give you good gifts.
- *You are noticed. Your heart matters. Your Father adores you.*
- The crucial thing about the stage of the Beloved Son—any of the stages, for that matter—is that it not be cut short, assaulted, unfinished, stolen in any way. We were designed to experience belovedness and boyhood, soak in it *for years*, learn its lessons, have them written indelibly upon our hearts, and then pass through this stage to the next, carrying all its treasures with us.

WHEN I WAS A BOY, MY FATHER WORKED AS A TRAVELING SALESMAN, IN paper goods and then garden supplies. I was his only son, with two older sisters, and come summertime Dad would take me along with him as he called on accounts across the western states—Oregon, Idaho, Colorado, Wyoming, Montana. It was a time of great adventures. Together. I was his navigator, poring over the road maps, which in those days you could get for free at any gas station. (They pumped your gas and checked your oil then, too—how many of you remember that?) My dad loved to fish, and as the weekend drew near he'd plan the route so as to land us near a lake or stream. We'd camp for the weekend, and fish to our hearts' content. Meaning, sunup to sundown. He'd make us fried-egg sandwiches for dinner, or sometimes Spam, which I loved. We slept in a tent. And if we didn't catch anything, Dad would swing me by Happy Jack's Fish Farm to make sure I landed a few. (It was decades later, as a father myself, that I learned you actually *pay* for the fish you catch there.)

Summertime to a boy seems eternal. Echoes of the endless days of wonder in Eden. It seemed to me that we'd be on the road for months and months, just me and him, sleeping at the Roadway or the Holiday Inn or, better, little places like Moe's Alpine Chalet Cabins with a creek running right behind them. No homework. No chores. We'd eat at the A&W (we both loved root beer). We were rock hounds then, too, pulling into every little nook to search for snowflake obsidian and geodes called thunder eggs. After what seemed like six months of "travels with my father," Dad would make the loop back home and pass through eastern Oregon, to his father's cattle ranch, where I would be dropped off for the rest of the summer. In the time of my boyhood, the ranch was a place of unending adventures. Later, it would become a key place for the raising of the Cowboy. My grandfather had horses and cattle, barns and tractors, and a yard with a huge lawn that seemed to go on forever.

There was a pond nestled back in one of the pastures on the property, a small pond half filled with cattails, a place of mystery and delight to a boy. There were bullfrogs there, and sometimes a great blue heron, standing so utterly still, like a lamppost, waiting to seize an unfortunate catfish. There must have been hundreds of fish in that little pond—too many in fact, for they never grew much past seven or eight inches long—but size didn't matter to me. It was abundance I was after. I'd dig for red worms in the soft, moist earth lining the irrigation ditch by the house, and carry them in an old Folgers coffee can to the pond, where I would fish with a hook and bobber. I loved watching those old red-and-white bobbers, sitting nearly motionless on the surface, waiting for it to tug, tug, tug then plunge suddenly beneath the surface, letting me know my prize was on the line.

Find a quiet place where you'll find it easy to reflect, and take some time, perhaps more than you'd immediately allot, and recall your boyhood (it may even be helpful to look through old photos).

What was your boyhood like?

Where did you grow up, what did you enjoy doing, what captured your time and imagination? Hobbies? Sports?

Who were your friends, what were they like?

What was your father like? Did you have special times with your father or a father figure?

A WORLD THAT IS SAFE

WE NOW BEGIN OUR JOURNEY BY LOOKING BACKWARD, TO WHAT OUR LIVES as boys were like, and, more important, what they were *meant* to be. For so much of the way we now approach life as men was set in motion in our youth—some of it for good, and some not so good. We want to recover what was good, and find healing for all that was not.

Boyhood is a time of exploration and wonder, and to be a boy is to be an explorer, from the time when the little guy figures out how to crawl up the stairs to the time he discovers that if he jumps over the back fence he can get down to Jimmy's house, where they have a secret fort.

Was this true of you? What are your recollections of exploration and wonder?

Oh yes! I spent what felt like a lifetime at our neighbors, the Walschmidt's, digging the quintessential cave. It wasn't a mere cave, but a cavern with every imaginable necessity and convenience—Hostess Twinkies, baseball cards, a couple of pocket knives, a canteen and of course an Army Ranger Flashlight (it's a miracle it didn't collapse and kill us!). I roamed the mountainside above Lake Mary knowing there were abandoned gold mines somewhere, searched for by many, and that I would have the good fortune to find and exploit them. There was a secret fishing hole on the American River that no white man had ever found but me and my cohort of explorers. To get to it required trespassing through a pear orchard and crossing at your own peril, and navigating the ever-dangerous hobo camp along the railroad tracks. (Craig)

When God set Adam in the Garden of Eden, he set his son in a world that was, at the very same moment, safe and secure yet full of mystery and adventure. There was no reason whatsoever to be afraid, and every reason to dare. Evil is—for now—held at bay. Such is the world God intended for the boy. And that world is created under the sheltering strength of a father who makes you feel safe. For this is the time in life when we were meant to come into the knowledge that we are the Beloved Son, the apple of our Father's eye.

Was your world growing up safe? Is it now?

How would you be different now if you had grown up in a world more like Eden?

What do God's intentions for a boy say about God's heart for you?

My friend Bart once told me, "I think I was four or five, and I spent all my days with my father on the family farm . . . He'd get me up in the morning and take me with him. I remember the tractor—this was back in the early fifties and they didn't have the big cab then like they do now—you rode out in the open, all those moving parts thrashing around, which just fascinated me as a boy. A little fearful to me, yet I felt so safe between the legs of my father. Holding on to the steering wheel, he'd make me think I was really driving this big, powerful piece of machinery."

They lived in west Texas, and Bart recalls a time when they were visiting his uncle's farm about twenty miles away when tornado warnings came in. "His family was pulling mattresses down into the storm cellar, getting ready to ride it out, and they urged us to stay. But my dad wanted to get home to my mom and brother."

While they drove the back roads home, they saw a twister heading across the plains about a mile away. "My dad took me out and held me in his arms as we sat on the fender of the pickup and watched this tornado just destroy the town of Cotton Center, Texas. He put his arms around me, and just being in the arms of my father, I felt so safe."

Safe in your Father's arms—*that* is what it feels like to be the Beloved Son.

What do Bart's recollections of being safe in his father's arms stir up in you?

Are you kidding? I want to cry, to gasp. I'm envious and lost, longing for something I never had—a father and his love. Bart's surreal stories stir up such a strong desire and it's pretty clear that I missed something I'd love to have had—and hope or wish I could have even now. (Craig)

How would knowing you are the Beloved Son of your Father have affected the way you've lived your life? How would it have affected your relationships, confidence, the major decisions you've made, career direction, etc.?

THE SAFETY THAT A FATHER'S STRENGTH PROVIDES ALLOWS A BOY TO *BE* A boy, creates the universe for a boy's heart to come fully alive. For a number of years Stasi and I raised our boys in a house with a second story. I think there were maybe thirteen stairs leading to the upper level. Often in the evenings, just before bedtime, the boys in their jammies with feet in them, we would play a game where they would get as far back on the landing as they could, get a running start to leap off the stairs, and fly through the air into my arms below. I was blown away by their trust in me, such abandoned confidence. When a boy has this confidence, this security and safety created by masculine strength over him, the whole world opens before him. He is able to live *as a boy*—an explorer and adventurer.

Were you able to "live as a boy"?

What's been the history of your masculine heart?

How is your heart now—today—as you read this question?

A VISTA JOURNEY

a view that enhances the journey

A film that illustrates how intent the enemy is to separate us from our Father is the mythic story of *The Lion King*. In the story, the lion cub Simba is separated in his youth from his father through a murder engineered by his uncle, Scar, the character symbolizing the evil one in our story. Scar arranges for the cub to be caught in a stampede of wildebeests, knowing that his father, Mufasa, will risk his life to save his son. He does, and Simba is saved, but Mufasa is killed. Scar then turns on Simba and accuses him, at such a vulnerable and desperate moment, of causing his father's death. Brokenhearted, frightened, racked with guilt, Simba runs away from home.

Another film worth viewing would be *Life is Beautiful.* There is a remarkable picture of a sense of safety and security a father gives his son in this Italian movie. The story is set in WWII. The boy is perhaps five years old, son of a Jewish father and Italian mother. When his family is taken away to a concentration camp, the father hides his son among the men being taken to the all-male camp, so that he will not be separated from the boy, and so that he might protect him. For many months in the camp, the father shields the son from the enemy, and the ruthless evil around them. There, in the midst of darkness, the boy shows a stunning immunity to it all, trusting fully in the goodness of his father, playing the endless games they make up together.

A WORLD OF ADVENTURES AND BATTLES

THE HEART OF A BOY LONGS FOR DARING ADVENTURES, BATTLES, UNCHARTED territory to be discovered. Spend an afternoon watching boys at play, and you will see something of what God intended when he created man as a man, when he created maleness, masculinity. The boy is also a warrior, and all those games he plays and battles he imagines are preparation for the day he enters the stage of the Warrior in its fullness.

A boy wants to be powerful. That's what's behind the superhero thing. To be powerful, and dangerous, a force to be reckoned with—that is the heart of the Warrior emerging.

How did your wanting to be a Warrior express itself when you were a boy?

I grew up in a Boomer neighborhood. We were the sons of WWII and Korean War vets. There had to be seventy young boys on our block of 7th Avenue. I was a sergeant of a small platoon of friends. We wore our fathers' helmets and aluminum canteens, our weaponry consisting of pop-gun rifles that could propel dirt clods and pockets filled with tangerine-grenades. We patrolled the area, setting up bunkers and ambushes in the hedges and ivy landscape. It would be a mistake to refer to this as "playing" army—we were living out our young masculinity as we protected our mothers and sisters from evil while the men were away at work. (Craig)

Does the Warrior heart find expression in your life now?

Who were your superheroes as a young boy? Who did you want to be like?

Sgt. Vince Saunders in the TV series Combat!, The Disney Series Davy Crockett, and of course John Wayne as Davy Crockett in The Alamo. Mickey Mantle, Roger Maris, and the numerous heroic fighter pilots and infantry men in the war novels and stories I read. (Craig)

Who are your superheroes now?

What's true of a boy is true of a man. To review or read a bit more on what it means to be an image bearer, to bear the image of God and the place of adventure and battle, see *Wild at Heart*, pages 19–38.

A WORLD OF SURPRISES

THERE'S A TOUCHING STORY A MAN ONCE TOLD ME ABOUT A RITUAL THAT would take place every evening when his father got home. The father would change out of his work clothes—a business suit—and into his "house clothes," and the children would get to dig deep into his pockets for whatever "treasures" they might find in his work trousers—a quarter, a pen, a cuff link, a stick of gum. The treasures were theirs to keep. So Daddy coming home was always an event that brought excitement and anticipation. Which is a wonderful thing to have linked with fatherhood, especially as we make the connection to God as Father, from whom, the Scriptures say, comes "every good and perfect gift" (James 1:17 NIV).

Do you find it hard to believe, or has it been your experience, that God wants to surprise you with joyous treasures and gifts?

What do you see as some of the treasures and gifts God has given you?

A FEW OF US WERE TALKING ABOUT OUR FATHERS THE OTHER NIGHT, AND sharing some of the good memories we have of them. Morgan told us of something like the story I just recounted that pertained to his father, who had a ritual of a poker game each week. The kids would be sent to bed long before their father got home, but the next morning they'd wake to find his winnings on the kitchen table, divided into piles for each of his children to take as their own. Treasure. Booty. For no other reason than "you are my beloved sons and daughters." Gary then remembered a time when he was very young, and his father told him, "After you take a nap, when you wake up I have a surprise for you." He had put up a rope swing for Gary, hanging from the tree in the front yard. "I felt like he was thinking of me, wanted me to be happy." This, too, lays a foundation in the heart of the boy, for he comes to learn that life is not something you have to arrange for. There is someone who cares, someone who wants to give you good gifts.

What gifts did your father give you when you were a boy?

Regardless of the successes or failures of your earthly father, have you found God to truly be a Father to/for you? Someone who cares and wants to give you good gifts?

What are the key things you're trying to arrange for or orchestrate in life?

BELOVED SON

IT IS EXPERIENCES LIKE THESE THAT SPEAK TO THE HEART OF A BOY. *You are noticed. Your heart matters. Your father adores you.* For we must remember that above all else, boyhood is the time of Affirmation, the time when a boy comes to learn and learn deeply that he is the Beloved Son.

How comfortable are you being referred to as "the Beloved Son"?

I love the concept. I want to be a beloved son of God's. I may be comfortable with it as I go farther into this journey. But yikes, it just feels like an extremely exclusive term expressing God's great love for Jesus alone. It's not the same love for me. Right? I may be a small caps beloved son, but not (large caps) the Beloved Son. So, I guess I'm a little uncomfortable believing God's love for me is that great. (Craig)

I EXPLAINED IN *WILD AT HEART* THAT EVERY MAN AND EVERY BOY IS asking one core question: "Do I have what it takes?" It's why, when the boys ride their bikes with no hands, or learn to do a back flip on the trampoline, they want me there to see it. And all that crazy stuff young men do—cliff-jumping into the river, riding motorcycles, all the competition of sports—that is fueled by the same drive. That is the expression of a man's need for validation. *Do I have what it takes?* is a core question to be sure, and I still hold that it is the vital question of the masculine journey. But there is a deeper and prior need, one that comes first—in this stage—and one that must be met first, or the boy cannot move with confidence into any of the other stages.

A boy yearns to know that he is prized.

How does your heart immediately respond to the question *Am I prized?*

Does the question *Am I prized?* seem deeper and prior to the question *Do I have what it takes?* How would you answer that?

Yes! Sitting here at this moment I can with a confident humility say, Yeah, I've got what it takes. I have learned a lot, have common sense, am basically competent, have a few gifts, and the trump card of God having spoken those words to me. So that question, Do I have what it takes?, feels answered, while I still have much to learn and grow in. But, the question, Am I prized? feels very different. It's on a deeper, more vulnerable, needy, defining level of my being. And in some ways it feels unanswered. Theoretically I know God loves me, that I'm liked, even loved by a number of people—but am I prized? Egads! Yes, kinda, maybe, hope so! (Craig)

THIS IS MORE THAN JUST BEING LOVED IN A GENERIC SORT OF WAY. "OF course I love you—you're my son." A boy can see right through anything false in that. He yearns to know he is *adored. Uniquely.* That he holds a special place in his father's heart, a place no one and nothing anything else can rival. Without this certainty down in the core of his being, the boy will misinterpret the stages and lessons that are to come, for as a young man (Cowboy) he will soon be tested, and he will face battles and challenges as a Warrior, and those tests and challenges often feel to men like a form of rejection or cold-heartedness on the part of God, because he does not first know in his heart of hearts that he *is* the Beloved Son.

Have you faced trials, betrayals, hardships, or failures that you took as rejection or cold-heartedness on the part of God? If so, what were those difficulties and what did you expect God to do?

If you knew, truly knew, God uniquely and personally adored you, that you held a special place in his heart, that you are the Beloved Son, how might that alter the way you interpret the difficulties of life?

NOW, YES, A MOTHER PLAYS A CRUCIAL ROLE IN A BOY'S LIFE. FROM HER A boy learns mercy, tenderness, and unconditional love. But in a core way that is essential to the masculine journey, the bestowing of the mantle of Beloved Son needs to come from the father. That father might be a man other than your biological father, a man who is father to you in truer ways. Paul calls Timothy his beloved son, and you can imagine it meant the world to his young apprentice (1 Cor. 4:17; 2 Tim. 1:2).

How was your mother's role in your masculine development different from your father's role?

Without diminishing the role of a mother or the value of her love, have you found it to be true, that the mantle of Beloved Son needs to come from a man?

Why, for you, would a man's validation be so important?

My grandfather fathered me, too, in some very important ways. He called me "Johnny," and he was the only one ever to call me that. Oh, how I loved those summers at the ranch. We'd wake early in the morning and head down to the small diner in town for coffee and milk and donuts. Nina's Diner was the gathering place for ranchers, seated along the counter, swapping information about the weather or cattle prices. My grandfather would sit me right there beside him, right in the action, at his side. I was proud he was my "Pop" and I could tell he was proud I was his grandson, his Johnny. I was prized by a man I loved. This is the greatest gift any boy ever receives.

Who were the other men, besides your father, who "fathered" you?

Who are the men, even now, who in some way are fathering you?

Come back for a moment to Jesus' probing questions regarding our feelings about God as Father. He almost seems puzzled. "Are you not much more valuable than they? Will he not leave the ninety-nine on the hills and go off to look for the one that wandered off? How much more will your Father in heaven give good gifts to those who ask him!" In other words, don't you know how your Father feels about you? Jesus did. He walked through the world knowing he was the Beloved Son, the favored One. It's what enabled him to live as he did.

This relationship was meant to be our secret, our joy also. We were meant to know this, too. First through our earthly fathers, and then, by the extension of fatherhood, to our Father in the heavens. But there are few who came through their boyhood with such knowledge intact, without a trace of doubt.

In summary, write out how God, your Father, feels about you.

WOUNDED

IT WAS THE BEGINNING OF THE COLLAPSE OF MY FAMILY. THE SUMMER TRIPS came to an end. The fishing came to an end. Mom had to go to work. I went to Boy Scouts alone, came home to an empty house. I felt abandoned. My world ceased to be a safe place. Emotionally, physically, spiritually, I became an orphan. And a terrible lie settled deep into my heart: *You are on your own.* A boy without a father, in a dangerous world. The days of the Beloved Son cut off, and I never knew why. Perhaps it was something I did. Perhaps I could have prevented it.

When did your boyhood end and your world cease to be safe? What ended your boyhood?

I was eleven or twelve. I cannot recall what precipitated it, but my stepdad, in the hall between his bedroom and the bathroom, was so angry with me he could barely control his rage. The yelling, cursives, and expressed disappointment I've forgotten, but what I can't shake is his saying that he was so mad he could kill me, and unless my mom had intervened restraining him I'm certain he would have wailed on me. I felt like I was now living with an enemy, not a father. (Craig)

THE CRUCIAL THING ABOUT THE STAGE OF THE BELOVED SON—ANY OF THE stages, for that matter—is that it not be cut short, assaulted, unfinished, stolen in any way. We were designed to experience belovedness and boyhood, soak in it *for years,* learn its lessons, have them written indelibly upon our hearts, and then pass through this stage to the next, carrying all its treasures with us. We were meant to move on, *with the help of our fathers,* into the next stage of masculine initiation.

Which of these words/phrases describe your stage of the Beloved Son:

Cut short . . . not soaking in it for years
Assaulted
Unfinished
Stolen
Soaked in it for years
Learned its lessons
Passed through this stage carrying all its treasures with you

A BOY'S HEART IS WOUNDED IN MANY WAYS. HE IS WOUNDED WHEN HE DOES not live in a world made safe by his father, when he is not free to explore and dare and simply *be* a boy, when he is forced to grow up too soon. He is wounded when he *does* have that world, but it ends with a sudden loss of innocence. And most especially, a boy is wounded to the core when he does not know that he *is* the Beloved Son. Sometimes the wounding is intentional, oftentimes it is not, but this is the story of many a boy, and many a man reading this book, living in the world we have, so far from the Garden.

Which of these statements would be true of your boyhood:
Your world or your father was unsafe.
You weren't free to explore and simply *be* a boy.
You were forced to grow up too soon.
You weren't prized, uniquely enjoyed.

A COUPLE OF MONTHS AGO, I AND A FEW MEN I AM CLOSEST TO WERE sitting around a fire one evening, talking about our dreams for our lives. The subject on the table was, "What is the life you want to live?" It wasn't a conversation about yachts and the Bahamas. We were talking about finding God's purpose for our lives, wanting to live the life we alone were created to live. Craig in particular had a hard time going there. As we gently pushed into his reluctance, he admitted, "I just don't believe anything good ever really comes true." A core belief, he'll tell you, one that has shaped his life since he was eight years old. And there is a story with that as well. His father was killed in combat when Craig was four months old, a fact Craig learned about one afternoon when as a boy of eight his mother and the man he thought was his father sat him down in the living room and told him, "This man you call Dad is not your father. Your real father was killed in combat. This is your stepfather."

"I remember everything about the room that day—the way the couch looked, the parakeet in the corner. Time had stopped. Looking back, I can see that was the turning point in my life. In some horrible way the defining point. I died then." A sudden loss of innocence, a boy's world sent careening off its orbit, sometimes never to be recovered.

There is a wound that comes when the boy knows very well he is *not* the Beloved Son. Just this weekend I was talking to a man who at the age of fifty-five is now coming to see this. His parents were missionaries in South America, his father gone most of the time on "church business." He said, "I felt as though they [the Bolivian people] were more important to him than I was. He never played with me, was rarely home. I always felt like if my father had a picture of a boy in his wallet, it would be a Bolivian boy." He never, ever felt prized by his father. To this day this man struggles with turning to God as a good and loving Father. Why? "Because he took my dad away."

This sort of rejection can be subtle, hidden by a father busy about "more important matters," or simply by a dad who is checked out. But the message was clear: "You are not prized. I don't care a bit about you. You are not now, nor ever will be, my Beloved Son."

And then there are the violent stories, the boys raped by their fathers or beaten by them. The boys who endured years of emotional abuse, being yelled at night after night, "You are a worthless piece of crap." Whatever the details of the story might be, the boy is robbed both of his father and of the deep and fundamental blessing that he is the Beloved Son. It is the evil one's first and most devastating blow against the soul of a man.

Men at times are reluctant to acknowledge that they have been in any way wounded. There's that macho misperception that to admit a wound is to somehow admit, in essence, that you're not a man . . . because a real man would never really hurt, complain, or play the victim. Push past that misperception and think about this question: How were you wounded as a boy?

How did your wound change your boyhood, your world, your life?

A PAUSE IN THE JOURNEY

an opportunity to reflect on the ground you've just covered

Look back again at pictures of your boyhood. Look at your face in the pictures, your eyes, countenance, posture . . . what do you see?

What did you feel about life then?

THE EVIL BEHIND ALL EVIL

THIS IS THE ENEMY'S ONE CENTRAL PURPOSE—TO SEPARATE US FROM THE Father. He uses neglect to whisper, *You see—no one cares. You're not worth caring about.* He uses a sudden loss of innocence to whisper, *This is a dangerous world, and you are alone. You've been abandoned.* He uses assaults and abuses to scream at a boy, *This is all you are good for.* And in this way he makes it nearly impossible for us to know what Jesus knew, makes it so very, very hard to come home to the Father's heart toward us. The details of each story are unique to the boy, but the effect is always a wound in the soul, and with it separation from and suspicion of the Father.

How has the enemy attempted to separate you from the Father?

So many things come to mind, but it seems one of the common underlying themes is how he uses my wound and the message I took from the wound to establish a foothold that puts a wedge between the Father and me. The message of my wound is, "You have nothing to offer, there is something terribly and deeply wrong/filthy/shameful about you." When I agree with this web of lies, I simply cannot and, perhaps more accurately, will not believe God's love for me is true, unique, personal, deep, and passionate. So I balk at drawing near to him and hesitate at his moving toward me. (Craig)

Have you heard these whispered lies from our adversary: *You see—no one cares. God doesn't prize you. You're not worth caring about. This is a dangerous world, and you are alone. You've been abandoned. This is all you are good for.*

How are these lies affecting you even still, as a man?

BUT GOD IS NOT WILLING TO SIMPLY LET THAT BE THE END OF THE STORY. Not in any man's life. Remember what Jesus taught us about the Father's heart in the parable of the lost son: "But while he was still a long way off, his father saw him and was filled with compassion for him; he ran to his son, threw his arms around him and kissed him" (Luke 15:20 NIV). Filled with compassion, our Father God will come like a loving Father, and take us close to his heart. He will also take us back to heal the wounds, finish things that didn't get finished. He will come for the boy, no matter how old he might now be, and make him his Beloved Son. So it might be good to pray at this point:

> *Father, what did I miss here, in this stage? Did I know I was the Beloved Son? Do I believe it even now? Come to me, in this place, over these years. Speak to me. Do I believe you want good things for me? Is my heart secure in your love? How was my young heart wounded in my life as a boy? And Jesus, you who came to heal the broken heart, come to me here. Heal this stage in my heart. Restore me as the Beloved Son. Father me.*

As you finish this chapter, what do you sense God saying to you about being the Beloved Son? Capture those thoughts now, for they will be quickly forgotten or stolen.

4

Raising the Beloved Son

"Is not Ephraim my dear son,
the child in whom I delight? . . .
Therefore my heart yearns for him;
I have great compassion for him," declares the Lord.
—Jeremiah 31:20 NIV

BEFORE STARTING

Before you dive into this chapter, and all it will rouse in you, is there any more time, thoughts, or prayers that would deepen the impact of the previous chapter? More important than an artificial deadline to get through the material is your encounter with God and all he has for you in each chapter. Take some time to review all that "jumped" out at you in the chapter "Raising the Beloved Son," and ask God if there's more he'd like to say to you on these things before moving on.

I have entitled this chapter "Raising the Beloved Son" for two reasons. First, because many of you who are reading this are raising sons even now, as I am, and hope to find in these pages wisdom for doing it well. We want to raise boys who get to *be* boys, and who know beyond any shadow of doubt that *they* are the Beloved Son. But there is another meaning to the title of this chapter. To be raised also means to be *resurrected.* Brought back from the dead. There are many, many men who never knew the happiness and security of being the Beloved Son, and therefore never really got to be a boy in fullness and freedom. They might be angry, they might be uncertain of themselves; they may have looked to the woman for love, or to another man. They may be overachievers, or dropouts. They need to be raised from dead, from their woundedness, and given the life they haven't had, the life of the Beloved Son.

There *are* times a picture is better than a thousand words. A dramatic picture worth viewing is *Antwone Fisher.* Take the time to view it and watch one man's masculine journey into realizing he is the Beloved Son (and yes, there are some sections and themes we would not endorse, but try to look past them and let the story capture you). At the end of this manual, in the Appendix, you will find some observations and notes to refer to as you view the film.

FIRST REACTIONS

Having reread this chapter, were there any "*aha*" moments where something struck a deep cord? New thoughts, questions, anything disrupting? Write out your first reactions to the material and anything God seemed to say.

KEY POINTS OF THE CHAPTER

- It is God himself who embraces us and tells us we are the Beloved Son. He will bring this to us through words spoken in our hearts, through Scriptures that suddenly take on new meaning, through events that bring to us his delight—we come to see that he is smiling upon us, that he wants to bring us close to his heart.
- No matter how old we are, our true Father wants us to experience being his Beloved Sons, and all the joys of boyhood that go with it. But this requires opening our hearts, which will take us back into some of our deepest wounds, into the cynicism and resignation that shut our hearts down a long time ago. God does this so that he might bring his love and healing to the fatherless boy within us, the boy that still needs to know he is the Beloved Son.
- When devastating things happen to us—especially when we are young—they have the power to break our hearts. Literally. Something in the soul is shattered, and it remains stuck at the age it was when the blow came. The heart is a tender thing and easily broken, especially when we are young. That is why Jesus offers to heal the brokenhearted.
- The heart of the boy can be resurrected, and no matter what our age now, we can *know* that we are prized, that we have a place in our Father's heart that no one and nothing else can rival. We *are* his Beloved Sons, and we can begin to experience that in deeply personal ways.

IT IS GOD HIMSELF WHO EMBRACES US AND TELLS US WE ARE THE BELOVED Son. He will bring this to us through words spoken in our hearts, through Scriptures that suddenly take on new meaning, through events that bring to us his delight—we come to see that he is smiling upon us, that he wants to bring us close to his heart.

What does it stir up in you to know that whether or not we had a father, or despite how good or evil he was, ultimately, what every man needs is to hear God speak to us that we are his Beloved Son?

Would the question/issue be settled if God alone embraced you and said to you, *"You are my Beloved Son"*?

> I know I'm supposed to say yes and I know that yes is the biblically correct answer, and I want to, I really, really want to say yes. BUT, there's that tangled thing in me that has believed for a lifetime that he would never embrace me and say such a thing. Until very recently, my answer would have been no! (Craig)

STARTING WITH MEN

AFTER READING *WILD AT HEART*, A MAN I KNOW WENT TO HIS AGING father and told him how desperately he needed his love and validation. He described to his father a scene he loved from *Braveheart*, where Wallace's closest friend, Amish, is blessed by his father: "I can die a happy man, to see the man that you've become." The man asked his father to do the same for him. His father's response? Silence. He was silent, looking down at the table. Then he said, "I can't. My father never did that for me."

Did your father ever tell you that he was proud of you, delighted in you, that you were his "Beloved Son"?

Have you ever thought to go to your heavenly Father with your question, *Am I prized, am I the Beloved Son?*

Now, at age 53, my father has been dead for 52 years. I never knew him, and as crazy as it may sound, I've lived most of my life wanting his pleasure, wishing I had it, and suffering from a deep paralysis of heart because I didn't receive it and never will. But despite the hopelessness of my quest, there is a deeply-rooted disbelief that God could really, in any legitimate sense, be a father to me. (Note, I have been a Christian for thirty-two years, pastor and proud expositor of the cardinal truths of God's Word). It's still very fresh and new, but just three weeks ago through an incredible experience at the funeral of a friend's father, something shifted. I turned from my dead father to a living Father for the deepest and oldest yearning of my masculine heart. At 53 I've found God bringing to me that which I wish I'd gotten when I was 13. (Craig)

Put your own name in this verse (Jer. 31:20 *The Message*), in the place of "Ephraim" (a name for God's people, and that includes you). Imagine that God's heart bursts with longing for you.

Oh! _______ is my dear, dear son,
my child in whom I take pleasure!
Every time I mention his name,
my heart bursts with longing for him!
Everything in me cries out for him.
Softly and tenderly I wait for him.

Let this be true of you. What does your heart say in response to this passage?

THIS IS THE MESSAGE OF JESUS: THERE IS A GOOD AND LOVING FATHER WHO cares so deeply and passionately for you. He yearns to be your Father now. He will draw near, if you'll let him.

No matter how old we are, our true Father wants us to experience being his Beloved Sons, and all the joys of boyhood that go with it. But it requires opening our hearts, which will take us back into some of our deepest wounds, into the cynicism and resignation that shut our hearts down a long time ago. God does this so that he might bring his love and healing to the fatherless boy within us, the boy that still needs to know he is the Beloved Son. The Father will do many things to try to get us back to this longing in our hearts—the longing for a father, the longing to be prized, to be the Beloved Son.

So much of what we long for in our relationship with God is precipitated by our opening our hearts, yet to do so we face our wounds, cynicism, and resignation that shut our hearts down a long time ago. As best as you know/discern now, what needs to be dealt with for your heart to be open to God? If you don't know, why not ask God to surface the obstacles? (Whether God chooses to speak now, or further in to your journey through this material, this would be one of those questions to highlight and consider again later.)

RESURRECTING THE BOY

WHEN DEVASTATING THINGS HAPPEN TO US—ESPECIALLY WHEN WE ARE young—they have the power to break our hearts. Literally. Something in the soul is shattered, and it remains stuck at the age it was when the blow came.

Haven't you had that experience, when suddenly some part of you feels very young? Maybe somebody gets mad at you, threatens to leave you—just like what happened when you were a boy. Maybe you've been asked to give a talk before a crowd, and something in you freezes. A group of men are laughing and joking easily, but you just can't join in. Something happens that was all too much, like something that hurt you when you were young and in that moment, you don't feel much like a man at all. You feel like a boy inside. The reason you feel this way is that some part of you is still a boy.

In what circumstances do you feel very young?

Budgeting, investing, and managing my money. Fixing many things: Cars (unless it's a fuse, flat tire, dead battery, or out of windshield wiper fluid), computers, a toilet that keeps running (even after I've "successfully" replaced the entire internal plumbing twice). Filling out all the tax forms I need to. Being in the presence of some family members. Trying to purchase a one-day subway pass from a machine during rush hour in D.C. I could keep going but will stop here to limit the hemorrhaging of my pride. (Craig)

How old do you feel at these times?

Are you aware of what shattered your heart to stunt your growth in some area?

Do you see that you feel like a boy inside because some part of you still is a boy?

WE REMAIN UNFINISHED MEN, HAUNTED BY THE MEMORIES, CRIPPLED BY the wounds. The addictions remain, the fears remain, the lack of wholeness remains. The human heart was designed to grow up in a world of love and security, a world where we are known and prized each and every day—a world very, very different from the world anyone actually grows up in, living now so far from Eden.

The heart is a tender thing and easily broken, especially when we are young. That is why Jesus offers to heal the brokenhearted:

> The Spirit of the Sovereign LORD is upon me,
> because the LORD has anointed me
> to preach good news to the poor.
> He has sent me to bind up the brokenhearted,
> to proclaim freedom for the captives
> and release from darkness for the prisoners. (Isa. 61:1 NIV)

Understanding the proposition that a boy needs to grow up in a world made safe by his father—a world full of adventures and surprises and above all a father's love—understanding this is not enough for our restoration. Understanding that we might, in fact, have endured some painful things in our youth is not enough for our restoration. We need a different kind of medicine. We need God to come for the boy within.

Exactly how God comes to heal the human heart is a deep mystery, but it works something like this: He will often arrange for some event to make us feel just as we did when we were boys and our hearts were broken. Feeling again what we felt then, or perhaps suddenly a memory surfaces, we have an opportunity not to push it away, or run to the refrigerator, or get angry at someone (however it is we typically handle these emotions). Rather, we invite God to come to the broken place within us, come and find the orphaned boy within and embrace him. We ask the Father to come and heal our broken hearts, rescue the boy, and bring him home. I describe this process in much greater detail in chapter 8 of *Waking the Dead*; you might find it helpful.

Perhaps this prayer can be a beginning:

O Father, yes—I need you. I need your love, need you to come for the boy within. Wherever he is hiding, whatever holds him down, come for him, Father. I give you my permission. I renounce the ways I, too, have rejected him, pushed him away. I want to see him restored. Come and embrace him. Let me know I am your Beloved Son.

Linger here for a moment. Where does your heart need the healing ministry of Jesus? Can you name a time in your life when the wound came? Do you remember a certain age? Ask Jesus to come for *this* place in your heart. Linger and listen. Let him come.

THE FATHER'S HEALING COMES TO US IN MANY WAYS—SOMETIMES QUITE immediately, through healing prayer, other times over the course of many months as he speaks to our hearts, brings us gifts, opens our awareness of our hearts and reawakens memories. Our part is to remain open to the fact that there is often a boy inside that needs a Father's love, to cultivate an awareness of the yearning in our hearts to be prized, and watch for the ways our Father is bringing his love to the young places in our hearts.

AN OPENNESS

THINK ABOUT WHAT YOU LOVE, AND WHAT YOU LONGED FOR AS A BOY. When my friend Gary was a boy, his father gave him a "Rifleman" rifle, a toy based on the old Chuck Connors Western. "It was my favorite toy," he said. But a neighborhood bully broke it, simply took it out of Gary's hands and whacked it against a tree. "I think that's when I started to mistrust people," Gary said. Forty years later, last Christmas, Gary's family gave him a real 30/30. He has recovered a love for guns, and the Father has been fathering him in this intimate way. Gary will often go up to the shooting range all by himself, just with his rifle, to be with God.

The heart of the boy can be resurrected, and no matter what our age is now, we can *know* that we are prized, that we have a place in our Father's heart that no one and nothing else can rival. We *are* his Beloved Sons, and we can begin to experience that in deeply personal ways.

What did you love, and long for as a boy that, as in Gary's case, was stripped, stolen, or lost along the way? Describe.

I loved fishing small streams for trout, but a bad LSD experience as a teen seared that passion from my soul. My love of backpacking and handball were lost as a young man foolishly trying to live as a serious-type "A", with no time for personal pleasure, spiritually minded, exegetically and theologically gifted-and-called, evangelical, sure-to-be mega church pastor, and world renowned spiritual giant whose only rival would be the apostle Paul. Oh, and I gave up my love for 60's classic rock, which no one really walking with God could enjoy. (Craig)

Might God want to resurrect some of these lost joys and treasure as an expression of his heart for you in some way now? What would you love for God to restore to you?

Do you see an opportunity, a provision, or a chance to take one of these lost treasures back?

I've begun to fish again, I'm hoping to restart handball this summer. We'll see how it all unfolds. (Craig)

DISCIPLINE AND FREEDOM

DISCIPLINE IS AN ESSENTIAL PART OF RAISING THE BELOVED SON, AND IT will become an essential part of masculine initiation. I am not the first to point out that children—boys being the subject here—need two basic messages when they are growing up: You are loved more than you can possibly imagine, and, you are not the center of the universe. Without the first, a boy will grow up insecure, uncertain, looking for love and finding it difficult to believe that he is worthy of being loved, even by God. Without the second, he will grow up selfish and self-centered, assuming that everyone else's agenda bows to his own. No doubt you know both sorts of men.

As a young boy, what answers did you hear to the two basic questions every child has: "Am I loved"?

"Am I the center of the universe?" (Can I get my way?)

Discipline teaches us obedience, and immediate and unquestioned obedience is a great gift to endow a boy, a quality of character that will serve him the rest of his life. What importance did discipline have in your home growing up? How did you respond to it then?

My stepdad served a lifetime in the Navy (20+ years) prior to marrying my mom. He'd run a "tight" ship through two major wars and knew a thing or two about discipline. Discipline meant drudgery, chores without praise or reward, zero joy, exacting adherence to directions, and therefore, my being grounded for what felt like totally draconic periods of time. I rebelled, fled, cut corners, and grew to hate my dad (or anyone who expected too much of me, including teachers, coaches, cultures, governments . . . and God). (Craig)

How do you respond to God's discipline now? Do you welcome it? Balk at it or resist it?

Is there a need to confess and repent of your attitude toward God's attempts to raise you into a man?

Would those who know you well use the word "discipline" as one word to describe you?

IT IS AN ESSENTIAL TRUTH OF LIFE TO KNOW AND APPRECIATE THE FACT that the universe does not find you at its center. Rather, it demands things of you, requires you to live within its limits. No matter how much you wail and bellow, the rain will fall, summer will pass into winter, and a two-by-four will hurt you if you drop it on your toe. Welcome to reality. Learn to live within it. How much more true this is for a man before his God. You are loved immensely, and you must obey. That is the secret to Lesson One in the Christian book of spirituality. You are loved; you must obey. This is what the writer of Hebrews was getting at when he encouraged us to see God's discipline as an expression of his love. He cares. (See Heb. 12:5–11.)

At this point how would you answer these two basic questions:
"Am I loved"?

"Am I the center of the universe?"

DISCIPLINE CAN BECOME A RIGID SYSTEM, ESPECIALLY IN A RELIGIOUS HOME. I remember with a shudder a dinner conversation I had several years ago with a man who wanted to inform me of the way he and his family observed the Sabbath. In addition to church in the morning, followed by Sunday school, and church in the evening, he created a rule whereby his young children were not allowed to play in the remaining hours of the day. Rather, he had religious books for them to read, and that was the only permissible activity for the five hours between services, apart from prayer, which was also sanctioned. He told me the plan with no small self-satisfaction, then followed it by a lecture on how most Christians "do *not* observe the Sabbath." I was horrified.

There was something awful in his plan, something severe, made all the more pernicious because it was cloaked under Christianity.

What was the Christianity you were raised with? Describe it. Was it rigid, legalistic, smothering, severe, or lifeless?

If not, fall on your knees and thank God!

If so, how has it affected your ability to believe that God is a good, loving Father and that his heart for you is good, that he sees you as the Beloved Son?

WE NEED A BALANCE TO OUR SYSTEM. DISCIPLINE, AFTER ALL, IS ULTIMATELY the means to freedom. My boys don't clean their rooms so they can do it again; they clean their rooms so they can go *play*.

Let us remember: We are raising *boys*. We ourselves were meant to be raised *as boys*. By our very nature created for adventures and battles and wild places. Created for all the wonder and *freedom* of Eden. (I recall only one command being necessary there.) Discipline is simply to keep our sin from destroying all the life God wants for us. Life is the point.

Life is the point. *Wow.* Is that how you understand Christianity?

What do you think it would be like to be the son of the best father in the world? Would there be life? Joy?

SYMBOLS OF OUR AFFECTION

I BROUGHT A GO-KART HOME THIS SPRING. YOU CAN IMAGINE WHAT A HIT that was. Remember—unlooked-for surprises foster in the boy a belief that a father is a source of wonderful things—something we want them to know about God. The discipline of the go-kart is simple: "Don't run it at 6:00 a.m. when your mother is sleeping. Other than that, go for it." They quickly figured out that if they hit the brakes and turn hard on a slick spot, they can make it do a one-eighty. It wears the tires down. So? I buy a new set of tires.

Again, *life* is the point! Do you find yourself craving and praying for more life?

I love John's statement, "Discipline, after all, is ultimately the means to freedom." I want all the freedom and life God has for me, and my hunch is there is so much more freedom and life available for me in this life than I've imagined. And if discipline is either "a" means or "the" means, I want all the discipline I can muster, because I crave the life and freedom it brings. As I grow in Christ, I'm amazed that I'm beginning to understand holiness as a synonym for freedom (something I would never have imagined 20 years ago as a younger man). (Craig)

THE QUICKEST WAY TO KILL THE SPIRIT OF THE BOY IS THROUGH A RIGID moralism, which lacks any spontaneity, adventure, or freedom. For the boy is both a Cowboy and a Warrior in the making, and as such he needs adventures and dangers in order to thrive. When we provide them, far above and beyond discipline, we develop things in the boy he will later need, things like courage and curiosity, and we demonstrate that we know and love *his* heart.

What is it in the Christianity commonly practiced that has killed your spirit as a boy, as a man?

What areas of freedom or adventure and spontaneity might God want you to move into?

And what will you say to those who question your newfound freedom?

OUR FATHER'S HEART

I WAS WALKING IN THE WOODS YESTERDAY WITH MY FRIEND MORGAN, doing some scouting for elk before the opening of archery season later this month. Though it was a cool, rainy day, still, we did not expect to see any elk, for they rarely come out during the day. Our aim was simply to cover a lot of ground, looking for the signs of their haunts, mapping our way mentally up the mountain so that we might find it later in the dark hours of early morning. But we did see elk—first a cow, by herself in the woods, then my dog, Scout, jumped a calf lying low in a meadow, and then . . . five bulls, grazing together in a stand of aspen just beyond some dark timber. They were breathtaking.

On our way down the mountain Morgan and I were marveling at the gift of it, nearly incredulous, for we have spent a lot of time in the mountains pursuing elk but seen very few up close. Did we really just experience what we just experienced—five glorious bulls, thirty yards from us? At that moment Morgan reached down and picked up a six-point antler. We shook our heads, smiling, laughing. This was God's way of saying, "It was real. They are here." Honestly, I was happy for Morgan. I'd been looking for shed antlers for some time, but hadn't found any, and though I would have loved to have been the one to discover the hidden treasure, I wasn't envious in any way.

After about forty-five minutes of continued descent down the mountain, we broke out into the open sage near where we had parked. As we walked through the sage and tall grass, I looked down, and there lay another antler. I reached down to pick it up, and lifted a six-point antler not only nearly identical to Morgan's, but the mirror image from the left side of the rack. The two could have been a pair. We were . . . speechless. Stopped, literally, in our tracks. Yet another surprise from God. But more. A *sign*. My favor is upon you. You are my Beloved Sons.

I could tell you a hundred stories like that, intimate and unlooked-for ways the Father is trying to get it into my heart how he feels about me. Slowly—I'm sorry to say ever-so-slowly—I am beginning to realize how good the Father's heart really is, and that I do have a place there no one else can take. And so he is raising the heart of the boy in the soul of a forty-five-year-old man.

Father, I need to know that I am your son, and that there is a place for me in your heart no one else can fill. I need to experience your love. Raise the orphaned boy in me. Take me back to those places where I felt so missed, and show me that my heart matters to you. Give me eyes to see and ears to hear how you are raising the heart of the boy in me, raising me in belovedness even now. Heal and restore my soul as a son—as your Beloved Son. Give me the grace to believe it.

And show me now how to offer this to my son—what does he need with me at this time in his life? How might I have missed his heart? How can I come with love and delight now? Lead me, in Jesus' name.

Take a moment and listen now—let God speak. Let your own heart speak too. Ask God, "*What do you have for me, Father? What do you want me to have or to do, to experience being your Beloved Son?*" Write down either what you hear God saying, or simply what you find your heart yearning for. Now—make a plan to go do it!

5

Cowboy

And [the boy] grew in wisdom and stature,
and in favor with God and man.
—Luke 2:52 NIV

BEFORE STARTING

The next two chapters deal with the Cowboy Stage. As we begin, we want to remind you that you can presume falsely that you're past this stage, but be humble and don't presume. God may have some things for you that were missed, lost, or stolen along the way. That has been true for every man we've known. God has more for you.

On the other hand, be alert to the ways and means God was present in your life and how the memories of events, seasons, people, projects, hardships, and joys of your past will affirm how much God *has* done. He wants you to see it and know that he is involved and you may be further along than you know.

"Taking to the road" often plays a big part of the Cowboy (or Ranger) stage, as you see with the hobbits in *The Lord of the Rings*, with Balian in *Kingdom of Heaven*, and with a group of young men in an old Western favorite of mine, *The Cowboys*. John Wayne plays his typical crusty old self, in this case a rancher who can't find enough men to help him drive his herd the four hundred miles to market. He is forced to employ boys in their early to mid-teens, and the story is the coming of age of those boys. They take to the trail together on a high—and dangerous—adventure that calls forth daring and courage, and requires hard work and determination—things a boy-becoming-a-young-man needs to learn in order to face life head-on.

FIRST REACTIONS

As you read through this chapter on the Cowboy, what jumped out at you—new thoughts, questions, an immediate action item? Write out your reaction. What questions are you hoping will be addressed at some point?

KEY POINTS OF THE CHAPTER

- I would set the beginning of the Cowboy (or Ranger) stage in early adolescence—around age twelve or thirteen—and suggest it carries into the mid-twenties. A notable shift begins to take place in the boy's soul as he approaches his teens, a yearning for *real* adventure. Something inside tells him that he needs to prove himself, needs to be tested. And now the Question of a man's soul begins to present itself in nearly everything the boy-becoming-a-young-man does: *Do I have what it takes?* In the Cowboy stage the answer comes partly through adventure, and partly through hard work.
- Men, and boys, learn by *doing*; we learn through experience. The experience is both a revelation and a kind of authoring, in that it reveals to you what you are made of and writes the lesson on your heart.
- Life is hard. While he is the Beloved Son, a boy is largely shielded from this reality. But a young man needs to know that life is hard. Until a man learns to deal with the fact that life is hard, he will spend his days chasing the wrong thing, using all his energies trying to make life comfortable, soft, nice, and that is no way for any man to spend his life.
- The Cowboy heart is wounded in a young man if he is never allowed to have adventure, and it is wounded if he has no one to take him there. It is wounded if he has no confidence-building experiences with work. And on both counts, it is wounded if the adventure or the work is overwhelming, unfit to the heart of the boy, and if he repeatedly fails there.

ON AUGUST 1, 2002, WE FOUND OURSELVES HIGH ON A SOUTHERN RIDGE, in the early morning light, attempting the summit. Named for Glenn Exum, the man who first ascended it—alone and without protection—the Exum ridge is "undeniably one of the most spectacular routes of its grade anywhere in the world" as the guide service has it, with "sensational exposure." Meaning, there are places on the ridge where the drop is two thousand feet or more.

There were eight of us on the ridge, roped together in two teams—my son Samuel (thirteen at the time) and I, Morgan, and our guide. Then Gary and his son Jesse (fifteen), and another young man, Aaron, led by their guide. We climbed the Grand in two teams of four, using a hip belay. In a hip belay the lead climber ascends to a ledge or a shelf or someplace he can stand—or better, sit, his legs braced in front of him against rock so that should his buddy below take a fall he won't be yanked off the mountain himself. It's a choice made in favor of speed, being faster than using various climbing gear to set and then remove fixed protection at every belay station. And speed is one of the nonnegotiables on the Grand. You want to get up and off the peak before there are any signs of the afternoon thunderstorms so common to the West, which bring with them the deadly lightning strikes. The following summer, one climber was killed and several others critically burned by lightning on the Exum Ridge, right about where we were ascending.

Once you commit to the ridge there is no turning back, no down-climbing options available. The only way off is up. The faster the better. It adds to the drama of the climb, facing each tough move with no choice but to do it. Several times I would make a move or climb a section of a pitch and think to myself, *I hope Sam can do this—he's never made a move like that before.*

The expedition was planned as a part of Samuel's "vision quest year," a year devoted to his passage from Beloved Son into young manhood—into the stage of the Cowboy. (I'll tell you more about Sam's initiation in a coming chapter.) But what happened was, it proved to be crucial to every one of our hearts, for every one of us was yet in need of fathering here, in adventure, into a strength and courage we doubted we possessed but desperately wanted to know we had. So I would take my position, signal Sam to climb, and hope and pray that he made each move as I took in the rope that signaled his ascent. My favorite snapshots, most of which are captured in my mind, are of those moments when Sam would appear, big smile on his face, making his approach to my current belay station. We'd trade a quick high five and a word of encouragement, and usually by then Morgan was tugging on my end of his rope to say, "Get going."

What risky adventure of your own past does this story surface, stir in you?

ADVENTURE

I WOULD SET THE BEGINNING OF THE COWBOY (OR RANGER) STAGE IN EARLY adolescence—around age twelve or thirteen—and suggest it carries into the mid-twenties. Though I would be quick to remind you that the stages overlap. What little tike doesn't want adventure, as he races his sled down a hill or learns to climb a tree? What man of fifty doesn't need time away, in the outdoors? But a notable shift begins to take place in the boy's soul as he approaches his teens, a yearning for *real* adventure. Something inside tells him that he needs to prove himself, needs to be tested. He wants to learn how to do things—how to drive a car, to hunt birds, to build a loft in his room. And now the Question of a man's soul begins to present itself in nearly everything the boy-becoming-a-young-man does: *Do I have what it takes?* In the Cowboy stage the answer comes partly through adventure, and partly through hard work.

What was "adventure" in your early adolescence like?

Watching baseball, practicing baseball, playing baseball, fishing, hiking. I wanted to be either a professional ball player or a ranger prowling the High Sierra. In early adolescence life seemed good, fairly safe, and I was still a bit innocent and naïve. (Craig)

Where and how did you try and prove yourself as a teen? How were you tested?

I was good at baseball. To be an annual all-star and admired by the coaches was a young source of validation. Then the validation and testing came through wild, crazy wilderness adventures or surf trips to Mexico or Encinitas without any money. (Craig)

What did you suck at?

Playing musical instruments, math, basketball (which was a bummer—because of my height, everyone assumed I'd be good). (Craig)

What have been some of the memorable adventures of your life . . . those events or circumstances that required more of you than you realized you had? Were there elements of anxiety, fear, or apprehension involved? How did things turn out?

What place does adventure with high stakes play in your life now?

List some of your favorite "guy" movies. Who's the character you'd want to be? Why?

THE POWER OF EXPERIENCE

MEN, AND BOYS, LEARN BY *DOING*; WE LEARN THROUGH EXPERIENCE.

It's one thing to be *told* you have what it takes. It's another thing altogether to *discover* that you have what it takes, through some trial brought up in an adventure, or through some test that hard work demands. For masculine initiation is not a spectator sport. It is something that must be *entered into*. It is one part instruction and nine parts experience.

How has experience, testing, trials, or adventures answered your question, *"Do I have what it takes?"* Can you recall times and events that spoke to your Question as a man? How did it go—for good or for ill?

DAVID IS BARELY A TEEN WHEN HE GOES TO THE CAMP AND SEES THE TERROR that Goliath is inspiring in the Israelite camp. He offers to fight the giant, at which point he is brought before the king, who in turn attempts to dissuade the lad. "You are not able to go out against this Philistine and fight him; you are only a boy, and he has been a fighting man from his youth" (1 Sam. 17:33 NIV). Sound advice, the likes of which I wager any of us would offer under the same circumstances. David replies:

Your servant has been keeping his father's sheep. When a lion or a bear came and carried off a sheep from the flock, I went after it, struck it, and rescued the sheep from its mouth. When it turned on me, I seized it by its hair, struck it, and killed it. Your servant has killed both the lion and the bear; this uncircumcised Philistine will be like one of them, because he has defied the armies of the living God. The LORD who delivered me from the paw of the lion and the paw of the bear will deliver me from the hand of this Philistine. (vv. 34–37 NIV)

Being a shepherd, as I explained earlier, is the Cowboy stage, and David learned lessons here that would carry him the rest of his life. The life of the shepherd was not a sweet little life with lambs around. It was a hard job, out in the field, months camping out in the wild on your own. And it had its effect. There is a settled confidence in the boy—he knows he has what it takes. But it is not an arrogance—he knows that God has been with him. He will charge Goliath, and take his best shot, trusting God will do the rest. That "knowing" is what we are after in the Cowboy Ranger phase, and it only comes through experience. And may I also point out that the experiences David speaks of here were physical in nature, they were dangerous, and they required courage.

Do you find yourself diminishing your life and calling by saying to yourself something along the lines of, "*Pfhh* . . . God would *never* ask something that large of me. And *if* he did, there's *no way I* could do it, no way at all"? If you are hearing these messages, where do you think they are coming from?

The message of my wound is, You are nothing and you have nothing . . . nothing to offer, nothing to say, so sit down and shut up. That lie is the foundation of the adversary's attempts to have me disbelieve and distrust God's heart and my place in his Larger Story. If I give in to the lie (usually by making an agreement with it) I walk off the field and find a cozy seat alongside everyone else on the bench. (Craig)

What is yet to be done in your life so that, like David, you can step into the epic story God has for you?

Younger man, you have a mythic part in God's Larger Story, to play an epic role is what God has for you. Given that, do you see how important your training, your development is?

Older man, have you lived with a small story for most of your life, a story that doesn't require an epic risk? It may be because you missed some of the valuable building blocks God intended you to get in this stage. Are you ready for a Larger Story and all that's required to walk in it?

HARD WORK

I WANT TO BE QUICK TO SAY THAT THE TIME OF THE COWBOY IS *NOT* meant to be merely one of unending adventure. Many fatherless young men find life in some adventure like kayaking or snowboarding, and they stay there and make it their world. They are modern-day Peter Pans, refusing to grow up as men. On the surface they seem alive, and free, and daring. Beneath, they are uncertain and ungrounded. And they have broken the hearts of many young women who loved the adventurer, and didn't understand why he wouldn't go on to be the Warrior, and the Lover, and the King.

Younger men, what makes you feel most "alive" ?

Have you moved beyond the adventures that once consumed you, giving you a sense of transcendence ? What "grown up" things frighten you?

Older men, have you refused to grow up in any area? What "grown up" things are you avoiding?

What in your youth was transcendent for you? What happened to that activity?

THE BALANCE HERE TO ADVENTURE IS THAT THIS SEASON IN A YOUNG MAN'S life is equally a time of learning to work. No doubt David had many adventures in the field, as anyone knows who has spent time outdoors. Adventure has a way of finding you out there. But the context of those months and years was *hard work*. Was Jesus an outdoorsman? We have no record, but we do find him often turning to the wilderness during his ministry years, and it is not a long reach to assume that those walks in the desert and nights on the mountain didn't start out of the blue when he took up the ministry. That he turns there for comfort and refreshment and to be with his Father indicates a history of doing so. We do know he worked in the carpenter's shop, and that is more significant than most profiles of Jesus understand. Working with wood and tools, side by side with your father, does things for a young man that few other situations offer.

Did you have models of men who worked hard growing up?

If so, who were they and what did they do? What did you learn about life from their work ethic?

If not, did you develop a good work ethic or have you struggled when it comes to hard physical work? What impact has this had on you?

List all the physically harder jobs you held. Which were the ones you enjoyed most?

A job unloading cement bags from railroad freight cars. A summer job at a Christian camp in food delivery that required fifteen hour days. Being a warehouse worker. A job hanging sheet rock. Remodeling the interior of a home as a side job. (Craig)

In which jobs did you grow the most? Why?

Both the summer job at the Christian camp and remodeling the interior of a home. Though separated by a few years, both required more of me than anything I had previously done. The summer job was physically exhausting and required a discipline to accomplish. The remodel required me to learn and apply a number of carpentry skills I had no knowledge or experience in. When I was finished the house looked awesome and I felt like I could host a TV home improvement show. It was an incredible experience. (Craig)

LIFE IS HARD. WHILE HE IS THE BELOVED SON, A BOY IS LARGELY SHIELDED from this reality. But a young man needs to know that life is hard, that it won't come to you like Mom used to make it come to you, all soft and warm and to your liking, with icing. It comes to you more the way Dad makes it come to you—with testing, as on a long hike or trying to get an exhaust manifold replaced. Until a man learns to deal with the fact that life is hard, he will spend his days chasing the wrong thing, using all his energies trying to make life comfortable, soft, nice, and that is no way for any man to spend his life.

You can learn this prematurely (as a boy) or too late (as a man of fifty). When did you learn this lesson?

As a young boy without a guide/father/interpreter, the conclusion I came to was not that life is hard, but that life is overwhelming. (Craig)

How has your life been hard?

How have you tried to make life comfortable, soft, nice?

Younger man, is your career path entirely based on a strategy to make life "fun," or is it to live in your giftedness and calling?

Older man, what is it you want in retirement . . . comfort or impact?

UNDEVELOPED AND WOUNDED

THE COWBOY HEART IS WOUNDED—OR AT LEAST, UNDEVELOPED, BUT MORE often wounded—in a young man if he is never allowed to have adventure, and it is wounded if he has no one to take him there. It is wounded if he has no confidence-building experiences with work. And on both counts, it is wounded if the adventure or the work is overwhelming, unfit to the heart of the boy, and if he repeatedly fails there.

In the area of adventure:
Were you wounded or are you undeveloped by not having adventure as a young man?

Or was all the adventure you had either overwhelming, unfit for your heart, or an experience of repeated failures?

Do you have adventure in your life now? Are you comfortable playing sports with men or going on a trip with some men who are adventurers? If not, might that be because you were wounded in this stage?

I BELIEVE I'VE TOLD THE STORY BEFORE OF A MAN I KNEW WHOSE MOTHER would not let him, as a boy, ride on a roller coaster. He could see it there, day after day, because they lived across an empty field from the amusement park. But he could never win permission to join his friends in the adventure. That is emasculating, and it applies to those parents who never let their boys ride bikes on a dirt path, forbid them to climb a tree or jump on a trampoline, keep them indoors most of the time. They might say they are only acting out of love and concern for the boy, but the message is, "You'll get hurt. You can't handle it. You don't have what it takes." Often this is the voice of the mother, whose nature is mercy but who must learn to let her son face danger.

When have you heard the words of caution quoted above? In what areas of your life do you still hear them?

FOR THAT MATTER, A BOY IS WOUNDED WHEN HIS PARENTS SIMPLY LET HIM live in front of the TV, or the computer, or the video games young men love. I have nothing against computers or video games per se (with the added warning that some games are very wicked in their content and ought to be sent to the Abyss). In general they are benign, and boys love them because they work in the same way a boy's brain works, with spatial relationships and all that, but I am *very* concerned when they take the substitute of a *real* adventure.

In his study of the development of male homosexuality, Joseph Nicolosi is especially worried about the boys who are too frightened to go outside and play with the other lads in the neighborhood. He calls them "kitchen window" boys, who stay inside and merely watch. Some boys are more inherently fearful than others; some are made fearful by overprotective parents. Either way, it is a wound to let a boy stay there.

It is emasculating to shelter a young man from everything dangerous.

How sheltered were you? How do you currently avoid danger? Why?

YES, THERE ARE RISKS INVOLVED, AND AS THE YOUNG MAN MOVES INTO HIS mid- to late teens, those bodily risks increase dramatically. I don't let my sons go ninety miles an hour on an ATV, though they would like to. There is wisdom in parenting, but we must accept the fact that there is risk also. You might recall the line from the movie *Seabiscuit*, during the debate of whether to let Red even ride again after his accident, because he might further injure himself. It is another jockey who warns them, "It's better to break a man's leg than it is to break his heart."

On the other hand, I just heard the story of a young man this weekend who worked with his father on a ranch when he was growing up. They spent their summers in the high country, at a cow camp with no running water, and they'd climb in the saddle before dawn and ride until after dark. The father brought no food or water along, and when the boy complained of thirst the father would tell him to "suck on a rock." The boy was ten years old. That is abuse of the first order, putting a boy through paces that would break a grown man. When it comes to work, the principles are the same. Too little is a wound, as is too much.

We hope, as you are reading this, you're aware that nobody gets through their youth without being wounded. This reality is not meant to take you to depression, cynicism, or hopelessness. Rather, as we begin to see our woundedness and its impact, we can look to God for the redemption and restoration that are central to the very heart and mission of God. It's amazing that what we want to deny or minimize is the very thing that can open the door to the life we were designed and desire to live.

In the area of work:
Would you have described yourself as a confident teenager? Why or why not?

Would you describe yourself as confident now? Confident in broad terms, or is it a confidence in selected areas (your job, or hobby etc.)?

Are you comfortable handling tools, fixing things around the house?

Were you wounded or are you undeveloped because of not having confidence-building experiences with work as a young man? Or was all the work experience you had either overwhelming, unfit for your heart, or an experience of repeated failures?

A YOUNG MAN'S HEART IS WOUNDED WHEN HE HAS NO ONE TO TAKE HIM into the adventures his soul craves, no one to show him how to shoot a free throw or jump his bike or rock climb or use a power tool. This is how most young men experience fatherlessness—there is no man around who cares and who is strong enough to lead him into anything. His father might be physically present, but unavailable in every way, hiding behind a newspaper or spending hours at the computer while the young man waits for the father who never comes. Much of the anger we see in young men comes from this experience, because he is ready and fired up but has no outlet, no place to go. So it comes out in anger. And a young man's heart is wounded when he repeatedly fails. Of course, failure is a part of learning and every cowboy gets thrown from his horse, so to speak. But there needs to be someone at his side to *interpret* the failures and setbacks, to urge him to get back on the horse.

Who have you had in your life to interpret the failures and setbacks, to urge you to "get back on the horse"?

Looking back, my stepdad was a good man. Battle-scarred (literally from two wars) and overwhelmed with the requirements of an adoptive dad and providing for five kids, I have nothing but compassion for him. Nonetheless, I was wounded, and for his every wound I have fully forgiven him. He simply wasn't present for me. But there were two men who were at the time. One was an uncle (Uncle Willy) who loved life, had a sense of humor, was incredibly fun to be with, and had a ton of patience. The other was a family friend, Don Dickson. I experienced him as a strong man who was interested in me. He asked questions, was sincere, and invited me into adventures and conversations no one else did. Neither of these men saw my failures, rebellion, or shortcomings as an obstacle to relationship or maturity. As I write this, I want to tell Don the role he played in my life, and my guess is that he has no idea. (My Uncle died several years ago.) (Craig)

If you don't have an interpreter, what have you done with your failures?

Assumed there's something wrong with you?

Blamed God?

Gone to resignation or disengagement with life and/or God, others?

Developed a strategy of self-protection?

IF YOU AREN'T THE BELOVED SON, THE TESTING THAT COMES WITH THIS stage can feel unkind, cruel, a sort of rejection—especially if you are on your own.

The masculine soul needs the trials and adventures and experiences that bring a young man to the *settled confidence* David showed before Goliath—the lion and the bear experiences. All of these experiences of the Cowboy stage are driving at one basic goal: to answer his Question. The boy-becoming-a-young-man has a Question, and the Question is, "Do I have what it takes?" It is a father's job to help him get an answer, a resounding *Yes!* that the boy himself believes because it has come through experience. The father provides initiation by arranging for moments—through hard work and adventure—when the Question is on the line, and in those moments help the young man hit it right out of the park. The father is to speak into his son's heart deep affirmation. *Yes, you do. You have what it takes.* He needs a hundred experiences that will help him get there, and he is wounded and emasculated when he is kept from those experiences, or left on his own to interpret them, or when no one is there to help him succeed.

Father, take me back, back to the Cowboy stage and finish the unfinished business I need here in my soul as a man. Heal the wounded Cowboy in me. Take me into adventure and danger, and hard work. Simple work. Take me into the shop and into the field, to the places where the soul of a young man is made strong. Father me here.

And give me the grace to father my sons, and the young men around me, as true Cowboys. Help me to initiate them, even as you are initiating me.

A PAUSE IN THE JOURNEY

an opportunity to reflect on the ground you've just covered

So, as you finish this chapter, what do you sense God saying to you about being the Cowboy? Capture that thought now, for it will be quickly forgotten or stolen.

6

Raising the Cowboy

Be men of courage; be strong.
—1 Corinthians 16:13 NIV

BEFORE STARTING

Before you dive into this chapter, and all it will rouse in you, is there any more time, thoughts, or prayers, that would deepen the impact of the previous chapter? Before you begin to work through this chapter of the manual, consider:

- The temptation will come to kind of breeze through this second chapter on the Cowboy. The notion that you've already spent a considerable amount of time and soul work could lead you to the mistaken notion that you're finished on this topic. There's more. More for you as a Cowboy. Don't get distracted.
- While there is much in this chapter about *raising* or *fathering* a Cowboy that a dad will immediately relate to and benefit from, the exercises are written from the perspective that every man still needs fathering. This is about *you* as a Cowboy.
- What movies, books, or stories come to mind that have a good model of a Cowboy?

FIRST REACTIONS

As you've done previously, what's your first reaction to this chapter?

KEY POINTS OF THE CHAPTER

- You have a strength, and it is needed. When you feel that to be true of yourself you will rise up and engage like a man.
- The stages of your life build on one another, and a good foundation of mercy and unconditional love needs to have been laid in your soul as a boy so that your transition into the Cowboy does not feel overwhelming, or premature, or unkind.
- Adventure calls us out and builds confidence. You need adventure.
- The heart of a man hungers to be part of something epic. You need an epic story.
- There is a humility and a seasoned wisdom to be learned in the natural world. You need an encounter with nature.
- A man needs a fellowship of men to help him interpret his failures. You need a fellowship of men.
- Hard work gives a man a sense of strength and confidence. You need hard work.

WE HAVE A TRADITION OF DOING A FLOAT TRIP DOWN THE SNAKE RIVER for a day, a beautiful float through some gorgeous country, with the occasional moose or buffalo along the banks, and eagles in the trees. There is always a lunch stop on a sandy beach where we hike back up the river about a quarter mile and jump in with our life jackets on, floating down in the bracing water like a flock of ducks or a pack of otters. As for canoeing, when the boys were young they simply rode along in the middle of the canoes; then, around the age of twelve or thirteen, they got to take a turn at the bow, putting their strength into the paddling; finally, two years ago, we asked the older boys—Sam and Jesse, fifteen and seventeen—to pilot their own canoes, with passengers, since they were both capable at this point and the experienced ones in the group.

The only real white water on the trip comes at the end, and, given that our canoes are usually loaded down with people and coolers, we typically swing around the worst of it. This summer, however, we decided—at the last moment, about a hundred yards upriver—to run it head-on. Blaine, Luke, and I were in the first canoe, and though we took on a little water, we shot right through. Stasi and Sam were behind, and they hit the big wave in the middle at just the wrong angle, so that their canoe rolled, pitching Mom, son, cooler, and gear all over the river. Sam swam after most of the gear and had brought it to shore by the time I got my canoe landed. But Stasi was trying to rescue their canoe, now submerged, and was floating by us fast, headed past the last take-out spot and into stronger white water below. In a flash Sam was back in the water, swimming strongly for her, and once he got hold of the canoe he pulled it to shore, freeing Stasi to swim on her own. Meanwhile, Blaine went to help her.

The rescue was a great moment, for both boys were seen for what they had become—young men—and their strength was needed and they came through.

Have you had a "great moment" where your strength was needed and you came through? Describe it.

THE SHAPING POWER OF ADVENTURE

You have a strength, and it is needed. When a man feels that to be true of him, he rises up and engages like a man. What are your strengths? Or what would you like them to be?

(If you're having a difficult time identifying your strengths, this is probably a stage you're either going to enter or revisit, because that is very much what you discover in the Cowboy stage.)

Knowing and believing you have a strength is one thing; believing that your strength is really needed is another.

As a boy begins to become a young man, there are some key issues at stake. He needs to know he possesses a genuine strength, and he needs to know that strength is ultimately for others.

Where or for whom is your strength currently needed? What's at stake, or what will be lost if you don't offer it?

THERE IS A BRAVERY THAT MUST BE CULTIVATED IN HIM, FOR IT WILL BE called upon in every other stage of his life. Adventure comes into play to develop the masculine soul, because adventure calls us out, requires us to be something we want to be but aren't sure we are. Adventure nourishes and strengthens a man's heart in ways that cannot be articulated, must be experienced. It works like nothing else I know.

What adventures has God, is God, using to call you out and validate your bravery and courage? Are there any?

If you cannot think of any, are you willing to ask him to strengthen your heart through adventure? If so, ask him now.

Older men, how has your courage, your bravery, developed over the years through the various stages of life?

Where do you feel frightened or uncertain, as a man?

Are there "adventures" you are avoiding—adventures you very much need in order to face those fears?

AS I EXPLAINED IN *WILD AT HEART*, ADVENTURE IS A SPIRITUAL LONGING set in the heart of every man. Adam wasn't created in Eden; he was created from the dust of the earth, in the outback. And notice that in the tales told in Scripture, whenever God gets hold of a man he takes that man into an adventure of the first order. Abraham, called out of Ur, to follow this God to a land he has never seen, never to return. Jacob, wrestling with God in the wilderness in the dead of night. Peter, called out of the boat to Christ in a raging storm. Paul, called out of his prominent role as the ultimate Jew, to become apostle to the Gentile world of east Asia. The stories of his journeys are one narrow escape after another.

What kind of adventures do you long for (or did you long for, as a younger man)?

There are adventures we choose for ourselves and then there are adventures God chooses for us. What adventures has God, or might God, choose for you that you might not choose for yourself?

What have you interpreted as a "trial" that God might have intended as an "adventure" to promote your growth?

In standing up for a team, I led a much needed opening of Pandora's box of dysfunctional church leadership. The following two years of conflict over the character, qualifications, and calling of the senior pastor which led to the dismantling of the Pastoral Staff was the most brutal trial of my character, integrity, and heart to date. The far reaching impact of this season forever altered my family, friendships, and view of the church. It most definitely was a trial. And, at the same time, it was a once-in-a-lifetime season of God initiating me, validating me, and inviting me into an epic story that transcends the severe losses. (Craig)

Older men, what unwelcomed adventures do you look back on as the times of incredible growth and validation?

TEDDY ROOSEVELT'S STORY WOULD BE WORTH READING. HIS LIFE AS A BOY was emasculating—overweight, pampered rich, poor eyesight. His mother even dressed him as a girl when he was young. When he began to come into manhood, he knew he needed to develop *as* a man, knew he needed initiation. He left the refined culture of the upper-class East Coast elite and headed west, bought a ranch in what was then simply called the Dakotas. He began to camp, ride horseback, hunt, not only for the personal pleasure they brought him but for the *effect* it all had on his soul. Eventually he became a big-game hunter in Africa, bringing down bull elephants and male lions on the charge, only moments from his own death.

Let the man who thinks himself "average" take special note—Roosevelt, a man who struggled with his weight, had poor eyesight, and was never initiated by his father, was able to develop that confidence we see in David before Goliath. He went and found initiation, and embraced it. Too many men I know missed the Cowboy stage; too many boys are not being guided through it. So we must go back and pick up where we left off, intentionally, as Roosevelt did. He went on to become a Warrior, by the way, a Lover and a great King, in my opinion, and all that was built on this Cowboy stage.

John said, *"Too many men I know missed the Cowboy stage; too many boys are not being guided through it."* Younger man, who could you turn to as a guide through this stage in your life?

Like Teddy Roosevelt, what would it look like for you to go out and find it now, to embrace initiation?

Older guys, have you missed much of the Cowboy Stage?

Like Teddy Roosevelt, what would it look like for you to go out and find it now, to embrace initiation?

NOW, THE SCALE AND NATURE OF THE ADVENTURE NEED TO FIT THE BOY, and the man, fit his stage of the journey. Ride in the canoe; paddle in the bow; pilot one yourself. There is a progression. Take the boy into adventure, and give him an increasing measure of freedom and responsibility there. My boys just headed out for a night on the mountain behind our house. I looked out the window as they were gearing up—meaning, gathering as many snacks as they could carry—and I saw thunderstorms rolling in. I offered them the use of my four-season Northface tent. "We've got a tarp—we'll be okay." "A *tarp*?!" I urged wisdom, warned that they'd be wet and miserable if they didn't take the tent. "Dad," Sam said, "how can we learn from our mistakes if you don't let us make any?" Right.

But make sure the test or trial fits the young man's heart.

What are some of the "foolish mistakes" you've made as a cowboy? What did you learn?

A friend wanted to do a sort of passage event for his son, who was fourteen, so he arranged for some men to join him and his son on a wilderness trek. The boy asked his father, "What is this all about?" and the father said, "It's about your becoming a man." The boy replied, "I don't want to be a man. I want to be a boy." His story leading up to the event had been full of wounds, and the father knew he was a great part of that. His absence from the boy's life, his own brokenness and sin as a man, had forced the boy to be responsible too young in life. And though the father had repented and begun to live as a truly good father, the boy needed some recovery. He needed to be the Beloved Son he did not get to be, and in his case the invitation into the Cowboy stage was premature.

The stages build on one another, and a good foundation of mercy and unconditional love needs to be laid in the soul of the boy so that this transition does not feel overwhelming, or premature, or unkind.

The adventures and work that we choose must fit the soul of the boy. One young man's adventure would be terrifying to another.

How have you seen the mercy and love of God in the adventures and tests he has brought you?

As I grow in my relationship with him, more and more I see his heart of mercy and love lurking in all that I do. Sometimes it's immediate, and sometimes I see it a little later. Last month, I attended a military funeral for a good friend's father at Arlington National Cemetery. God showed up and I felt like I was six years old attending my father's funeral, God gently nudging me out of grief and more into life. The following weekend, I visited my folks in Northern California. As I was driving the rental car through Gold Country, God showed up and spoke to so many questions that have been haunting me lately with a volume and clarity I'm not familiar with, speaking as a father would. The following week, I was mountain biking in Moab. I was busting my butt, pedaling up and down mountains with a few of my closest friends, and suddenly God was there, returning to me a gift that got misplaced somewhere down the road—strenuous adventure with other men. I've never been happier. (Craig)

To miss the genuine heart of God for you in all that unfolds may indicate more is needed in knowing you are the Beloved Son. To see this is God's kind guidance to what is most needed at this point in your journey.

AN OBSTACLE TO THE JOURNEY

something that could hinder your journey

Now, I need to clarify something. The place of adventure in a man's journey is very, very important. Unfortunately, we live at a time when adventure has become big business. Magazines are filled with photo essays of the latest gear, the coolest places, the most extreme adventurers—men and women kayaking off waterfalls, kite boarding, looking for the ultimate big waves. Much of this adventure is not initiation at all; it tends to be merely exotic (often extreme) play, nothing more than adolescent indulgence. The characters that often fill these pages are postmodern Peter Pan types.

Without a *context*, adventure is for the most part . . . just adventure. Nothing wrong with it per se, but I know from experience, and you can hear in an honest interview with professional adventurers, that it is empty.

A VISTA JOURNEY

a view or rabbit trail that enhances the journey

There are levels of adventure, from casual to crucial to critical. Casual adventures are mostly what fill the pages of those magazines. I believe they *can* develop a boy and a man for more important adventures, and they can be a key part of initiation *if they have a context*, and *if they are intended to be a first step* toward more important adventures. You don't go from being a couch potato to a strong man in a day. But we mustn't get the idea that masculinity is just one outing after another.

SOMETHING EPIC

IN THE SURFING CULTURE, WHEN YOUNG SURFERS HAVE A DAY OF uncommonly big waves and high adventure, they call it "epic." As in, "It was epic, man. You had to be there."

So much of the thrill-seeking we see in young men is a search for a deeper experience, one that is spiritual in nature, though they don't know how to put words to it. Notice that as a boy grows older, his longing for adventure typically grows more extreme.

He is seeking something epic. Just look at the movies young men love—the *Star Wars* films, *Braveheart*, *Gladiator*, the *Matrix* films, *Black Hawk Down*, *The Lord of the Rings*. The heart of a young man hungers to be part of something epic.

What epic movies stir you? And why?

Saving Private Ryan, Glory, Gladiator, Braveheart. In each movie, the hero/main character is caught up in something larger than his own safety and comfort. For others he gives up his life . . . what's more epic than that? (Craig)

What epic adventure were you a part of earlier in life? What epic adventures lure you? Do you see a search for God in that?

WE NEED TO HELP HIM FIND IT IN CHRISTIANITY. WE NEED TO FIND IT with God ourselves. So many times we miss this yearning in a young man's life by telling him to "calm down," when what we should be doing is hooking that yearning up to God. Now, "going to church" does not meet this need. It can help to *convey* an epic story, if that is the Christianity being offered there, but in and of itself going to church is not the Epic Story, nor does it alone suffice to communicate that Story. The spirituality we offer a young man must be epic, or we'll lose him.

Younger man, how have you been told to "calm down" with your yearning for an epic adventure/spirituality?

As an older man, what have you done with the desire to be a part of an epic? Buried it? Denied it? Labeled it "fleshly" and killed it? Substituted it for something else?

MY ADVICE IN THIS REGARD IS THREEFOLD.

First, take a look at the Christianity you are living. Is it epic? Or is it just good morals and a few prayers?

Remember that in the Scriptures, whenever God gets hold of a man he takes him into an epic story, one full of danger and drama and meaning. Abraham, Joseph, David, Jesus' disciples, Saul. The stories we read there are not meant to simply impress us with another man's life. There are examples of what can happen when we abandon ourselves to God—which for any man means, among other things, that we stop hedging our bets, playing it safe.

Second, when it comes to raising a young man, it is crucial that his father's life (and Christianity) be epic at heart.

Have you abandoned yourself to God?

I am abandoning (present tense) myself to God. It seems both like a genuine daily reorientation, and an occasional deeper experience that takes place several times over the seasons of a man's life. God is asking me for an abandoning of new places previously unexposed. I want to be fully surrendered, totally yielded and am asking God to take me there. (Craig)

If so, was it hard to stop hedging your bets and playing it safe?

It is both the easiest and most difficult thing to do. (Craig)

If you haven't abandoned yourself to God, what do you fear in doing so? What does your hesitancy say of your belief in God's heart toward you?

Old or young, have you heard the messages *"It's not time to make a change; Just sit down, take it slowly; You're still young; There's so much you have to go through"*? If so, what has that done to your heart, your confidence that you have what it takes?

THE ROLE OF NATURE

A NUMBER OF MEN HAVE WRITTEN TO ME THAT AT FIRST THEY WOULD NOT read *Wild at Heart* because they "don't go for all that outdoor stuff." They love the city, not the wilderness. They'd rather spend a Saturday reading or going to the movies. They never hunt, have no desire to. They work indoors, in an office, and enjoy it. Yet they went on to tell me that upon reading *Wild at Heart*, they discovered a great deal for their soul, and realized that the themes of the masculine heart *are* universal. For that I am grateful. And I want to say that it is not necessary that a man become a mountaineer, a hunter, or a whitewater rafting guide to experience what I am describing in this book.

However, there is something vital and, yes, necessary for the masculine soul that can be found only in wilderness.

What is your reaction to the thoughts in the preceding excerpt?

FIRST, IT WOULD BE GOOD TO REMEMBER THAT THE WORLD OF NATURE IS the world God created and set us in. The created world, with all its beauty and diversity and wildness, this is the world God intended for us to live in relationship to. Scripture makes it clear that many lessons are woven into the fabric of that world, lessons God intended nature to teach us. As Paul said, "For since the creation of the world God's invisible qualities—his eternal power and divine nature—have been clearly seen, being understood from what has been made, so that men are without excuse" (Rom. 1:20 NIV).

What have you discovered of God in wilderness? Or, why haven't you been drawn to the wilderness?

THERE IS A HUMILITY AND A SEASONED WISDOM TO BE LEARNED *IN* THE natural world, as they are learned no other place. Yes, I have learned humility from my computer. But it pales in comparison to all I have learned from the mountains. And there are many other lessons there too.

A LENS OF LIFE FOR THE JOURNEY

There is a way things work. That is one of the great lessons nature has for us. *There is a way things work.* You cannot simply walk through this world any old way you want. Turn a canoe sideways and it will tip. Approach an elk upwind and it will spook. Run your hand along the grain of wood and you'll get a splinter. *There is a way things work.* Oh, what a crucial lesson this is for a man. In the realm of nature, you can't just order room service, or change the channel, or write a new program to solve your problems. You can't ignore the way things work. You must be taught by it. Humility and wisdom come to a man when he learns those ways, and learns to live his life accordingly.

On the other hand, the artificial world is a world that is primarily under our control. And that's why we like it—we men like to have things under our control. Remote control, whenever possible. But that is not good for the masculine soul, nor is it good for a man's spirituality. God is not under our control, and one of the ways a boy and a young man come to begin to realize that is through the natural world. It is big enough, and bold enough, and awe-inspiring enough to begin a sort of fundamental reorientation. You are not the center of the universe. There are forces that command your respect. Learning to live in harmony with them is essential to your survival, not to mention your happiness. So you find that nearly all masculine initiation done down through the centuries took the young men *outside*, for long periods of time.

What immediately comes to mind as something that is out of your control?

SO, YES, I AM SAYING THAT AN ENCOUNTER WITH THE NATURAL WORLD—THE world God set us in—is essential for masculine initiation. I'm not saying that every man needs to love to fish and hunt. But yes—there are things to learn through nature, lessons that simply cannot be learned anywhere else. It might be out on the open sea. It might take place bicycling through farmlands. Does this mean that a man who loves the city cannot enter into masculine initiation and maturity? Not at all. C. S. Lewis was not an outdoorsman. He spent his days with books, in the academies of England. But I find it important that he felt his day was never complete without a walk outside. Not a fifty-mile backpacking trip. A walk in the woods. Time spent in the field. It's worth a try, and I'll guarantee God will meet you there, if you'll let him.

Where are the woods, field, beach, park, or stream you could enjoy and learn lessons from?

Prior to reviewing the next chapter, can you spend some time in nature and simply observe, listen, and learn?

INITIATION

Read the story of Luke's initiation through horseback riding on pages 104–106 in *The Way of the Wild Heart.* Remember how I said that the Cowboy heart is wounded when he repeatedly fails, or when there isn't anyone there to *interpret* his failures and help him get back on the horse? How much of your life have you been misinterpreting?

I've given my wounds and failures a large podium to speak of shame and condemnation while diminishing the weightiness of my strengths and gifts. (Craig)

How many things have you just written off as hassle or "life is hard," or even as warfare, when in fact God was in it, in the difficulty, wanting to Father you?

What's the "horse" God would have you remount?

Can God come through in this area?

AS A FELLOWSHIP OF MEN

Read this section in the book again. What do the accounts of these young men being surrounded by a company of men stir in you?

Does the story of Walt Harrington, an older man who found a fellowship of men he would never have expected to, give you hope?

FAR TOO MUCH HAS FALLEN ON THE SHOULDERS OF THE FATHER ALONE. IT takes a company of men to bring a boy into the masculine world, and to bring young men along in their maturity.

The fellowship of those old hunters changed Harrington's life. Rescued him. And he's the first to admit how rare masculine fellowship is. I've been intentional about fighting for friendships with men over the years—you have to be, to find them and keep them.

Who's your company of men?

Many men desire this yet have great difficulty finding it. Leaning into the good heart of your Father, why don't you ask him something along these lines:

Father, my heart's desire is to be among a fellowship of men whose lives and words will draw me deeper and deeper into a relationship with you and the masculinity you have for me. Open my eyes to these men as you bring them across my path.

HARD WORK

Read this section again in its entirety on pages 109–111 in *The Way of the Wild Heart.*

NOW, THERE IS A RHYTHM TO THE EARTH, AND TO MAN'S LIFE UPON IT. AT its best, the rhythm is a harmony of Discipline and Freedom. Harvest and Sabbath. School year and summer vacation. Monday mornings and Friday nights. Clean your room and go out to play. We teach a boy—and we who are being initiated also learn this most vital lesson—by mixing the years of the Cowboy with both adventure and hard work.

The wisdom for adventure is the same for work—where is the hesitation in the boy or man? Go there. What will develop in him a sense of strength, and courage, and confidence? Go there. And finally, how will you counter that essential selfishness inherent to man, how will you teach him to serve others?

What could you do, where could you "go," this week/month that would be exposing yourself to initiation in terms of hard work? (You older guys might want to clean your own carpets, as a way of accepting some initiation, and not just pay to have someone else do it for you.)

Dang! Suddenly a whole list of things I've been assuming I'd hire out come to mind! (Craig)

AS HARRINGTON LEARNED THE LESSONS OF THE FIELD, HE BEGAN TO SEE HOW he had missed all sorts of opportunities for masculine initiation over the course of his adult life:

I didn't even know how to replace my own car muffler. When I came to own a house, I wasted money on plumbers to fix leaky faucets and electricians to repair broken light switches. I hired a nursery to lay down the landscaping and a gardener to trim and tidy it all up twice a year. Even if he could have afforded it, my father would never have ceded so much mastery of his world over to hired hands. But I had done what young men in America are supposed to do. I had risen in society. I had eaten dinner with the president. Funny, but despite my social ascent, my simple and deepest hope came to be that I could teach Matt [his son] some of what my father had taught me about being a man. He taught me that a man kills and eats animals. Animals bleed. Live with it. He taught me that a man strives to master his world, whatever that world is. He doesn't sit and whine—he acts. Most important, a man is never powerless, no matter how powerless he is. Maybe that philosophy is rooted in hard circumstances, but its noble qualities of grace and strength, resilience and eccentricity are self-evident. (The Everlasting Stream)

React to Harrington's observations.

What are some skills you wish you'd learned as a Cowboy that you would love to learn now?

How can you put yourself in a context to learn them (take a woodshop class, ask a neighbor or uncle, just give it a try)?

MENTORS AND GUIDES

NOW, I KNOW, I KNOW. IF IT HASN'T HAPPENED YET, IT WILL HIT AGAIN SOON, and hard, right in the lonely place in your heart—"But who will do this for me? For my fatherless son? How can I find this now that I am thirty-eight . . . or sixty-two?"

Who will do this for you?

Does your answer reflect despair, resignation, a determination to make it on your own, or a turning to God?

My answer has irritated many men, and I don't know why. God. Your Father will do this for you. Are you irritated by my response? Why or why not?

I'VE SEEN SO MANY MEN WALK AWAY DISAPPOINTED WHEN I'VE TOLD THEM this. Perhaps it was from an unhealed father wound. Perhaps they don't realize that there is an intimacy available with God far better, much closer than what they've heretofore experienced. But my brothers, do not despair. God *wants* to father you. Has been fathering you for sometime—you just haven't had the eyes to see it. In fact, even the best father can only take you so far. He was never meant to be your all-in-all. Rather, he was meant to bring you to *the* Father.

A man who's gone through the Cowboy stage knows this to be true. Do you?

If you found this to be true, that God wants to father you and is, indeed a good father, what does this stir in your heart for him? Express it. And if you don't yet know this, then ask God to come and father you here—as a Cowboy (no matter your age!).

GOD WILL, AT TIMES, PROVIDE MEN TO "FILL IN THE GAPS." THE FISHING guide along the South Platte being one of a hundred stories I could tell. I learned to work on my Squareback by watching a mechanic I'd take it to, and talking with him about it. I learned to climb from another man, learned to love Shakespeare from my high-school drama teacher. Some of my mentors have been dead for years—C. S. Lewis and George MacDonald, Saint John of the Cross and Thomas à Kempis. I've learned so much from them. It comes to us in many ways. You might find a mentor to walk you personally through many stages, but we all know by now that he's hard to find. Don't insist that it come from one man.

Who are the men God has provided for you to "fill in the gaps"?

John Muir, A.W. Tozer, a part-time college professor of American History (I've forgotten his name), Larry Crabb, Gerald May, Kevin Huggins, D. Martyn Lloyd-Jones, John Eldredge, Stephen Ambrose. (Craig)

MY EXPERIENCE—CONFIRMED BY THE STORIES TOLD ME BY MANY MEN—IS that God mostly wants to do our initiating directly, personally, himself. He wants the same relationship with us that Jesus—as a man—experienced with him during his journey on this earth. Remember—you *are* the son of a kind, strong, and engaged Father, a Father wise enough to guide you in the Way, generous enough to provide for your journey, offering to walk with you every step. Whatever else might *seem* true, this is what is *most* true.

IT IS HAPPENING ALL THE TIME

WHAT SEEMED LIKE A BAD NIGHT BROUGHT ON BY THE *LACK* OF MASCULINE wisdom and strength turned out to be an act of initiation, an *affirmation* of masculinity. It wasn't just trial and hardship. God was in it, and his interpretation of it allowed this man to hear words we all long to hear. I believe this sort of thing is happening in our lives more often than we know, and *will* happen even more clearly as we allow God to take us back through stages like the Cowboy to finish what needs to be finished in us.

Can you see this happening in your life now, or maybe in the past year? What hardships have you been going through? Ask God what he is up to with it—in terms of your initiation.

Father, take me there. Take me back to things that were lost, or unfinished, or never even started. Take me into the Cowboy phase and do this work in my soul. Father me here. Give me eyes to see, both where you have been fathering me and I didn't know it, and where you are initiating me now, though I might be misinterpreting it. I want to be brave and true. I want a strength, and I want to offer it to others. Lead me on.

And help me to offer this to my sons, and the men you have brought into my life. Give me eyes to see what they need, and creativity in offering just that. Show me how to help them in their journeys, even though mine is still very much under way.

A PAUSE IN THE JOURNEY

an opportunity to rest/reflect on the ground you've just covered

- The last two chapters have dealt with the Cowboy Stage. In your own words, summarize what it means to be the Cowboy.

- While the stages overlap, and there is some aspect of them in every phase of a man's life, there is also a time in a man's life when one of the stages is prominent. Is this stage, is the Cowboy:

  A stage you anticipate going through in the future?
  The stage you think you're currently in?
  Did this read like a map for the journey you're currently on?
  Or a stage you feel you have passed through?

With heart and eyes wide open, be keen to all God has for you. He will affirm, validate, convict, heal, and call you more deeply into all the lessons and growth he has for you in this stage of life. And you, as well, don't prematurely assume you're ready to move on. God orders the seasons of a man's life and in his perfect way, your graduation *will* come.

Did God remind you of the people, events, hardships, and joys of this stage to affirm that indeed you have passed through this stage well. And while saying that, be willing to allow God to speak of the "more" he'd like to do in you as a Cowboy. You may as well find a number of things you missed in this stage . . . The good news is that it's never too late. Be expectant, there's more for you.

7

Sam's Year

And the child grew and became strong; he was filled with wisdom, and the grace of God was upon him.

—Luke 2:40 NIV

BEFORE STARTING

In this chapter, John tells the story of Sam's Vision Quest year, in hopes that it might serve both as an example for ritual and effort, and as a sort of parable to shed light on what God may be calling us to experience even as men of thirty-one or seventy-two.

As the father of a son(s), you'll be keenly aware of either the possibility of doing something similar for your young son, or if you're the father of an older son, perhaps even an adult son, you'll no doubt be thinking of what you could still do to validate him as a father.

However, this chapter is a model of what God wants to do (and is doing) in your life to initiate you. And, it is also an inspiration for what you could do yourself—for your own journey and perhaps with a few men you know.

FIRST REACTIONS

What did this story of Sam's year stir up in you? What are your reactions, thoughts, impressions, or questions?

KEY POINTS OF THE CHAPTER

- The masculine journey has many mile markers to it, many critical moments of transition. One of *the* most significant is that point in time when a boy leaves behind him the stage of boyhood, and enters into the world of men. I believe this takes place early in the Cowboy stage, and I believe it is one of those transitions meant to have far more intentionality given to it than most of us experienced.
- A "vision quest" ought to involve ritual and effort, a variety of tests and challenges, love and validation.
- Our guide is the Holy Spirit, whom the early Celtic Christians like Patrick called the Wild Goose. They knew he could not be tamed. Ours is merely to trust and follow his haunting call, and he will take us on the adventure he has for us. "Those who are led by the Spirit of God are sons of God."
- A man's need for validation is one of his most desperate longings. Until we have that validation, we live with an uncertainty down deep inside. As men, we need to know who we truly are, and what we are destined to become. And the only really reliable source for that is the God who made us. So we need to hear from God what *he* thinks of us. (John 17:6, 11–12 NIV)

THE MASCULINE JOURNEY HAS MANY MILE MARKERS TO IT, MANY CRITICAL moments of transition. One of *the* most significant is that point in time when a boy leaves behind him the stage of boyhood, and enters into the world of men. I believe this takes place early in the Cowboy stage, and I believe it is one of those transitions meant to have far more intentionality given to it than most of us experienced. "The ancient societies believed that a boy becomes a man only through ritual and effort—only through the 'active intervention of the older men,'" as Robert Bly reminds us. Ritual, and effort—that is what I mean by intentionality.

The Sioux were intentional about initiation for their young men—as were all Native American tribes, so far as I can tell, as were nearly all pre-industrial revolution cultures around the world since the dawn of time. For a young Sioux brave this included the "vision quest," whereby he would set out on his own into the wilderness for a period of fasting and prayer, seeking from his gods the vision, or calling, of his life.

In *Crazy Horse and Custer*, author Stephen Ambrose writes,

For the Sioux male, the vision quest was central to life. It was usually preceded by a fast, complicated purification rite, and a series of lectures from a holy man. The teenagers then stayed alone in some sacred place, forcing themselves to remain awake until the vision came. A holy man interpreted the dream and it became the guiding star for the remainder of the dreamer's life. From the vision the Sioux drew their inspiration. Their dreams might lead them to become medicine men, or warriors, or horse catchers, but whatever the vision proscribed for the dreamer, it was *wakan* and never to be disregarded. The vision gave a man his power. Without it, he was nothing; with a vision he was in touch with the sacred forces.

In your dreams as a pre-teen or a teen, who did you dream of being? What did you dream of doing?

To be in an elite military unit, to be an all-star ball player, an incredible fisherman, a forest ranger who backpacked all week long, a rock star. (Craig)

How do they compare to your dreams now?

Do you know God's dream for your life, or, in other words, do you know your calling?

Do you have a vision for your life?

The curtain continues to be pulled back. I like what I've seen so far. (Craig)

IN *HOW THE IRISH SAVED CIVILIZATION*, THOMAS CAHILL WRITES ABOUT St. Patrick's journey through the stage of Beloved Son and then being hurled into the Cowboy or Ranger stage, where he encountered God:

> "Tending flocks was my daily work, and I would pray constantly during the daylight hours. The love of God and the fear of him surrounded me more and more—and faith grew and the Spirit was roused, so that in one day I would say as many as a hundred prayers and after dark nearly as many again, even while I remained in the woods or on the mountain."
>
> Patricius endured six years of this woeful isolation, and by the end of it he had grown from a careless boy to something he would surely never otherwise have become—a holy man, indeed a visionary . . . On his last night as Miliucc's slave, he received in sleep his first otherworldly experience. A mysterious voice said to him, "Your hungers are rewarded: you are going home."

Thus begins the story of Patrick's remarkable escape from Ireland, his return home, and how—through another vision—he was to receive his call as a missionary back to the very people who had once been his captors. God speaks to young men—through trial, prayer, and fasting, and most often in the wilderness. What he speaks becomes a guiding force for their lives.

Have you had a season set apart to seek God's calling for your life?

Several of different lengths and intensity, each in periods I saw major choices or issues approaching on the horizon (Craig)

If so, how has he directed you . . . what did he say?

If not, how would knowing your calling change your life?

IT WAS BACK IN 1997 WHEN MY DEAR FRIEND BRENT CURTIS PRESENTED TO me the idea of doing a sort of "vision quest" for our sons around the time they turned thirteen.

We talked about how it ought to involve ritual and effort, a variety of tests and challenges, love and validation. As Samuel approached the age of twelve, I thought his vision quest year should begin and that way it would culminate on his thirteenth birthday, with a special ceremony. But as I prayed I sensed God saying, *No—wait another year.* I was disappointed, frankly, but how right and timely that counsel proved to be. It proved true for Sam, and then for Blaine—a shift took place on its own, not in their twelfth but in their thirteenth year, a shift from boyhood into young manhood, a time for active intervention.

Whether you are a young man or an older man, God has chosen to use ritual, effort, a variety of tests and challenges, love and validation as the components for your masculine journey. Recall and write out the mile markers in your masculine journey, those moments or events that marked a transition from boyhood to manhood.

Were any of these the intentional active intervention of older mature men?

YOU ARE MY DELIGHT

I WROTE TO HIM IN THE OPENING PAGES OF A LEATHER JOURNAL I'D GIVEN him for his quest. Those words shall remain private to Samuel alone, but the gist of what I wanted to say was, first, to explain the year and why we were devoting this year to his passage into young manhood, and, second, that I would guide him. His part was to be open to all that God was doing, and trust me along the way. Father, to son. Then I prayed, *What is this trip about, Jesus?* There were so many things I wanted to talk to Samuel about—girls, courage, prayer and God, and becoming a man.

Your delight in him. That's what I heard. Your delight in him. But of course. That is Lesson Number One. You are the son of my right hand, my delight, my Beloved Son, in whom I am so well pleased. That is the building block for everything else.

Honestly, I felt a sense of relief. Like so many boomer-generation fathers, I'm trying real hard to do what was not done for me, and we can get a little driven about it and pile on too many "lessons" and "values" and "teachable moments," and miss the heart of the boy altogether. You are my delight. Okay. I can do that. The weekend was magic, filled with laughter and adventure and joy. We fished in the pond, rode horses together in the woods, ate out. We stayed in Otis's old cabin, and though the master bed was downstairs I slept upstairs in the loft with Sam. You are my delight. I love just being with you.

Of all the things God could say, how would it feel to hear him say, *"You are my delight. I love just being with you."* Have you heard that from him?

Yes, in words and common graces and gifts. (Craig)

This is the issue you simply must resolve . . . you are the Beloved Son.

THE WILD GOOSE

WHEN ONE OF MY BOYS TURNS TWELVE, THAT IS THE YEAR THEY CAN COME with the men elk hunting. Not to hunt themselves yet—that is a privilege to be earned—but to tag along and "be with the men," eating with us, listening to the banter and the stories, following us step-for-step through the mountains in search of the elusive game, enduring the rigors of elk hunting. Up well before daybreak, hunt all day, home after dark to eat something hot and fall into bed utterly exhausted, only to feel as though you've just laid your head down when the alarm goes off again for another round, like a prizefighter called from his corner by the bell.

Harrington called this sort of invitation "the honor of entrée the men had offered me," and he comes to realize that though the men taught him to "kill rabbits pretty well," that in itself "turned out to be the least of their hunting knowledge and the least of what I would learn from my years of hunting with the men."

As a young man, what did you receive or what would you have liked to have received by being with good mature men over several seasons?

As I mentioned earlier, I began reading this book with a sense that God would answer some of my questions about my masculine journey and the sense that I was seriously damaged and deficient as a man. I began this book thinking I have been entirely on my own, convinced that I'm probably about twenty miles away from where I should be at my age/stage. Going through the material a number of times, I've found myself remembering past events that God seems to be saying, See, I was fathering you back then. Do you see in that memory how I was initiating you? God's brought *back the memory of physically demanding jobs I held, of adventures, challenges, and tests I never viewed as key to my masculine development. He's reminding me of men who did play a role in my life. Oh, there's much I missed out on, and I wish so many things were different; however, God is graciously affirming that he was present. I've thought so much of my journey was simply me alone bouncing off the walls of a narrow alley going nowhere. As I've been reading this, God has been revealing his hidden hand is so very much of my life. He was there, he was engaged, I wasn't alone, and I've realized that I've gone through more than I might immediately think. (Craig)*

At this stage of life, however old you are, what would you see yourself receiving by being with older mature men over several seasons?

How can you begin to make that happen?

ON SAMUEL'S FOURTEENTH BIRTHDAY WE HELD A CEREMONY CELEBRATING his year, and welcoming him into the fellowship of men. I began the evening with this story, and said, "Samuel played the man. He didn't let fear come in. He kept up a man's pace through wicked terrain in the dark, and he kept his spirits up as well. I am *very* impressed with this young man." I hadn't set out to make this a milestone in his passage; but that is the way of the masculine journey. After all, our guide is the Holy Spirit, whom the early Celtic Christians like Patrick called the Wild Goose. They knew he could not be tamed. Ours is merely to trust and follow his haunting call, and he will take us on the adventure he has for us. "Those who are led by the Spirit of God are sons of God" (Rom. 8:14 NIV). As Chesterton said, "An adventure is, by its nature, a thing that comes to us. It is a thing that chooses us, not a thing that we choose." How we respond to that adventure shapes us into the men we become.

Can you really orchestrate the masculine journey God has for you?

What is either comforting or discouraging about this reality?

While our intentionality and pursuit of initiation is pivotal, God ultimately is responsible for our journey. It's some mysterious combination of God requiring nothing of us and everything of us . . . and even still it's entirely a work of God. This, to me, is both comforting and hopeful. (Craig)

How would you like to respond to the adventures God chooses for you?

AN OBSTACLE TO THE JOURNEY

something that could hinder your journey

Forgetfulness. We are a forgetful people. Can you remember the milestones, the turning points of your life? Can you recall the lesson learned, how God was "in it," your convictions, reactions, and commitments? To forget those moments is to lose them and their impact upon you. A key practice in our walk with God is to keep a journal. To do so will encourage you and help you fight off the lies and accusations of the enemy down the road.

Do you keep a journal of the work and words God is bringing into your life? If not, consider beginning one now.

GOING ON MISSION WITH US

OUR MEN'S MINISTRY TEAM WAS HEADED UP TO WISCONSIN FOR A CONFERENCE, and for the first time Sam was coming with us. I wanted Sam to *experience*. He'd seen us play together, work together. Now I wanted him to see us fight together, listen to how we prayed, watch how we supported one another, moved into enemy territory to set captives free.

The important thing here was to see us on mission—watch how we operated with God and one another, listen to how we prayed to shut down the spiritual warfare, how we walked in humility in order to deliver the gospel. He wasn't a spectator—he had jobs to do, and we treated him like a member of the team. To see that we *do* live in something epic, and that Christianity is more than just Sunday school videos and Awanas. It's dangerous, it's costly, it's beautiful.

What "mission" can you participate in that would give you the opportunity to learn from and live in an Epic Christianity? If nothing comes to mind, ask God what he has for you. And *keep asking* over the next few weeks and months until something does surface.

SPIRITUAL LESSONS

SPIRITUAL TRAINING SEEMS MOST FRAUGHT WITH AMBUSHES. TEENAGERS have in incredible capacity to pick up even a hint of the shallow, goofy, hypocritical, or posing. And they haven't a moment's patience for lessons they can tell have nothing to do with real life. Sure—there's plenty of churchy stuff out there, but my boys see right through it. They've tasted enough of the kingdom of God to know the counterfeit when they see it, and while I love that about them, it also makes discipleship that much harder. There's just no faking it, no padding it with spiritual "filler."

Have you developed the helpful capacity to pick up "even a hint" of the shallow, goofy, hypocritical churchy stuff out there (especially in men's ministries)?

What do you do with it? Avoid the posing and live with the ache for a genuine fellowship? Get involved anyway because it's the only game in town while risking the "frog in the kettle" syndrome (the slow, imperceptible death of your masculine heart)? Or . . . is there another option?

What are you doing (in addition to working through this manual) to seek a *real,* authentic walk with God?

A MAN'S NEED FOR VALIDATION IS ONE OF HIS MOST DESPERATE LONGINGS. Until we have that validation, we live with an uncertainty down deep inside. As men, we need to know who we truly are, and what we are destined to become. And the only really reliable source for that is the God who made us. So we need to hear from God what *he* thinks of us (John 17:6, 11–12 NIV).

For more on hearing the Father's voice and the new name he may have for you, we'd encourage you to read/reread chapter 6 of John's book *Wild at Heart,* and listen to an audio CD we've recorded, *Developing a Conversational Intimacy with God.*

For some this disrupts your time line, but stop and take a good bit of time and ask God what he thinks of you.

What did you hear?

What affect does hearing this from God have on you?

POSTSCRIPT

SAM'S VISION QUEST YEAR WAS SOMETHING I PUT TOGETHER LARGELY ON my own, sometimes on the fly, and it had its highlights, and disappointments too. It seemed as though our time together was constantly opposed, and a month would disappear without our having spent significant time together.

How has your time with God and his initiation of you been opposed?

I KNOW I MISSED MANY OPPORTUNITIES, AND I WISH I HAD ANOTHER chance at the year. I've continued to develop the idea for my other sons, and we are learning as we go (Luke is next). We must be intentional about a boy's passage into young manhood, and it must be tailored to the boy and his needs. I believe whatever the details, it needs to involve test and trial of a physical, emotional, and spiritual nature. That it needs to be done by the father—if he is available—or another significant man, and that it occurs best in the fellowship of men.

As you anticipate the tests, challenges, and trials of a physical, emotional, and spiritual nature coming during this next season of your journey, what emotions surface in your heart?

At this moment, absolute excitement. I want it! (Craig)

I ALSO BELIEVE WE CAN OFFER SOMETHING LIKE THIS—BOTH INITIATION experiences like those Sam had in his year and a ritual event like that which culminated it—to men who never had any initiation offered them as young men. But it must have the same sincerity to it. Not as "encouragement," but as *validation* coming from men who know him and have journeyed with him. Man-to-man.

I believe there also can and ought to be other significant ritual moments as we move through the stages, such as graduation and marriage and others particular to the man himself. Seize those moments, my brothers, and find ways to make them opportunities for masculine initiation. Instead of the typical bachelor party, I've had friends take the groom on a white-water trip or skydiving (far more true to what he is about to enter by way of marriage) and then speak words of validation to him. Bart just held a very powerful ceremony for his son, Kris, who has been inducted as an officer in the Marine Corps. That would be another example of a watershed moment, and Bart seized it and invited the men in our fellowship to do a sort of "spiritual" commissioning over Kris, and to speak words of counsel and validation to him.

Are there men in your life (perhaps your son) who are ready for a validating ritual moment?

What would a meaningful vision quest for *you* look like?

What books, challenges, lessons, tests would you like to under go?

Who would be involved?

What would the celebration look like?

BUT I THINK IT'S IMPORTANT TO SAY THAT MUCH OF MY SONS' INITIATIONS—as with my own—will continue to be *informal*, sometimes even accidental, as in the Tetons canoe rescue and the Moab trips and the thousand other opportunities life presents to bring a boy along in his journey. When a father and a son spend time together, and when men spend time together—whether it's doing homework or shooting hoops in the street or working on the car or pheasant hunting—something passes between them, deep and unspoken, the truest form of initiation there can be.

Is inviting God into the everyday affairs of your life (i.e., spending time with your Father) something you want more of?

Father, I invite you into the everyday details of my life. I want to spend time with you and enjoy you. Come into my day, today. I open my eyes to see you in new places and new ways, I open my ears to hear you . . . speak through the events, circumstances, and people I cross this day. I am your son, you are my Father. I love you.

8

Warrior

Gird your sword upon your side, O mighty one.

—Psalm 45:3 NIV

BEFORE STARTING

Before you begin to work through this chapter of the manual, consider:

- ➢ Without referring back to the book, from your recollection and in your own words, describe the Warrior.
- ➢ While the stages overlap, and there is some aspect of them in every phase of a man's life, there is also a time in a man's life when one of the stages is prominent. Is this stage, the Warrior:

A stage you anticipate going through in the future? If so, read it knowing God is preparing you now, in your current stage of the masculine journey, for what's to come. Give yourself the grace to learn, benefit, grow, and take in all God has for you in this season of life without either jumping the gun or getting anxious about the next season.

The stage you think you're currently in? If so, read it as a map for the journey you're currently on. With heart and eyes wide open, be keen to all God has for you. He will affirm, validate, convict, heal, and call you more deeply into all the lessons and growth he has for you in this stage of life. Don't prematurely assume you're ready to move on. God orders the seasons of a man's life and in his perfect way, your graduation *will* come.

Or a stage you feel you have passed through? If so, God will no doubt remind you of the people, events, hardships, and joys of this stage to affirm that indeed you have passed through this stage well. And while saying that, be willing to allow God to speak of the "more" he'd like to do in you as a Warrior. You may find a number of things you missed in this stage . . . The good news is that it's never too late. Be expectant; there's more for you.

FIRST REACTIONS

What were you struck by in this chapter? Were there any "aha" moments or new thoughts as you reread it? Did God speak?

KEY POINTS OF THE CHAPTER

- Our God is a warrior, mighty and terrible in battle, and he leads armies. It is *this* God that man is made in the image of.
- Our God is a Warrior because there are certain things in life worth fighting for, must be fought for. He makes man a Warrior in his own image, because he intends for man to join him in that battle.
- We live in a world at war. We are supposed to fight back.
- The heart of the Warrior says, "I will not let evil have its way. There are some things that cannot be endured. I've got to do something. There is freedom to be had." The heart of the Warrior says, "I will put myself on the line for you."
- Above all, the Warrior learns to yield his heart to nothing. Not to kill his heart for fear of falling into temptation, but to protect his heart for more noble things, to keep the integrity of his heart as a great reservoir of passionate strength and holy desire.
- The Warrior heart has been wounded.
- We have a Father who is a great Warrior, and he will raise us as Warriors, if we'll let him, if we will embrace the initiation that comes with this stage. There is a Warrior in you, by the way. However it has been handled up to this point in your life, it can be restored, recovered, and made strong. The promise of Scripture is that the Father is raising us to be sons just like Jesus, meaning, you shall be as valiant as he was.

When Alexander the Great died, his massive empire was divided among several high-ranking officers in his cabinet. What we would refer to as the Middle East, including Israel, came under the rule of the Seleucids, who continued Alexander's mission to Hellenize the locals, making all the world Greek in its customs and values. What began as the seemingly innocent importation of Greek culture became increasingly hostile, and eventually violent. The Seleucid overlords took a special hatred of the Jewish insistence on worshiping one God, seeing it—as have so many dictatorships since—as a threat to their regime. In 165 BC a Greek officer holding command over the village of Modiin—not too far from Jerusalem—ordered the Jewish villagers to bow to an idol and eat the flesh of a slaughtered pig, acts that struck at the heart of Judaism, at the heart of the people for whom such a command was unthinkable. Blasphemy.

The people refused, an argument ensued, and the Jewish high priest Mattathias killed the officer with a sword. The villagers—led by Mattathias's five sons—took up arms against the rest of the soldiers and killed them as well. Mattathias and a growing number of his followers fled to the hills, from there launching a resistance movement against their Hellenistic oppressors. Meanwhile, Antiochus IV (current heir to the Seleucid Empire and a cruel enemy of the Jews) seized control of the temple in Jerusalem, set up in the Holy of Holies a statue of Zeus, and commanded the Jews to worship him. Those who refused to abandon God and his commands—including circumcision—were persecuted, mothers put to the sword with their infants hanging round their necks.

Meanwhile, Mattathias had died, leaving command of his growing forces to his son Judah Maccabee, who led his outnumbered and outarmed troops against a far superior force (ten thousand Jews against more than sixty thousand Greeks and Hellenized Syrians) and eventually routed their enemies from Jerusalem. They cleansed the temple, tore down the desecrated altar (including the idol) and rebuilt one from uncut stones, after which they held a feast of worship and dedication. Of course, I am referring to the origin of the Jewish Festival of Lights, Hanukkah. Historian Thomas Cahill observed that "there are humiliations a proud people—even one oppressed for generations—cannot abide."

Indeed. It may take time, and require repeated provocation, but eventually a man must come to realize that there are certain things in life worth fighting for. Perhaps, when we appreciate the truth of this, we can better understand the heart of God.

Did you ever get into a fight as a young boy? Who did you fight, and what were the issues you were fighting over? How'd you do?

Some may have never gotten into any fights. If that's your story, why do you suppose you didn't?

How have your battles evolved as you've grown older? How are your fights different; what's changed from when you were younger? Looking ahead, do you anticipate your battles getting easier or harder? Why or why not?

What things in life—and in your life—would you say are worth fighting for?

A WARRIOR GOD

THE LORD IS A WARRIOR; THE LORD IS HIS NAME. (EX. 15:3 NIV)

The LORD will march out like a mighty man, like a warrior he will stir up his zeal; with a shout he will raise the battle cry and will triumph over his enemies. (Isa. 42:13 NIV)

But the LORD is with me like a mighty warrior; so my persecutors will stumble and not prevail. (Jer. 20:11 NIV) [The NASB translates mighty warrior "dread champion." Goliath was a dread champion; the mighty men of David were dread champions. King James has it as "a mighty terrible one."]

Lift up your heads, O you gates; be lifted up, you ancient doors, that the King of glory may come in. Who is this King of glory? The LORD strong and mighty, the LORD mighty in battle. (Ps. 24:7–8 NIV)

How new to you is the concept of God's being a warrior? What does God's being a warrior evoke in you . . . is it comforting or disturbing?

Until five or six years ago, I would have understood any reference to God being a warrior as a reference to an Old Testament view of God, which, by New Testament standards was primitively undeveloped and trumped by the greater revelation of God through Christ, which clearly presented God as compassionate and merciful. After an appropriate hesitancy (for a theologically conservative I've-got-the-truth-and-the-truth-don't-change pastor) I found myself shouting "YES" to God being a Warrior. It's beyond comforting, it's the basis of all my hopes and desires—my Father is the leader of angel armies and he will fiercely defeat Satan and victory will be ours. (Craig)

OUR GOD IS A WARRIOR, MIGHTY AND TERRIBLE IN BATTLE, AND HE LEADS armies. It is *this* God that man is made in the image of. I spoke of this in *Wild at Heart*, but some things bear repeating, because a man will be in a much better place to enter the stage of the Warrior if he knows this is thoroughly grounded in Scripture, supported by Scripture, *compelled* by Scripture.

John points out a number of scriptural examples of "the Spirit of the Lord" coming upon a man when that man went to war. What does this tell us about the God the Spirit is?

When you're in a difficult circumstance or agitated about something and you ask God to fill you with His Spirit, what typically are you anticipating will happen? Are you expecting God to fill you and move you into battle/war mode?

I'm cracking up, because most of the time what I anticipate happening is that God will fill me with his Spirit, then convict of me of my shameful heart and attitude, and then he'll overpower what I often label as fleshly sinful anger. He calms me with a peace and contentment that will *allow me to turn my cheek again and again and again. Any urge to fight is most certainly pugnaciousness (a clear fruit of the flesh). (Craig)*

What battles/fights has God directed you into in the past? How did you handle them?

What might be the battles God would have you fight currently? Would you be ready?

Now . . . how about Christ as a warrior? Our image of Jesus as a man has suffered greatly in the church, but perhaps no more so than our image of Jesus as a Warrior.

What was it that made Jesus so outraged that he sat down, and in an act of premeditated aggression, built for himself a whip of cords and then, having built it, used it on the merchants occupying the temple courtyards (John 2:13–17). "Zeal for your house will consume me" (John 2:17 NIV).

Is this the kind of behavior you'd expect from the Jesus you've been told about?

What picture of Christ did you have growing up? Or even now?
Christ as a gentle shepherd with a young lamb draped over his shoulders?
The masculine carpenter with the warm broad smile?
Mr. Rogers with a beard?
A skilled and fierce warrior?

YES, JESUS COULD BE IMMENSELY KIND. BUT WHAT IS THIS OTHER SIDE TO him we see in the Gospels? "Woe to you, teachers of the law and Pharisees, you hypocrites! You travel over land and sea to win a single convert, and when he becomes one, you make him twice as much a son of hell as you are" (Matt. 23:15 NIV).

THE REASON FOR THE WARRIOR

OUR GOD IS A WARRIOR BECAUSE THERE ARE CERTAIN THINGS IN LIFE worth fighting for, must be fought for. He makes man a Warrior in his own image, because he intends for man to join him in that battle.

When do you feel like a Warrior?

What are the things that rouse the Warrior in you?

In which of these areas do see yourself as being in a war/battle?

Your marriage
Your children
Friendships
Your church
Those you work for or with

Take anything good, true, or beautiful upon this earth and ask yourself, "Can this be protected without a fight?" Can it?

A VISTA JOURNEY

a view that enhances the journey

There are a number of movies mentioned in this book that capture the warrior stage in a man's development. Think of your favorite movies. How many of the movies you really love include a battle of one form or another? (Would watching one of those "favorites" again right now be good for your masculine heart?)

One of my all-time favorite stories comes at the end of *The Lord of the Rings.* The Beloved Sons are toughened as Cowboy Rangers, and they go on to become Warriors in their own right. After helping Aragorn, their king, win the last great battle for Middle Earth, the hobbits make their way home. Then comes one of my favorite chapters in all the books: "The Scouring of the Shire" (totally overlooked in the movie). For when the hobbits finally return at the end of their quest (and initiation), they find their beloved Shire in the hands of the evil one. The trees are cut down, the rivers polluted, their people are enslaved, the charming inns shut down or replaced by jails. The wolf is not merely at the door. He has made himself at home. They will not stand for it. Tolkien writes,

This was too much for Pippin. His thoughts went back to the Field of Cormallen, and here was a squint-eyed rascal calling the Ring-bearer "little cock-a-whoop." He cast back his cloak, flashed out his sword, and the silver and sable of Gondor gleamed on him as he rode forward. "I am a messenger of the King," he said. "You are speaking to the King's friend, and one of the most renowned in all the West. You are a ruffian and a fool. Down on your knees in the road and ask pardon, or I will set this troll's bane in you!" The sword glinted in the westering sun. Merry and Sam drew their swords also and rode up to support Pippin . . . the ruffians gave back. Scaring Breeland peasants and bullying bewildered hobbits had been their work. Fearless hobbits with bright swords and grim faces were a great surprise. And there was a note in the voices of these newcomers that they had not heard before. It chilled them with fear.

The Beloved Sons had returned as Warriors. And a good thing for the Shire, too, and its gentle inhabitants. Sometimes the battle has to strike close to home in order to rouse the Warrior in a man. Perhaps that is why God often allows it to strike so close to home.

What battles have struck close to home for you through the years? Were you a reluctant Warrior who had to be roused to battle?

Are there battles you face now that you're balking at entering?

PASSIVITY

ONE OF THE SADDEST OF ALL THE SAD STORIES IN THE HISTORY OF THE people of God comes shortly after the dramatic Exodus from Egypt, as they stand on the brink of a whole new life in the land God had promised:

> But you were unwilling to go up; you rebelled against the command of the LORD your God. You grumbled in your tents and said, "The LORD hates us; so he brought us out of Egypt to deliver us into the hands of the Amorites to destroy us. Where can we go? Our brothers have made us lose heart. They say, 'The people are stronger and taller than we are; the cities are large, with walls up to the sky. We even saw the Anakites there.'" Then I said to you, "Do not be terrified; do not be afraid of them. The LORD your God, who is going before you, will fight for you [Not "comfort you." Not "be with you in your distress, defeated by your enemies." *Fight for you*], as he did for you in Egypt, before your very eyes, and in the desert. There you saw how the LORD your God carried you, as a father carries his son, all the way you went until you reached this place." In spite of this, you did not trust in the LORD your God . . . Then you replied, "We have sinned against the LORD. We will go up and fight, as the LORD our God commanded us." (Deut. 1:26–41 NIV)

But it was too late. Their decision *not* to fight is what led to their wandering in the wilderness for forty years. We often cite that part of the story, talking about our own wilderness experiences, embracing the wilderness saga as if it were inevitable. No, that is not the lesson at all. We have forgotten *it was avoidable*. The reason they took the lamentable detour into the wilderness was because they would not fight. To be more precise, the wilderness was a punishment, the consequence of refusing to trust God, and fight.

Are there things in your life you could have changed by fighting?

Do you see passivity in yourself? In what ways? How has your passivity hurt others?

What is it in human nature that just won't face the reality of war?

WHY, MY SON HEARD IT AGAIN JUST THE OTHER DAY, IN HIS BIBLE CLASS OF all places. "We are not supposed to resist Satan. That's God's job." That is dangerous thinking, and unbiblical.

Resist the devil. (James 4:7 NIV)
Resist him. (1 Pet. 5:9 NIV)

We live in a world at war. We are supposed to fight back. It is apparently a difficult reality to embrace, as witnessed by the passivity that marks much of modern Christianity. We just want the Christian life to be all about the sweet love of Jesus. But that is not what's going on here. You may not like the situation, but that only makes it unattractive—it does not make it untrue.

We live in a world at war. Do you live as if this were true?

What's been the impact of this war upon you?

AGGRESSION

WHEN IT COMES TO THE RECORD OF MEN IN PARTICULAR, OUR WORST moment has to be Adam's failure and the introduction of original sin, which got us into this whole mess in the first place. It was a failure marked by *passivity*. Eve was deceived, says Paul, but not Adam (1 Tim. 2:14). He sinned for other reasons, unspecified, but when we look at the story we have some evidence to go by. Adam doesn't engage, doesn't intervene, doesn't do a damn thing. He is created to act, endowed with the image of a mighty God who acts and intervenes dramatically. Adam did not, and whatever else got passed on to us men from the first man, we know that *paralysis*—another word for *passivity*—is certainly one of them.

When are you like Adam, disengaged, passive?

> First off, it's hard for me to admit I'm ever passive. That feels like I'm admitting to being a weasel. But I am passive at times. It surfaces quickly in situations where I don't think I have what it takes. Either because of how I view myself, or by a perceived dismissal by someone (my wife, a friend, a colleague), I retreat, disengage, and turn limp. Actually, this is probably one of my most common failings. I always have some justification for being passive that makes it seem less . . . passive. (Craig)

WHAT ARE THE REGIONS OF A MAN'S WORLD THAT HE ALLOWS TO BECOME A sort of DMZ, an "I won't bother you if you don't bother me" land of capitulation and passivity? It might be the family finances, or a struggle with in-laws. It might be a growing conflict in his church or community. We look for the path of least resistance, and that is rarely the right path to take. It is essential that a man overcome this inherent passivity, this paralysis we got from Adam that lies deep in our bones. To be a man we must, with the help of God, overcome it intentionally, repeatedly, on front after front across the seasons of our lives.

What are those regions you allow to be in an area of capitulation and/or passivity?

For a start: Addressing extended family dysfunction. The detrimental relational behaviors/actions of those close to me. Personal weight or health issues. Family financial management. (Craig)

THE ASSUMPTION IS THAT WHATEVER ELSE A MAN MIGHT BE, HE OUGHT TO be a fighter. Scripture assumes that a man acts, a man intervenes. Passivity has no place in the lexicon of true masculinity. None. And to overcome passivity, God has set his warrior heart in every man.

Would turning to him for help in this area be something to do now? Perhaps expressing to him something like this:

Lord, deliver me from passivity, from the sin of Adam. Rouse me to discernment, to action, to strength, and to fight when necessary. I repent of my passivity and turn to you for the masculine life I long to live.

THE HEART OF A WARRIOR

AS I EXPLAINED IN *WILD AT HEART*, THE WARRIOR IS HARDWIRED INTO every man. This is true because he is made in the image of God, who is the Great Warrior. Like Father, like son. It is also true because it constitutes a great part of man's mission here on earth—to join the Great Warrior in his battle against evil. It is this aggressive nature that will enable us to overcome the passivity and paralysis we inherited from Adam. In fact, we are siding with one or the other—the Warrior or the paralyzed man—in every decision we make, every day. Encouraging the Warrior as it begins to come into full force in a young man's life will be a great help to him as the years unfold, for you and I know how hard the battle is if we've spent years in passivity.

Can you recall how the Warrior nature expressed itself when you were young?

Viscously fighting neighborhood evil by "playing" army. The competiveness I had in sports. My misguided but passionate social and political activism as a young man. My fierce self-righteous posture as a doctrinal cop in and following seminary. (Craig)

Was its development encouraged as it began to come into full force in your life?

I AM NOT SAYING EVERY MAN MUST JOIN THE MILITARY, THOUGH THAT IS A noble calling; there are many ways for the Warrior to emerge. Over the ages the pen has proved mightier than the sword, as the old saying goes. What I am saying is that there is an inherent aggressiveness written in the masculine soul. So it shouldn't surprise us—though many parents are still a bit unnerved—when you see the Warrior emerge in the boy when he is very young. As for the stage of the Warrior, I believe it begins in the late teens—about the time we send a young man to war. The heart of the Warrior says, "I will not let evil have its way. There are some things that cannot be endured. I've got to do something. There is freedom to be had." The heart of the Warrior says, "I will put myself on the line for you." That is why it must come before the Lover stage, for he will need to do that time and time again in his marriage, and it is passivity that has broken the heart of many women. The Warrior nature is fierce, and brave, ready to confront evil, ready to go into battle. This is the time for a young man to stop saying, "Why is life so hard?" He takes the hardness as the call to fight, to rise up, take it on. He learns to "set his face like a flint," as Jesus had to do to fulfill his life's great mission (see Isa. 50:7).

React. How does it strike you to be described as aggressive?

I like it, I love it, I want some more of it. (Craig)

How must the Warrior nature express itself at this point of your life?

What must you stand up to? Where is the evil you can no longer endure?

Younger man, your error could be fighting either too many battles, the wrong battles, or battles you are not yet trained for. Which do you think would be your tendency?

Older man, your error could be retreating from the battles believing that this stage of life is meant to be a season of peace, when the peace you're looking for comes later . . . in heaven. Or you may have never battled and now would be the time, to enter in and fight for those things you've been passive about for years. Do either of these descriptions fit?

UNYIELDING

WE ARE TOLD THAT JESUS HAS FASTED FOR FORTY DAYS. STOP RIGHT THERE—it is the Warrior in a man that enables him to do that. How much hardship a man will endure, how long and tenaciously he will persevere, is determined by the amount of Warrior within him. A young man may have a job he hates, under an arrogant boss, but if he sees it as Warrior training, he will endure. A man in a difficult marriage can persevere only if he finds the Warrior inside.

What hardships have you endured that God may have been using as Warrior training?

What hardships have you folded in probably because you lacked a bit as a Warrior?

If enduring hardships has been difficult for you, this may be an indicator that you missed some of the lessons of hard work in the Cowboy stage. Could this be true of you?

THE TIME OF THE WARRIOR IS THE TIME OF LEARNING DISCIPLINE, A concentration of body, mind, and spirit. Of course, all our military boot camps are saturated with discipline, because they know that when all hell breaks loose on the battlefield, a man has to have something to fall back on other than emotion. Spirits are high before you actually meet the enemy, but in the chaos of warfare high spirits can vanish in an instant. This is true far beyond the sands of Iwo Jima, and especially true in spiritual warfare.

For many men "discipline" is not a popular word; we want an easy life. What did you grow up learning about discipline?

What stirs in you when you hear a sermon or someone suggests that you need more discipline?

Given that scenario I quickly think of more rules (usually arbitrarily chosen by men who don't really live by them either), pressure, and ultimately more failure, shame, guilt, and an anger that if it's so important, why is it so hard to come by. Something in me wilts when I hear that discipline is essential. (Craig)

THE CHURCH HAS LARGELY PRESENTED DISCIPLINE AS "KILL YOUR HEART and just do the right thing." That is terrible. It wearies the soul, and ends up destroying the heart—the very faculty you will need in the face of great trial and testing. Good discipline *harnesses* the passions, rather than killing them. When Jesus "set his face like a flint" toward Jerusalem, he manifested an inner resolve that came *from* deep within, from his heart. He would not be deterred from his mission. A young man will need this strength of heart, whether to finish his PhD, or to hold fast his convictions under persecution, or to master an art form—all of which take great discipline, fueled by passion.

In what ways may you have killed your heart by "just doing the right thing"?

What passions fuel you? What passions would you love to have?

THIS INNER RESOLVE IS WHAT IS SO SORELY TESTED IN JESUS AS SATAN COMES to him in the wilderness, probing his defenses, looking for some angle, some hook to get Christ to give in and yield to temptation. He does not. This is absolutely essential to the Warrior, to develop an unyielding heart. This is where we will be most profoundly tested.

Above all, the Warrior learns to yield his heart to nothing. Not to kill his heart for fear of falling into temptation, but to protect his heart for more noble things, to keep the integrity of his heart as a great reservoir of passionate strength and holy desire. That was Jesus' battle in the wilderness, as Satan tried this way and that to get him to surrender his integrity.

Where is this "test" of your heart going on right now in your life?

How have you cared for, protected your heart? Nurtured it?

What needs to change for you to better, more consistently care for your heart?

WOUNDED

The heart of the Warrior is wounded in a boy and in a young man when he is told that aggression is flat-out wrong, unchristian, that niceness equals godliness. In what ways have you heard this message?

HE IS WOUNDED WHEN HIS ATTEMPTS TO RISE UP AS A WARRIOR ARE mocked, or crushed. He is wounded when he has no one to train him, no king to give his allegiance to and no cause to fight for.

Can you remember this happening as a young man? A teen? As an older man?

THE HEART OF THE WARRIOR IS WOUNDED IN A YOUNG MAN WHEN HE attempts to be a Warrior and is shamed.

When were you shamed in your attempts to be a Warrior (perhaps by parents, classmates, friends, your spouse)?

NEVER WINNING AT ANYTHING, GETTING BULLIED, PUSHED AROUND, outright beat up has crushed many a young Warrior's heart, sent him into passivity.

What did you win at? What did you suck at? What sent you into passivity?

THE WOUND IS DOUBLED WHEN THE BEATING COMES FROM HIS OWN father, or perhaps an older brother. For that matter, the Warrior is wounded when a boy has to become a fighter too soon.

Was your father or a sibling abusive?

Did you become a fighter too soon? If so, what led you to that?

ON THE OTHER HAND, IF THE FATHER IS PASSIVE, HOW WILL THE YOUNG man learn to be a Warrior? Nothing rouses anger, frustration, and mounting disrespect in the heart of a boy as does his father's passivity.

How would you describe your father: a Warrior or pretty passive?

How much like him are you?

FINALLY, THE HEART OF THE WARRIOR IS WOUNDED, OR ABANDONED, OR sometimes let loose in very bad ways, when the young man does not have a King and a cause to serve. For years I was angry at older men who would not act like Kings. It cuts deep into our fatherlessness.

Who have been the Kings in your life?

What was the effect upon you of either having Kings or not having them in your life?

BUT THERE IS HOPE. JESUS NO LONGER HAD JOSEPH AROUND WHEN HE entered his Warrior stage. On a human level, he was fatherless. But we know he was *not* alone. We, too, have a Father who is a great Warrior, and he will raise us as Warriors, if we'll let him, if we will embrace the initiation that comes with this stage. There is a Warrior in you, by the way. However it has been handled up to this point in your life, it can be restored, recovered, and made strong. The promise of Scripture is that the Father is raising us to be sons just like Jesus, meaning, you shall be as valiant as he was.

Father, show me where I have lost heart as a Warrior. What did I miss here? What was wounded, and what was surrendered? Take me back to those times and places when the Warrior in me was shut down. Wake the Warrior heart in me. Train me. Show me what I have surrendered, where I am walking in passivity. Teach me an unyielding heart. Rouse me. I am willing. I am yours.

And help me to raise my sons and the young men around me to be Warriors in your image. Show me where the warrior is emerging in them, how to strengthen it, call it forth, and make it holy.

A PAUSE IN THE JOURNEY

an opportunity to rest/reflect on the ground you've just covered

So, as you finish this chapter, what do you sense God saying to you about being a Warrior? Capture that thought now, for it will be quickly forgotten or stolen.

9

Raising the Warrior

It is God who arms me with strength . . .
He makes my feet like the feet of a deer;
he enables me to stand on the heights.
He trains my hands for battle.

—Psalm 18:32–34 NIV

BEFORE STARTING

It's so easy to push through this manual too quickly and in doing so miss some of the profound work God would love to do in your life. Before jumping into this chapter, did you go back to those times and places in your own story when the Warrior was wounded? Did you invite Christ to take you there, and speak, and bring the healing you need? Some of you just need to live as the Beloved Son for a while, and then experience your initiation as a Cowboy. Then you can enter the Warrior stage.

Ask yourself, what does God want to do in me to further me in my development as a Warrior?

As a parent reading this chapter, ask yourself: What does my son need at this time?

What is required of me as a father, or what kind of father do I want to be? What do I want to offer, protect, guard, and resist on behalf of my son?

Watch the movie *Seabiscuit.* Don't be mistaken to believe this is merely the story of a horse. The movie transcends its main character to speak to each of us about the rebirth, the rescue, and the restoration we each need.

FIRST REACTIONS

What were you struck by in this chapter? Were there any "aha" moments or new thoughts? Did God speak?

KEY POINTS OF THE CHAPTER

- We are at war, and our Father and elder Brother are great Warriors, and much of what we encounter is in fact either our Warrior training or a battle we must fight, or, most often, both at the same time.
- In the Cowboy Ranger stage, we seek to answer the Question: *Do I have what it takes?* In the Warrior stage, there is a new lesson to be learned: *You are dangerous and powerful. Use it for good.*
- "How does God raise the Warrior in a man?" Hardship. I think this is where we have most misinterpreted what God is up to in our lives. As long as we are committed to the path of least resistance, to making our lives comfortable, trial and tribulation will feel unkind. But, if we are looking for a dojo in which to train as a Warrior, well then—this is the real deal. What better means than hardship? What better way to train a Warrior than by putting a man in situation after situation where he must fight?

In my ninth-grade year, two years after the bully knocked my teeth out in gym class, I got into another fight. This one was even more accidental, for me at least. A few of us guys were goofing around before class, and I threw a grapefruit into a crowd and it hit a guy I didn't mean to hit, didn't even know I'd hit him at all, and as I was walking away he attacked me from behind. He was six feet tall; I was five-feet-five. Needless to say, he pretty much got to just pound on me until a teacher broke it up. Shortly after that a couple of friends asked if I wanted to take a karate class from a local guy offering lessons in his backyard. You'll understand why there was not a moment of hesitation. By now I felt like a total wuss inside, unable to defend myself, unable to help the defenseless. I felt weak. Had I words for it at the time, I'd have said, *I am not a Warrior, and never will be.*

Did you ever come to this same conclusion: *I am not a Warrior, and never will be?*

How have you lived as if that were true?

YOU'LL REMEMBER ALSO THAT I SUCKED AT SPORTS. ENTERING SERIOUSLY into martial arts changed all of that. I found my coordination, got a sense of living in my own body. It took some time, but I grew strong, and fast. My buddies and I trained under a young Warrior for about a year, and then we went on to train by ourselves for maybe two more. Finally, we found an older man who could take us to the next step. He was a fourth-degree black belt with a kind and tender heart—a father figure to fatherless young men. I had no idea what rank I might qualify for. He had me test before him and awarded me a brown belt and within the year I had earned my black. The funny thing is, I never got into another fight.

I'm thinking of the scene in *The Kingdom of Heaven* where Godfrey and Balian have taken to the road, and we find them at camp in the woods. Godfrey begins to train his son in the way of the Warrior. He throws a sword on the ground next to Balian—"Pick it up. Let's see what you're made of." Balian tries to defend himself as best he knows how as Godfrey suddenly comes upon him. "Never use the low guard. You fight well. Come over here. Let's work on your skills." The academy in the woods has officially opened. "Take a high guard, like this." Godfrey raises his sword overhead, with a two-handed grip. "The Italians call it 'la costa de falcone.' The guard of the hawk. Strike from high. Like this. Do it." Balian attempts to imitate his father's skill. "Blade straighter. Leg back. Bend your knees. Sword straighter. Defend yourself."

The Warrior is being called out, trained for battle.

This is what we long for.

And if we accept the invitation I believe God is extending to us, to become his sons under initiation, if we intentionally make that mental shift that says, My Father will provide, then we will find that he indeed has already begun our training. God will train us as David said God trained him; he will bring what we need for our training. The shift begins when we accept a new way of looking at the world, and our place in it. We are at war, and our Father and elder Brother are great Warriors, and much of what we encounter is in fact either our Warrior training or a battle we must fight, or, most often, both at the same time.

There's an invitation from God for him to initiate you as a Warrior. What's your response?

I accept it. I long to charge the fields with cunning, skill, and passion! (Craig)

If you haven't yet accepted his invitation, why is that? Is there a fear? Perhaps you've got unfinished business from an earlier stage of your journey. What do you think it is?

If you have accepted the invitation your training will require several shifts:

You are at war.
The God whose image you bear is a Warrior.
God will provide all you need to be the Warrior you truly are.
Much of what you encounter is either Warrior training or a battle you must fight, or both at the same time.

We'd suggest you take some time right now to consider these shifts. Do you believe them to be true? Are you ready to live in the reality they express? What do these shifts require of you and how you live?

Express to God in prayer, journal, or both, your intention and desires regarding his invitation and these shifts.

THE BOY

YOU DON'T HAVE TO PUT THE WARRIOR IN A BOY—IT'S THERE, HARDWIRED into him. Yes, some boys seem to have more "Warrior" in them than others, but if we believe gender runs deep (as Gen. 1 implies), and if we believe a man is made in the image of a Warrior God, then we will find the Warrior if we look for it, and then we must be intentional to encourage it and direct it into maturity.

When the boy is young, encouraging the Warrior is pretty simple: Just don't shut it down. Wrestle with him, often, play games with him *and let him win*. Not all the time—he needs to know Dad is still a strong man to be respected. But more often than not, let him triumph.

Provide him with Warrior stories. There are plenty in the Bible, and those will capture the imagination of the boy, show him that God is exactly the kind of King he's looking for. (A Christianity of "just be a nice boy" has emasculated many a man, and it will not capture the heart of a boy.) The books and movies you choose—make sure they have noble Warriors in them.

What are the stories or movies you turn to for encouragement as a Warrior?

Stephen Ambrose's writings, Jack Bauer of the TV series "24," reading biographies (I'm currently finishing American Caesar, an influential story of General Douglas MacArthur), The History Channel, Kenneth Scott Latourette's The History of Christianity. (Craig)

In the Cowboy Ranger stage, we seek to answer the Question: *Do I have what it takes?* In the Warrior stage, there is a new lesson to be learned: *You are dangerous and powerful. Use it for good.* That's where we're headed.

Are you dangerous and powerful for good?

If you overheard someone describing you as "dangerous and powerful," what would you hope they meant by that?

YOUNG MEN

I WRITE TO YOU, DEAR CHILDREN,
because your sins have been forgiven on account of his name.
I write to you, fathers,
because you have known him who is from the beginning.
I write to you, young men,
because you have overcome the evil one.
I write to you, dear children,
because you have known the Father.
I write to you, fathers,
because you have known him who is from the beginning.
I write to you, young men,
because you are strong,
and the word of God lives in you,
and you have overcome the evil one. (1 John 2:12–14 NIV)

The old apostle John offers some insight into the stages in this passage. We see that the dear children are Beloved Sons. They know the basics of the gospel—that they are forgiven, and that God is their Father. Older men are referred to as fathers here—these are Kings and Sages. They know "him who is from the beginning," and I'll speak to that when we reach their stages. Let us focus on the young men, whom we see are the Warriors. They are strong (or valiant), the word of God lives in them, and they have overcome the evil one. That's good. To cultivate this in a young man (and in ourselves as older men), it might help to think along three lines: Bravery, Conviction, and an Epic Story.

Clearly there are developmental stages in our stories. Cultivating the ability to overcome the evil one involves Bravery, Conviction, and an Epic Story. How does bravery express itself in your life now?

What are the convictions that define you? (This will take some thought and time. Give yourself to it and write them out.)

As you've done these last three questions, where did your heart go? What surfaced about you and the life you're living now?

BRAVERY

WINSTON CHURCHILL BELIEVED THAT COURAGE WAS THE FOREMOST OF ALL virtues, because he saw that all other virtues depend on it. It takes courage to love, because we all know loving means you will be hurt. Repeatedly. It takes courage to have faith, because we all know that your faith will be sorely tested. It takes courage to be honest, and so on. Raising a young man to be brave is essential. And, may I add, there are several types of bravery—physical, emotional, and spiritual.

Read any biographical account of battlefield heroes, or heroes of any kind, and what stands out is their physical bravery. Physical bravery is cultivated in great part by adventure, and sports, by intentionally putting yourself in dangerous situations. As he grows, the adventures of the Cowboy Ranger stage become more serious, and they provide a context for the Warrior to be roused in him.

Are you physically brave? Is there a story that comes to mind?

Describe what your being physically braver would look like *a year from now*. How would it express itself in your life?

Where can you take a step to cultivate this in your life? What adventures lie in your imagination or desire that God may be using to lure you into situations that call forth a physical bravery?

EMOTIONAL BRAVERY IS DEVELOPED IN MOST CASES OF PHYSICAL BRAVERY, for he will have to master fear, but it is also formed when a young man takes risks in relationships. It might mean risking embarrassment by making a speech in front of a class, or running for an office. It might mean risking rejection by making a new friend, or confronting a good friend on some issue. It will require him to leave a party when the kids start doing things they shouldn't be doing. He will need emotional bravery in large measure when he enters into marriage, for Adam's paralysis seizes many a man when he finds himself in the mysterious interior of a woman's soul.

The important thing in cultivating emotional bravery is helping the boy learn not to quit, teaching him to rise above setbacks and heartbreaks.

Are you emotionally brave? Is there a story that comes to mind?

Describe what your being emotionally braver would look like *a year from now.* How would it express itself in your life?

Where have you quit that you need to reengage? What setbacks and/or heartbreaks do you need to rise above?

There are relationships that I've shed I'd like to move towards again. Ugh . . . it requires sooo much work, humility, repentance, and forgiveness . . . and bravery. (Craig)

Where can you take a step to cultivate this in your life? What adventures lie in your imagination or desire that God may be using to lure you into situations that call forth an emotional bravery?

SPIRITUAL BRAVERY IS CULTIVATED WHEN WE TAKE RISKS OF FAITH. THIS IS the greatest bravery, as far as I'm concerned. Think of the many martyrs, like Polycarp going to his execution. He had been warned in a vision that he would be burned at the stake, but he would not let fear seize him. Refusing to confess Caesar as Lord, the old saint went to his death willingly, even to the point of telling his tormentors it would not be necessary to nail him to the stake, that he would remain there by the grace of God. For he heard a voice from heaven say, "Play the man," and play the man he did. We will hear thousands of stories of such bravery at the Wedding Feast of the Lamb.

How do you raise a young man to be that kind of man? It begins with simple things, like risking to ask God for something in prayer—for if God does not answer, what is the young man to do? He must persevere, hold fast, not give up so easily. He must guard his heart against the Accuser. The breakthrough might come later, or in answer to a different prayer, in a different situation. He must be encouraged to take a stand for his faith. He must be taught to confront the evil one, as Jesus did in the wilderness, and to command him to flee when he is under spiritual attack.

Are you spiritually brave? Is there a story that comes to mind?

Describe what your being more spiritually brave would look like *a year from now.* How would it express itself in your life?

Is there anything risky unfolding in your life right now God may be using to call out a spiritual bravery?

Where can you take a step to cultivate this in your life?

DEVELOPING A BRAVE HEART COMES DOWN TO THIS—WHEREVER THE BOY IS frightened, wherever you see a hesitancy or uncertainty in him, gently take him there, over time, and help him conquer his fear. The place we want to come to ourselves, as we learn to press through our own fears. I believe it is why God continues to take us into situations that arouse fear in us. The enemy would say we've blown it, or that we've been abandoned; the Father says, "You can do this—play the man." This is how courage is developed.

Your Father wants to gently take you into whatever it is that frightens you, wherever he sees a hesitancy or uncertainty in you so that he can call out and validate a bravery you truly have. He wants to say to you "You can do this—play the man." This is how courage is developed.

React to this. What are the fears God wants to take you into?

Write out your prayer regarding your fears and desire to follow God into those fears to develop courage/bravery.

Remember what you must believe in this season of training as a warrior:

You are at war.
The God whose image you bear is a Warrior.
God will provide all you need to be the Warrior you truly are.
Much of what you encounter is either Warrior training or a battle you must fight, or both at the same time.

CONVICTION

IN *THE KINGDOM OF HEAVEN*, THERE IS A SCENE WHERE, THROUGH ANCIENT ceremony and ritual, Balian is given the oath and office of a knight. As he kneels, Balian's father gives him his oath: "Be without fear in the face of your enemies. Be brave and upright, that God may love thee. Speak the truth, always—even if it leads to your death. Safeguard the helpless and do no wrong. That is your oath." And a noble oath it is. My boys love scenes like this. I love scenes like this. There is something in a noble oath, a code, a cause, that stirs the heart of a man. To learn, for example, that *samurai* means "to serve." To be dangerous and powerful in order to serve. As with the samurai, nearly every warrior society down through the ages had a code of some sort. After all, we aren't raising reckless warriors; we are raising men who fight *for a cause*.

So, again, for what is God raising you up to be a Warrior?

AS JOHN SAYS OF THE YOUNG MEN WHO HAVE OVERCOME THE EVIL ONE, "And the word of God lives in you" (1 John 2:14 NIV). It was in my twenties that I developed a passion for the Word of God. I've seen this to be true in other young men—they come to take their faith seriously at this stage. It is no longer "my parents' faith," it is mine now. It might happen in high school, but more often in college. We should not attempt to rush this. It needs to come organically, from within. How do we not just know, but *love* the Word of God? Rote memorization won't do it, and I've counseled too many young men whose souls grew numb to the Scriptures *because* of Bible class. It ought to sober us that the Scribes and Pharisees knew more Bible than you or I ever will, and yet they couldn't recognize Jesus. The greatest enemy of true faith has always been religion (notice who Jesus reserves his harshest words for), and a religious attitude is *not* what we are after. Let them see your love for the Scriptures. Let them see the Word of God dwell in you richly. Talk about it naturally, as you bring it into daily life. Teach the young man to have time with God that is real and meaningful.

It's easy to either get very defensive or feel a ton of shame when the issue of God's Word comes up. But let's be honest—how passionate and alive is God's Word to you?

Shame? What Shame? I profess the Word of God to be my anchor, my "fixed point", the inerrant authority for my life and faith! What I practice for longer-than-I-want-to-admit seasons of my life is a "hot" and "cold" cycle of passionately profound immersion in God's Word and then a bout of spiritual amnesia where I've practically forgotten there is a God and that he has spoken. (Craig)

If it isn't, could it be? Ask God to give you a hunger and thirst for his Word.

AN EPIC STORY

THERE IS SOMETHING IN THE HEART OF A YOUNG MAN THAT SAYS, "GIVE ME a cause. I am supposed to fight." He is made for battle, and he must be given a Christianity that includes a great battle. The battle to behave yourself—the Christianity of "just don't do anything bad"—will not suffice, I assure you. Minding your manners needs no Warrior. The young man becoming a Warrior needs a bigger story. I remember Larry Crabb saying the one thing that impressed him as a boy was that his father loved something and Someone more than he loved anything else, even his family. It was not a form of rejection, for the boy knew he was loved. It was a mystery and an invitation to discover what that Something was all about.

Younger men, the cause you'd like to be a part of will require seasons of training, character development, and preparation. How patient or impatient are you with God's timing for your life?

Older men, isn't it easy to settle into the lifestyle, direction, and causes you've chosen without renewing or reevaluating with God the changes he might want to make? Is there something new, greater, epic that he would have you step into? What would keep you from changing directions at this point in your life?

I'VE EXPLAINED WHAT I BELIEVE TO BE THE EPIC GOD IS CALLING US TO IN other places, so I won't go into that here. How desperately we need to recover a Warrior culture among men, if only on behalf of the young men who need Someone and Something to look up to. It may never happen in our churches—oh, how I pray it does—but it can happen in our fellowships of men. Above all, the boy needs to see his father is a Warrior, caught up in a great battle.

If you are unfamiliar with the Epic God is calling us to, we'd encourage you to read a short book John wrote titled *Epic*. It's actually written in a way that nonbelievers as well can clearly understand this story we've found ourselves in and our role in it.

RAISING THE WARRIOR IN A MAN

And so it might be best for a man to go back to those times and places in his own story when the Warrior was wounded. Invite Christ to take you there, and speak, and bring the healing you need. Some of you just need to live as the Beloved Son for a while, and then experience your initiation as a Cowboy. Then you can enter the Warrior stage.

Pause, and ask God, "When was the Warrior wounded in me?" Write down the events that come to mind. Next, try to name the message that came to you in that wounding (e.g., "You are a coward," etc.).

Then one by one invite Jesus into those events to heal and restore the Warrior heart in you, and to break the power of those messages.

WARRIOR TRAINING

As I thought about this chapter—and our fatherlessness and our predicament—I wondered, *How does God bring that to a man, when there is no sort of training for spiritual warriors like this?*

Then it felt as though the Holy Spirit was gently but firmly directing my thoughts to my own life. As I thought back over the past twenty years, I saw that nearly everything I've learned as a Warrior, I've learned on the field of battle, in the school of reality, the classroom of my life. I realized the answer to the question: "How does God raise the Warrior in a man?"

Hardship.

Something in you knows it's true. I think this is where we have most misinterpreted what God is up to in our lives. As long as we are committed to the path of least resistance, to making our lives comfortable, trial and tribulation will feel unkind. But, if we are looking for a dojo in which to train as a Warrior, well then—this is the real deal. What better means than hardship? What better way to train a Warrior than by putting a man in situation after situation where he must fight?

What are the hardships you've misinterpreted as simply being examples of the fact that "life is hard," when it may very well have been God's means to train you as a Warrior?

What fight is he putting you in now as training?

YOU *WILL* BE TESTED. LIKE JESUS' DESERT TRIAL, THE ENEMY COMES, PROBING the perimeter. He knows your story, knows where the weak spots are. But this *is* our training. This is how we develop a resolute heart. We make no agreements with whatever the temptation or accusation is. We repent the moment we do stumble, repent quickly, so that we don't get hammered. We pray for strength from the Spirit of God in us. We directly—and this is the one thing so many men fail to do—we *directly* resist the enemy, out loud, as Jesus did in the desert. We quote Scripture against him. We command him to flee.

BE INTENTIONAL

Life will provide a thousand sessions for the raising of the Warrior. Turn your radar on during the day, and intentionally *don't* take the path of least resistance. Take the road less traveled. If you are the kind of man who just hates any sort of conflict, then walk into some. When an awkward subject comes up at work—or at home—don't run. Move toward it. Ask hard questions. Hold your ground. The phone rings, and you can tell by the caller ID it's someone you don't want to talk to. Pick it up. Engage. That's the key word—*engage*. So, as I said in the Cowboy stage, head into something that will really test you, and you'll see the Warrior emerge.

Be decisive. Every time a man makes a hard decision, the Warrior in him is strengthened. Notice those places you are normally passive, and do the opposite.

Reading this, what are you moved to do?

FACING YOUR ENEMY

EVENTUALLY WE FIND THAT WE MUST FACE OUR ENEMY HEAD-ON. NOW when it comes to direct conflict with foul spirits and the kingdom of darkness, I know many men who have avoided this far too long. Good men, for the most part, but intimidated from any direct conflicts with the enemy, and preferring to stay in the human realm.

We have the example of Jesus in the wilderness as a model for how we must resist Satan (and all foul spirits—for Satan has many subordinate demons working for him). Jesus treats him like a real person (not a human being, but a fallen angel with an intellect and personality). He doesn't treat the temptations and accusations and assaults simply as if they are weaknesses within himself; nor does he act as though they will go away if he tries to ignore him. He directly confronts the demon present out loud, with authority, and with Scripture.

Acts 16:16–18 gives us the biblical basis of our authority as believers over all foul spirits:

> Once when we were going to the place of prayer, we were met by a slave girl who had a spirit by which she predicted the future. She earned a great deal of money for her owners by fortune-telling. This girl followed Paul and the rest of us, shouting, "These men are servants of the Most High God, who are telling you the way to be saved." She kept this up for many days. Finally Paul became so troubled that he turned around and said to the spirit, "In the name of Jesus Christ I command you to come out of her!" At that moment the spirit left her. (NIV)

Direct confrontation will become more and more necessary as you rise up as a Warrior, and take back ground that you have surrendered, and begin to advance the kingdom of God.

Why have you avoided the spiritual battle John refers to above?

I've let the extreme wackiness of some dictate my theology or understanding of spiritual warfare. I haven't wanted to be labeled or viewed by others as one of those over-the-top biblically excessive loonies; thus I've thrown the baby out with the bath water. (Craig)

Many men live most, if not all their lives running, hiding, compromising with their enemies. What will you look back on, years from now, and regret losing *if* you don't face your enemy head-on now?

Below, list your conflicts and the devil's assaults against you, then how you must resist him (which may be some combination of prayer and specific action).

Conflict: The Devil's Assault Against You	How You Will Resist

You'll want to read up on this. Ed Murphy's *The Handbook of Spiritual Warfare* is excellent, as is *Victory Over the Darkness* and *The Bondage Breaker* by Neil Anderson, as well as *Spiritual Warfare* by Timothy Warner.

SOME COUNSEL FROM THE BATTLEFIELD

One Battle at a Time

THE ENEMY'S FIRST PLAN IS TO KEEP A MAN OUT OF THE BATTLE ALTOGETHER—through fear, or self-doubt, through bad theology or ignorance, through his wounds, or through the passivity we inherited from Adam. If that doesn't work (and it's worked with many a man), and a man rises up to be a Warrior, the enemy switches to dog piling, trying to bury you in battles.

Do you have to take on every battle that comes your way?

What are the battles you're engaged in now that you should drop, and which are you to stay engaged in? (Ask Jesus, *Do you want me to fight this?)*

Fight Your Battles Once

YOU DON'T WANT TO GET WORN OUT THROUGH HOURS OF SPECULATION, working over and over in your mind how some event is going to go. You don't know how it's going to go, and I have never once found speculation helpful. It simply ties you in knots. Resist it. Don't fight your battles twice—once in worry and anticipation, and the second time when you actually enter into the event itself. Cross that bridge when you come to it, as the saying goes. This will require strength and resolve, resisting speculation like this, and it will strengthen the Warrior in you. It's another way of learning not to yield your heart—in this case, to worry and fretting.

Is your Father the source of your fretting and anxiety?

What do you need to let go of, stop speculating about?

During Any Important Event, Assume It's Warfare

IN NORMAL DAY-TO-DAY LIVING, HASSLES, ACCIDENTS, OR SETBACKS MIGHT simply be that and nothing more. A flat tire is a flat tire. But during an important event, Stasi and I, and the fellowship we live in, have found it's nearly always warfare. Treat it as such. And by "important event," I mean anything redemptive—a mission, of course, but also a source of joy, like an anniversary. The enemy is out to steal your joy more than anything else.

Let's get real practical and deal with real-time spiritual warfare in the next few paragraphs and exercises. What's the warfare you're facing right now?

Resist it quickly . . . like now.

Resist It Quickly

DON'T LET THINGS GET A FOOTHOLD. HOWEVER TIRED YOU MAY BE, however distracted or inconvenient the moment, *now* is the time to fight. "Ye must be watchful," says à Kempis, "especially in the beginning of the temptation; for the enemy is then more easily overcome, if he is not suffered to enter the door of our hearts, but is resisted at the first knock."

When you pray, or resist, or act decisively *in the moments you least want to*, the Warrior in you is strengthened. Next time you'll be even stronger.

You Won't Feel Like a Warrior

THIS IS IMPORTANT TO KNOW, FOR WE LONG TO FEEL BRAVE AND POWERFUL in battle. But that is rarely the case. In the *midst* of battle, you will often feel confused, disoriented, perhaps overwhelmed, troubled with self-doubt. You will certainly feel the spirits that are present, and they will try to make you believe it's *you* that is angry, or prideful, or whatever assaults you. Set your face like a flint. It will clear, eventually, and you will again feel the presence of God and who you truly are. In the midst of it, war is chaos.

As you were resisting, what were the messages, thoughts, or discouraging ideas that crossed your mind?

Did you feel like a warrior as you resisted?

If not, those are the feelings and common experience of warfare John is referring to. You must set your face like a flint and continue the battle. Do you see this?

Stay With It

IT TAKES MORE THAN A SINGLE SKIRMISH TO WIN A BATTLE, AND A HATE-filled enemy usually will not yield at a single swing from us. Keep at it. The enemy is testing your resolve. Show him that no matter how long it takes, you fully intend to win.

On the immediate issue you've been praying over, do you need to "stay with it"?

It Will Make You Holy

THE ENEMY IS COMING, JESUS TOLD HIS DISCIPLES, BUT "HE HAS NO HOLD on me" (John 14:30 NIV). I love that, I just love it. Jesus is so clean, they've got nothing on him. It tells us something vital about warfare. First, that holiness is your best weapon. Spiritual warfare will make you holy. Trust me.

Why is the enemy using that particular angle on you at this particular moment? Is it an occasion for repentance? Deeper healing? Strengthening feeble places?

Invite Christ into that area of your life.

THE BATTLE WE FIND OURSELVES IN GIVES A WHOLE NEW PURPOSE TO holiness. The call is not to "be a moral man because it's decent." The call is to "become a holy man and a Warrior, for you are needed in this battle, and if you do not become that man, you will be taken out."

The recovery of the Warrior is absolutely crucial to the recovery of a man. All else rests on this, for you will have to fight, my brothers, for everything you desire and everything you hold dear in this world. Despite what you feel, or what you may have been told, you have a Warrior's heart, because you bear the image of God. And he will train you to become a great Warrior, if you'll let him.

We've included a copy of what we call "The Daily Prayer." As you read through it, you'll see that it is pretty much Scripture put into prayer. As a daily prayer we've found this reorients our hearts, minds, and souls to the realities of our day and the battles we face. Begin to pray this, or something like it, on a daily basis and see what difference it makes.

A DAILY PRAYER FOR FREEDOM (from *Waking the Dead*)

My dear Lord Jesus, I come to you now to be restored in you—to renew my place in you, my allegiance to you, and to receive from you all the grace and mercy I so desperately need this day. I honor you as my sovereign Lord, and I surrender every aspect of my life totally and completely to you. I give you my body as a living sacrifice; I give you my heart, soul, mind, and strength; and I give you my spirit as well.

I cover myself with your blood—my spirit, my soul, and my body. And I ask your Holy Spirit to restore my union with you, seal me in you, and guide me in this time of prayer. In all that I now pray, I include (my wife, and/or my children, by name). Acting as their head, I bring them under my authority and covering, and I come under your authority and covering. Holy Spirit, apply to them all that I now pray on their behalf.

Dear God, holy and victorious Trinity, you alone are worthy of all my worship, my heart's devotion, all my praise and all my trust and all the glory of my life. I worship you, bow to you, and give myself over to you in my heart's search for life. You alone are Life, and you have become my life. I renounce all other gods, all idols, and I give you the place in my heart and in my life that you truly deserve. I confess here and now that it is all about you, God, and not about me. You are the Hero of this story, and I belong to you. Forgive me, God, for my every sin. Search me and know me and reveal to me any aspect of my life that is not pleasing to you, expose any agreements I have made, and grant me the grace of a deep and true repentance.

Heavenly Father, thank you for loving me and choosing me before you made the world. You are my true Father—my Creator, my Redeemer, my Sustainer, and the true end of all things, including my life. I love you; I trust you; I worship you. Thank you for proving your love for me by sending your only Son, Jesus, to be my substitute and representative. I receive him and all his life and all his work, which you ordained for me. Thank you for including me in Christ, for forgiving me my sins, for granting me his righteousness, for making me complete in him. Thank you for making me alive with Christ, raising me with him, seating me with him at your right hand, granting me his authority, and anointing me with your Holy Spirit. I receive it all with thanks and give it total claim to my life.

Jesus, thank you for coming for me, for ransoming me with your own life. I honor you as my Lord; I love you, worship you, trust you. I sincerely receive you as my redemption, and I receive all the work and triumph of your crucifixion, whereby I am cleansed from all my sin through your shed blood, my old nature is removed, my heart is circumcised unto God, and every claim being made against me is disarmed. I take my place in your cross and death, whereby I have died with you to sin and to my flesh, to the world, and to the evil one. I am crucified with Christ, and I have crucified my flesh with all its passions and desires. I take up my cross and crucify my flesh with all its pride, unbelief, and idolatry. I put off the old man. I now bring the cross of Christ between me and all people, all spirits, all things. Holy Spirit, apply to me (my wife and/or children) the fullness of the work of the crucifixion of Jesus Christ for me. I receive it with thanks and give it total claim to my life.

Jesus, I also sincerely receive you as my new life, my holiness and sanctification, and I receive all the work and triumph of your resurrection, whereby I have been raised with you to a new life, to walk in newness of life, dead to sin and alive to God. I am crucified with Christ, and it is no longer I who live but Christ who lives in me. I now take my place in your resurrection, whereby I have been made alive with you, I reign in life through you. I now put on the new man in all holiness and humility, in all righteousness and purity and truth. Christ is now my life, the one who strengthens me. Holy Spirit, apply to me (my wife and/or my children) the fullness of the resurrection of Jesus Christ for me. I receive it with thanks and give it total claim to my life.

Jesus, I also sincerely receive you as my authority and rule, my everlasting victory over Satan and his kingdom, and I receive all the work and triumph of your ascension, whereby Satan has been judged and cast down, his rulers and authorities disarmed, all authority in heaven and on earth given to you, Jesus, and I have been given fullness in you, the Head over all. I take my place in your ascension, whereby I have been raised with you to the right hand of the Father and established with you in all authority. I bring your authority and your kingdom rule over my life, my family, my household, and my domain.

And now I bring the fullness of your work—your cross, resurrection, and ascension—against Satan, against his kingdom, and against all his emissaries and all their work warring against me and my domain. Greater is he who is in me than he who is in the world. Christ has given me authority to overcome all the power of the evil one, and I claim that authority now over and against every enemy, and I banish them in the name of Jesus Christ. Holy Spirit, apply to me (my wife and my children) the fullness of the work of the ascension of Jesus Christ for me. I receive it with thanks and give it total claim to my life.

Holy Spirit, I sincerely receive you as my Counselor, my Comforter, my Strength, and my Guide. Thank you for sealing me in Christ. I honor you as my Lord, and I ask you to lead me into all truth, to anoint me for all of my life and walk and calling, and to lead me deeper into Jesus today. I fully open my life to you in every dimension and aspect—my body, my soul, and my spirit—choosing to be filled with you, to walk in step with you in all things. Apply to me, blessed Holy Spirit, all of the work and all of the gifts in pentecost. Fill me afresh, blessed Holy Spirit. I receive you with thanks and give you total claim to my life (and my wife and/or children).

Heavenly Father, thank you for granting to me every spiritual blessing in the heavenlies in Christ Jesus.

I receive those blessings into my life today, and I ask the Holy Spirit to bring all those blessings into my life this day. Thank you for the blood of Jesus. Wash me once more with his blood from every sin and stain and evil device. I put on your armor—the belt of truth, the breastplate of righteousness, the shoes of the readiness of the gospel of peace, the helmet of salvation. I take up the shield of faith and the sword of the Spirit, the Word of God, and I wield these weapons against the evil one in the power of God. I choose to pray at all times in the Spirit, to be strong in you, Lord, and in your might.

Father, thank you for your angels. I summon them in the authority of Jesus Christ and release them to war for me and my household. May they guard me at all times this day. Thank you for those who pray for me; I confess I need their prayers, and I ask you to send forth your Spirit and rouse them, unite them, raising up the full canopy of prayer and intercession for me. I call forth the kingdom of the Lord Jesus Christ this day throughout my home, my family, my life, and my domain. I pray all of this in the name of Jesus Christ, with all glory and honor and thanks to him.

10

Lover

I found the one my heart loves . . .
—Song of Songs 3:4 NIV

BEFORE STARTING

Without referring back to the book, from your recollection and in your own words, describe the Lover.

While the stages overlap, and there is some aspect of them in every phase of a man's life, there is also a time in a man's life when one of the stages is prominent. Is this stage, the Lover:

A stage you anticipate going through in the future? If so, read it knowing the time will come when God will guide you through this season. But until then, be patient in your current stage of the masculine journey. Give yourself the grace to learn, grow and take in all God has for you in *this* season of life without either jumping the gun or getting anxious about the next season.

The stage you think you're currently in? Obviously be alert. Read these next two chapters as a map for the journey you're currently on. With heart and eyes wide open, be keen to all God has for you. He will affirm, validate, convict, heal, and call you more deeply into all the lessons and growth he has for you in this stage of life.

He will invite you into some difficult challenges and bless you with more intimacy with him. Don't prematurely assume you're ready to move on. God orders the seasons of a man's life; your graduation *will* come.

Or a stage you feel you have passed through? God will no doubt remind you of the people, events, hardships, and joys of this stage to affirm that indeed you have passed through this stage well. And while saying that, be willing to allow God to speak of the "more" he'd like to do in you as a Lover. You may find a number of things you missed in this stage. The good news is that it's never too late. Be expectant; there's more for you.

These questions are best answered with some spaciousness around them. Don't be blowing through the reflective exercises to quickly finish this chapter for whatever reason (your small-group discussion tonight, to keep your schedule of finishing this workbook, or out of a subconscious push to move past this because it's difficult). Take your time, give it some thought, and ask God to guide and protect your reflections.

FIRST REACTIONS

The Lover . . . well, what surfaced from your reading/rereading of this chapter? Were there any new thoughts, any *"whoa"* moments, something you'd like to ponder more, questions? Write out your first reactions.

KEY POINTS OF THE CHAPTER

- The great danger for the Warrior is not defeat, but success, for, as I said before, what the evil one then does to a good Warrior—if he cannot take him out, cannot keep him from entering the battle at all, as he has intimidated so many men—is to bury him.
- Down through its history the church has held up the good, the true, and the beautiful as a sort of trinity of virtues. As we think over the stages of the masculine journey, we find that the boy begins to understand Good as he learns right from wrong, and the Warrior fights for what is true, but when a man comes to see that the beautiful is the best of the three, then is the Lover awakened.
- It is very good for the Warrior to be arrested by Beauty. It provides a great balance to his soul, lest he simply be a fighter. The Celts had a phrase, "Never give a sword to a man who can't dance," by which they meant if he is not *also* becoming a poet, be careful how much Warrior you allow a man to be.
- That which draws us to the heart of God is that which often first lifts our own hearts above the mundane, awakens longing and desire. And it is that life, my brothers, the life of your heart, that God is most keenly after.
- While in other realms God will remain Father, and Initiator, when the Lover begins to emerge God invites the man to become his "intimate one." This is the crucial stage. The danger for the Warrior is that life becomes defined by battle, and that is not good for the soul nor is it true to our story, for there is something deeper than battle and that, my friends, is Romance.
- The awakening of his heart is essential if a man would truly love a woman.
- The heart of the Lover never gets to awaken or develop in a man so long as he rejects the heart, chooses to remain in the world of analysis, dissection, and "reason is everything."

TO SAY THAT I HAD COME TO THE MOUNTAINS, ALONE, TO BE WITH GOD, would sound as though I'd come of my own accord, making the journey seem noble, austere, spiritually gallant. But that would not be honest. I came to the mountains because I was *summoned*. Exhausted from months of battle and hard labor, I needed to get away, knew that I needed to get away, yet somehow could not bring myself to do it. You know how that is—you find yourself on the treadmill, hating it, but accustomed, even addicted to it, and getting off seems like an inconvenience, even if it will save your life. Thank God, something deeper in me was being called—a longing that is hard to describe, a compelling ache for Beauty. That is how God drew me.

The great danger for the Warrior is not defeat, but success, for, as I said before, what the evil one then does to a good Warrior—if he cannot take him out, cannot keep him from entering the battle at all, as he has intimidated so many men—is to bury him. Dog pile. Make it all about battle. Make it constant. One battle after another, like Jeremiah Johnson faces as his fame becomes known, like David faces because of Saul's jealousy and then because his enemies learn he is the man to contend with. Easy Company of the 506th in WWII kept getting one tough assignment after another because they could handle them. Like Jesus, who has to duck out of town because word has gotten out and everyone has come to the door with some need or another (see Mark 1:29–37).

We must not let the battle become everything.

So for several years I had made a practice of withdrawing to some remote place to be with God, usually for three days. Up till now my mode had been to backpack into wilderness in order to assure solitude and all that it brings. But this year I was just too tired to hike up any mountain like a packhorse with my camp upon my back. So I chose a place I could drive to, up a long four-wheel-drive road, hoping that would place me high enough in the mountains to be where my heart comes alive, which for me is above the tree line in the very high country. When I finally pulled over and parked, I was in a broad mountain meadow surrounded by glacial peaks, wildflowers in full bloom, the sun so hot because there was so little atmosphere left up there to filter it.

I forsook my usual ritual of first setting up camp, took my fly rod and walked out to the middle of the meadow, stood there for a moment, gave a deep sigh, and let it all go, all that I had left behind, in order to allow all this beauty some room to come in. The warmth, the smell of meadow grasses and wild mint, the sound of the little stream, the peaks all round—I stood there for some time to let the encompassing beauty enfold me. Then I began to fish.

The stream there runs about five to seven feet wide, making its way through the meadow rather whimsically, with twists and turns only nature can explain, in no apparent hurry to be anywhere. The brook trout that live in that stream are tiny, about six inches long, and despite a brief summer followed by long, harsh winters spent under snow and ice, they are vibrant and energetic. Delicate little creatures with green backs wormed crisscross with patterns the color of moss, red fins rimmed with white, and dozens of lavender spots along their sides, within which lies a bright pink dot. As Hopkins says, "Glory be to God for dappled things, for skies of couple-color as a brinded cow; for rose-moles all in stipple upon trout that swim." I caught a few, and held them in the glacial waters, amazed at their beauty and life, then returned them to make it through another winter. "Little poems" is what I called them. Living flashes of beauty.

Having lost a fly in the bushes—I wasn't casting well, partly because it had been a long time since last I fished, but mostly because I was distracted by so much beauty—I knelt down to tie on another, found myself kneeling in shallow water that rippled over a shelf of stones and pebbles on the inside of a bend in the creek. The water here was flowing only three inches deep—just enough to wet the stones into fullness of color, as you'll notice how a stone will leap to life when you wet it, as even the streets look their best after a rain. The pebbles beneath me spread out in a mosaic made of a thousand granite stones, the largest no bigger than a half-dollar and most of them between a quarter and a dime. Purples, browns of many hues from tan to chocolate, yellows, black, white, ground to utter smoothness by the glaciers, laid out like a Byzantine mosaic. Each stone was dappled, being granite, and together they made a dappled pattern, which was in turn dappled by the rippling waters rippling sunlight over them. I could have gazed at the fluttering mosaic all afternoon. It was captivating, and soothing, and intriguing—all the things that gentle, intimate, flowing beauty offers.

I was still kneeling in the shallow water, and as I looked down, my eye fell upon one small stone in particular, as if it were somehow illuminated, which is not quite right because it was one of the darker stones in the mosaic, almost black, so it could not have stood out for its brightness. But those of you who have had this experience will know what I mean, when in a crowd of people one face stands out to you almost to say *look at me*, or when you are reading a passage and one sentence causes you to stop and linger while all the rest of the page fades into the background but for that phrase. The stone was in the shape of a heart.

A kiss from God. A love note. I was being romanced. ☙

What are the most beautiful places you've ever been? You may not be a poet, but describe them. What does being in the midst of such beauty stir up in you?

THE AESTHETIC CONVERSION

NOW WE COME TO A FORK IN THE ROAD IN THE MASCULINE JOURNEY, A stage that is both essential and, sadly, often overlooked and bypassed by many a man. The stage of the Lover. By this I do not primarily mean that time in a young man's life when he falls in love with a girl. Though that is part of it, I don't believe it is the core of the stage or even its ultimate expression. ☙

If falling in love with a girl is not the core of the Lover stage or even its ultimate expression, what is the core?

THERE ARE MOVEMENTS IN THE YOUNG MAN'S SOUL THAT WOULD BE BEST TO take place *before* Eve steps into the picture, movements that often do take place but go unrecognized until she is there.

Down through its history the church has held up the good, the true, and the beautiful as a sort of trinity of virtues.

As we think over the stages of the masculine journey, we find that the boy begins to understand Good as he learns right from wrong, and the Warrior fights for what is true, but when a man comes to see that the beautiful is the best of the three, then is the Lover awakened.

When did the movement in your soul begin? When did beauty become an important category or virtue for you? If you can recall, describe your aesthetic conversion.

It may have been my first backpacking trip into the High Sierras. I was in eighth grade and I can recall being drawn to simply gaze at the alpine meadow brooks, their wild flowers, the moss, grasses, and lichen. This may have been the first time I stopped to notice a sunset, alpenglow, glaciated rocks, and the differences between pine trees. They were baby steps, but something began there and then. (Craig)

AS WITH THE OTHER STAGES, YOU'LL FIND EXPRESSIONS OF IT IN HIS YOUTH, but something happens about the same time a young man begins to become a Warrior, late in the Cowboy Ranger stage, late in his teens and into his twenties. Awakening with his passion for a battle you will often find another longing emerging, a longing for . . . he knows not what. An ache, often expressed in music, or perhaps poetry, a film or a book that stirs him like never before. His soul is undergoing a sort of second birth.

What was the first music, movies, poetry, or books you began to enjoy?

Photography was first. I enjoyed the photos in Life and National Geographic. I noticed and liked the subjects, composition, and colors of the pictures. Then music struck a deep cord, the Beach Boys, then the British bands—the Beatles and the far superior Stones. I could make distinctions in the beat and rhythm, lyrics began to move me, and I began to label songs "cool" or "groovy." Films lagged behind a bit after that. I think Patton was the first film I saw several times because of the story it told and it's profound affect upon me. (Craig)

HE BEGINS TO *NOTICE.* SEES MOONLIGHT ON WATER FOR THE VERY FIRST time. Is stopped by certain movements in a song he loves. Pauses to realize that a snowflake or a flower is really altogether amazing. Discovers authors that stir him with some special quality in their writings. Now, yes, it is often aroused by a woman. Woman is the personification of Beauty, and it often takes her to turn the young man's attention from adventure and battle, "turn his head," as the phrase has it, and his heart comes along for the turning too. But often the awakening comes in the world of Nature, especially if the young man has been allowed a generous season in the Cowboy stage. You see this in the poetry of David, whose lines are filled with the sun and stars, the dew of the fields, the brooks from which he drank so deeply.

This is very good for the Warrior, to be arrested by Beauty. It provides a great balance to his soul, lest he simply be a fighter. The Celts had a phrase, "Never give a sword to a man who can't dance," by which they meant if he is not *also* becoming a poet, be careful how much Warrior you allow a man to be.

And so, have you been arrested by Beauty? Are you both poet and warrior?

Yes, however, I've noticed that during those spells when I've stumbled back into the matrix of managing life and my relationship with God begins to run off the vapors of the season prior, that beauty is one of the first things to go. I'm in auto-pilot and no longer taste food, smell the mountains in the morning air, pause to watch a hawk, take a second look at a photo, or see the two-year-old smiling at me from her grocery cart in the market. My books get dusty and my heart atrophies a bit. (Craig)

If not, are you aware of the misbalance simply being a Warrior brings you?

Is there something that balks at being a "poet"? Why?

JOHN SHARES ABOUT A WONDERFUL TIME FLY FISHING ON THE SAN JUAN river with Brent. Captured by the waves of beauty unfolding, he says, My heart was awakened, wooed by the great Lover. It is often beyond our reach to describe to others the effect upon the soul that the fellowship of men upon a river, rod in hand, brings. More difficult still to capture the poetry, the beauty that sneaks upon us like the kiss of an evening breeze gently touching your face. But these moments are among the most treasured of memories, and they retain the power even still to lift my soul to Beauty, and eternity, to God. Catching a fish doesn't matter anymore, nor does the elk, nor the pheasant in the field, but only what they brought us here to find. As Thoreau said, most fishermen spend their entire lives without knowing it is not fish they are after.

In what beautiful place or experience have you found God wooing you in a similar manner?

If at this point you find yourself wondering about all this talk of beauty and poetry, and you're scratching your head and wondering, "What is he talking about?", could it be that I'm describing something wonderfully true but largely unexperienced by you? (Like hearing the superlatives about Kauai that don't move you until you've been to Kauai?) Let me suggest that if this all sounds a bit foreign to you it may be because either you haven't moved well through this stage or this stage was simply about the beauty of a woman for you.

THE POETIC AWAKENING

WE'VE HEARD AD INFINITUM THAT MEN ARE RATIONAL BEINGS, ALONG WITH the supporting evidence that our brains work differently than do women's, and this is true. Spatial abstractions, logic, analysis—men tend to excel in these because we are more left- than right-brained, and the commissural fibers that connect the two hemispheres appear in women in ratios far higher than in men. Women have an interstate uniting both sides of their brains. Men have a game trail. Thus men tend to compartmentalize, a capacity that allows men to handle the atrocities of war, and administrate justice. It also makes them excellent chess players and auto mechanics.

And yet . . . I don't buy it. Too many men hide behind reason and logic. A man must grow beyond mere rationale, or he will be stunted as a man, certainly as a Lover.

Do you hide behind reason and logic as many men do? How would others who know you answer this question regarding you?

In seminary I wanted to get a Ph.D. in Theology and blow people away with my grasp of the deep things of God. Being a "biblical" intellect was, to me, the top of the make-a-difference-for-God pyramid. Being the "Bible Answer Man" was godly masculinity. At that time I didn't have a full and accurate appraisal of my, ahh . . . intellectual capacities. So much of that was me longing to make a difference and looking for a way to do it while continuing to hide. Now, those who know me might very well accuse me of hiding, but I doubt that reason, logic, and intellectual pursuits would be where they accuse me of hiding. (Craig)

DAVID WAS A CUNNING TACTICIAN AS A WARRIOR, BUT HE WAS ALSO A POET of the first order. Jesus could hold his own in any theological debate, but he is also an artist (the Creator of this world of Beauty) and a poet (by whose Spirit David wrote the Psalms) and a storyteller. When he says, "Consider the lilies of the field," he does not mean analyze them, but rather, *behold* them, take them in, let their beauty speak, for "Solomon in all his glory was not dressed as beautifully as they are" (Matt. 6:29 NLT). He appeals to their beauty to show us the love of God.

The Lover is awakened when a man comes to see that the poetic is far truer than the propositional and the analytical, and whatever physiology might say, I've seen it happen in many men.

What do these thoughts rouse in you?

Is this the man you want to be . . . Warrior and poet? Sharp rational skills and abilities, as well as a comfort with mystery?

Is this the direction you're going or are you resistant or hesitant for some reason? If so, why?

I CAME TO CHRIST NOT BECAUSE I WAS LOOKING FOR A RELIGION, BUT because I was looking for the Truth, and, having found it, I knew it must be true across the realms of human culture. I yearned for an intellectually defensible case for Christianity, and I found it first in Schaeffer and then in the Reformed writers, to whom I remain very grateful. There are reasons to believe. My head was satisfied, but my heart yearned for something more. While I found logic in my theology (and went to war against my philosopher professor), I was being wooed by Beauty in the mountains and deserts, in literature and music. Why did they bring me closer to God than analysis? Why did the dissection of systematic theology cut all life out of the living Word? Then I discovered writers like Oswald Chambers, C. S. Lewis, and his Sage, George MacDonald. Smart men, all of them, quite capable of making a good argument. But that is not the essence of their glory. They speak to the mind, but also to the heart. More so to the heart.

Who have been the men you've admired and yearned to sit under? Those who merely speak to the mind or those who can make a good argument but also speak to the heart?

Knowledge isn't all it's cracked up to be. (Craig)

What has brought you closer to God—analysis or beauty?

What is the essence of your glory—your mind or your heart?

Older men, has there been a shift over the years? Should there be?

I HUNGERED FOR TRANSCENDENCE, FOR MYSTERY. I BEGAN TO PAINT, AND the gap between my heart's awakening and the arid propositions of so many self-assured rationalists no longer spoke to me. The riddle was solved when I learned that Chambers had first been an art student before he became a theologian. His biographer, David McCasland, wrote, "If there was a childhood trait that foreshadowed his gift and passion as a young man, it appeared in the realm of art." Ah, yes, that would explain it. Here is a man who knows the Way of the Heart because he knows and loves Beauty. Long before he went to the mission field (as a mature Warrior), Chambers wrote poetry, even a poem in defense of poetry, comparing "those divine essences we call Music, Poetry, Art, through which God breathes His Spirit of peace into the soul" with "mechanical monotony of so-called fact."

That which draws us to the heart of God is that which often first lifts our own hearts above the mundane, awakens longing and desire. And it is that life, my brothers, the life of your heart, that God is most keenly after.

What is it about *your* heart that it is *the* heart God is most keenly after?

Describe in terms of heart and mind the man you have been and the man you desire to be.

GOD AS LOVER

Who do you know that seems to truly be in love with Christ? Someone who truly has a personal, intimate relationship with Christ?

JOHN WESLEY WAS THIRTY-FIVE WHEN HE EXPERIENCED THE NOW FAMOUS "warming" of his heart—not his mind—toward Christ, and knew in that moment he had become not merely a Christian, but something more—a lover of God. Shortly after, he penned the hymn "Jesus, Lover of My Soul," whose first verse goes like this: "Jesus, Lover of my soul/Let me to thy bosom fly." Down through the years the hymn has left many a hymnologist reaching for a more palatable translation. "The difficulty," as John Julian said, "is the term *Lover* as applied to our Lord." Revisions now in hymnbooks read, "Jesus, Savior of my soul" or, "Jesus, Refuge of my soul," which are touching but nothing close to what Wesley meant. He meant *Lover*.

How comfortable are you with language referring to our Lord as our Lover? Explain.

I haven't been comfortable with such language. Initially I thought it was either an indicator of the feminization of the gospel or "buzz" phrases used by over-the-top "mystic" types that additionally are missing a chip and spirituality is their pose. Now, it's the very thing I long for and am beginning to enjoy. (Craig)

Is being described as a man who has fallen in love with God something you hope to be true of you?

DAVID WOULD HAVE HAD NO PROBLEM AT ALL UNDERSTANDING THIS. THE poetry that flowed from the heart of this passionate Lover is filled with unapologetic emotion toward God. He speaks of drinking from God's "river of delights" (Ps. 36:8 NIV), how his Lover has filled his heart "with greater joy" (4:7 NIV) than all the wealth other men have found, and he writes in many of his love songs how his heart sings to God. He cries through the night, aches to be with God, for he has found, really found, his life in God: "You have made known to me the path of life; you will fill me with joy in your presence" (16:11 NIV) to such a degree that his heart and soul "pants for you, O God. My soul thirsts for God" (42:1–2 NIV), his body even longing for God. These are not the words of a dry theologian or moralist. These are not the words of even your average pastor. For him, God's love "is better than life" (63:3 NIV). David is captivated by the Beauty he finds in God. On and on it goes. The man is undone. He is as smitten as any lover might be, only—can we begin to accept this? do we even have a category for it?—his lover is God.

Write your own psalm expressing your faith and love of God.

A VISTA JOURNEY

a view that enhances the journey

Take the time to read these psalms and note the relationship with God that David's vulnerable poetry presents: Psalms 36:8; 4:7; 6:6; 16:11; 42:1; 63:1; 63:3 27:4.

What do you find? What do these psalms stir within you?

IT MIGHT BE HELPFUL TO REMEMBER DAVID IS A GROWN MAN HERE, NOT A teenager, and he is also a battle-hardened Warrior with years of hand-to-hand combat experience.

What do we make of it, really? If a friend of yours in his forties told you he was losing sleep over a lover, crying all the time, writing poetry and love songs, wasting away until he could be with her again, wouldn't you feel that he'd lost all perspective; that yes, love is wonderful, but c'mon, buddy—pull it together?

Would you privately hold the conviction that he was a disaster?

And might you also wish you could experience the same?

HUMILITY URGES US TO TAKE A POSTURE TOWARD DAVID'S LOVE AFFAIR with God that goes something like this: I have no idea what he's talking about, but he's a far better man than I, and he's found something I need to know, need more desperately than I am probably even aware.

Take some time to express to God your heart for him, your desire for your relationship. You may want to read/pray the psalm you wrote to him. Ask him to draw you into an intimate loving relationship with him.

THE LOVER IS NOT AS RARE AS WE MIGHT THINK. IT'S JUST THAT WHEN THIS stage begins to unfold he is not sure how to speak of it, or even whom to tell.

At this stage a man's relationship with God opens a new frontier. While in other realms God will remain Father, and Initiator, when the Lover begins to emerge God invites the man to become his "intimate one." This is the crucial stage. The danger for the Warrior is that life becomes defined by battle, and that is not good for the soul nor is it true to our story, for there is something deeper than battle and that, my friends, is Romance. As Chesterton reminded us, "Romance is the deepest thing in life." Ours is a love story. Anything short of it is a Christianity of dry bones.

A dry bone Christianity or a Romance . . . what has been your experience, and what is your desire?

FALLING IN LOVE

HAVING SAID ALL THIS, WE CAN NOW SPEAK OF FALLING IN LOVE WITH A woman. We *must*. For God has said a man's life is not good without her (Gen. 2:18), so no matter how bold an adventurer or brave a warrior, the man is not living as a man should live unless he makes room for a woman in his life. And, in most cases at this stage, it usually is a woman who comes to awaken the heart of a man.

Now, often what he first sees is not a woman in particular, though he may be looking at her. What he sees is Woman, Beauty itself, tenderness and intimacy and allure, and that is what he falls in love with.

Hopefully, the young man will come to know an actual woman, not the universal but the particular woman across the aisle in chemistry class, or walking her dog in the park. They might begin as friends, and then suddenly one day he sees *her*. He notices. For the stage of the Lover involves seeing as only those in love can see.

When was your masculine heart first awakened by a woman?

When was it, who was it, and what did you feel? How did it affect you, your relationships with your buddies?

Initially it was my fifth grade teacher, Miss Evans. I was in love. I was sure she thought I was something special as well. Later that year it was Chrissy Orchard. It was then my young world was rattled. Suddenly, instead of my thoughts revolving around Stan Musial, Carl Yastrzemski, and the Dodgers, I began to think about her constantly—how I could show off, catch her eye, be with her, see her, belittle and dismiss the competition. I'll never forget the Saturday morning I rode my bike to her house to give her the water-filled baggie with the goldfish I bought her. I knew she was the one. My one concern was whether or not I broke the heart of Miss Evans. What started then continued to eventually govern much of my life . . . much too much of my life. (Craig)

THE AWAKENING OF HIS HEART IS ESSENTIAL IF A MAN WOULD TRULY LOVE a woman. Look at things from her point of view. What does she long for in a man? Every little girl dreams of the day her prince will come. Look at the movies women love—the hero is a *romancer*. He pursues her, wins her heart, takes her into a great adventure and love story. And notice—what is the great sorrow of every woman in a disappointing marriage? Isn't it that he no longer pursues, no longer romances her? Life has been reduced to function and problem solving. What she longs for is what you are meant to become.

How has the lack of awakening in your heart affected your relationships with women (dating, friendships, spouse)?

Which do you prefer—being the pursuer, the romancer, or being the one pursued and romanced? What's your history here?

React to the statement *What she longs for is what you are meant to become.*

SO WHEN IT COMES TO LOVING A WOMAN, THE GREAT DIVIDE LIES BETWEEN men as Lovers and men as Consumers. Does he seek her out, long for her, because really he yearns for her to meet some need in his life—a need for validation (she makes him feel like a man), or mercy, or simply sexual gratification? That man is a Consumer, as my friend Craig calls him. The Lover, on the other hand, wants to fight for *her*—he wants to protect her, make her life better, wants to fill her heart in every way he can. It is no chore for him to bring flowers, or music, spend hours talking together. Having his own heart awakened, he wants to know and love and free her heart. The sexual difference between Lover and Consumer is revealing—read Song of Songs and ask yourself, "Does this sound like our bedroom?" The Lover wants to "make love" to her. The Consumer—well, there are any number of crass phrases men use to talk about getting into bed with her.

Which most accurately describes the motives beneath your relating to woman, "lover" or "consumer"?

For decades it has been far and away that of "consumer." I am ashamed of the many years my governing passion was to "get" something versus "give" myself to Lori. She deserves a spiritual medal of honor! The shift began about twenty years ago, but has been slow in the making, and directly correlates to my finding validation in God and growing in my intimacy with him. (Craig)

Older men, have you seen the shift in your motives over the years?

Yes, thank God. (Craig)

Married men, does Song of Songs sound like your bedroom? Why?

OF COURSE THE STAGE OF THE LOVER BRINGS WITH IT GREAT PAIN AND suffering, because we are speaking of the heart, and the heart, as we all know, is vulnerable like nothing else. Resilient, thank God, but vulnerable. The heights of joy this stage ushers in are greater than any other, but with them comes the potential for sorrow as deep as the heights are high. That is why he must also be a Warrior, and that is why he must find his greatest love in God.

What sorrows and heartbreak have you experienced in your relationship(s) with the woman? How have those painful events altered for good or bad how you now relate to the woman?

What, for you, is risky about loving a woman?

WOUNDED

THE HEART OF THE LOVER NEVER GETS TO AWAKEN OR DEVELOP IN A MAN so long as he rejects the heart, chooses to remain in the world of analysis, dissection, and "reason is everything."

There are many reasons a man shies away from the world of the heart and from his own heart. It might be that he is shamed when he tries to go there by a father who thinks that art, creativity, and beauty "are girl's stuff." Thus, to him, the heart is a source of pain and embarrassment. He thinks a man cannot be a true man and live from the heart. It may be that he has simply never been invited to know his own heart.

But we must remember Adam's fall, and the fierce commitment fallen men all share: Never be in a position where you don't know what to do. Reason and analysis are predictable, manageable. They make us feel that things are under our control. I believe that is why many men stay there. It's safe—even if it kills your soul.

How was your heart treated or viewed as you were growing up? How have you treated or viewed your heart?

In what ways or areas do you need to move away from the world of analysis and into the world of your heart? What would that look like?

THE LOVER IS WOUNDED IN A MAN (OFTEN STARTING IN HIS YOUTH) WHEN he looks to the woman for that primary love and validation his father was meant to bestow. It is often wounded deeply through the breakup of a young love affair. And it is wounded when he has a sexual encounter far too soon.

Did you look to the woman for that primary love and validation your father was meant to bestow?

Definitely. If the home was a validating wasteland, what greater thrill and sense of "manliness" can a zit-faced squirrelly teen find other than a zit-faced wounded girl looking for someone to answer her question ("am I beautiful")? I was the guy I feared my two daughters would get involved with. (Craig)

THE LOVER MIGHT COME PARTIALLY ALIVE WHEN A MAN MEETS A WOMAN and falls in love, and for a time his heart seems alive and their romance blossoms. But things begin to fade, and neither he nor she knows why. The reason is that he stopped the progression, never went on to know God as Lover. No woman can satisfy this longing in a man's heart, and no good woman wants to try. When he makes her the center of his universe, it feels romantic for a while, but then the planets start to collide. It's not a big enough romance. He will find his heart awakening again when he opens his heart to God, and though he might have to journey there for a season, he'll find he has something to offer his woman again.

How do you see yourself looking to the woman for a love and validation that either your father or God alone can give you? Another way of putting this might be, can you see from your relationship(s) with women how wounded you are?

So what happens when the woman you're looking to cannot give you what only your father or God can?

Have you turned to pornography, an affair, to other men? Are any of these areas you need victory in? (This is where the Warrior would express itself in taking on the enemy of your being a Lover.)

FINALLY, THERE ARE THOSE OF US WHO HAD SEXUAL EXPERIENCES BEFORE our wedding nights, and I've never met a man for whom the fruit of that was good. It brings a terrible ambiguity into the heart of the Lover. So does early sexual experimentation. For years I was a cautious Lover toward Stasi, and it hurt her. Even on our wedding night she wondered, *Why doesn't he want me passionately?* It introduced a great deal of struggle that took years to heal. The caution had its roots. My first sexual experience was with a girl in high school, and she kept saying, "This will ruin everything." Things did not go well, and what does a young Lover's heart learn from that?

Recalling your early relationships with a girl/woman, is there a wound from either a breakup or a sexual relationship?

As I looked back over the relationships I had with girl friends since high school, I noticed a pattern that troubled me—I always waited until *she* pursued me. Knowing now that is not how a man should act, I wondered, *Where did that begin?* God took me back to my first love, a girl I fell absolutely head over heels for in middle school. I gave her my heart, and she broke it. The first cut is the deepest, as the song so truly says. And after that, I played it safe. Truth be told, I am playing it safe even still, and that has brought Stasi a great deal of hurt and confusion.

Many men who would come alive as a Lover feel stuck, their hearts pinned down long ago through some heartbreak. So it would be good to pray,

> *Father, God, awaken the Lover in me. Stir my heart. Romance me. Take me back into the story of love in my life, and show me where I lost heart. Show me where I have chosen safety over and against coming alive. Show me where deep repentance needs to take place. Heal the Lover heart in me. Awaken me.*

A PAUSE IN THE JOURNEY

an opportunity to reflect on the ground you've just covered

So, having completed this chapter on the Lover, what notes must you record about your life, God, action items, desires, and dreams? (It's important to note these thoughts, because so often, what impresses us in the moments we finish a chapter quickly is lost as we get back into the distracting realities of our day-to-day.)

11

Raising the Lover

Awake, my soul!
—Psalm 57:8 niv

BEFORE STARTING

Before you begin this chapter, our suggestion would be that you scan the previous chapter in this manual, chapter 10. Skim over your notes, responses, and thoughts . . . what was the main point God seemed to emphasize in that chapter? Is there any more time, thought, or prayer you should give to anything in chapter 10?

While there is much in this chapter about *raising* or *fathering* a Lover that a dad will immediately relate to and benefit from, the exercises are written from the perspective that every man, whatever his age, still needs fathering as a Lover.

As a parent reading this chapter, ask yourself: what does my son need at this time? What is required of me as a father, or what kind of father do I want to be? What do I want to offer, protect, guard, and resist on behalf of my son?

FIRST REACTIONS

And again, where did you find your heart going as you went through this chapter? What provoked your thinking . . . what immediate impact did simply reading this have on you?

KEY POINTS OF THE CHAPTER

- When he is a boy, the greatest gift he can be given is to know that his heart matters, matters very, very much. To live in a world of love when you are young enables you to love freely when you are grown.
- When the boy becomes a teen, the heart of the Lover may come out in force, as an intense longing he knows not how to name, but nearly always attached to a Beauty.
- The Lover emerges around the time of the Warrior, those stages overlapping, and let me add he continues right through to the end of a man's life, for the King must be a Lover as he must be a Warrior, and the Sage is a Lover long after he has handed the fighting of battles over to younger men. So what we are cultivating here is something that will grow all your life. We are opening a door that must never be shut.
- We must take in Beauty, often, or we will be taken out by beauty.
- Often her brokenness will remain hidden until she becomes engaged, or married, and then wham—it all comes out. Why is that? You'd think now that she is safe, now that she knows she's loved, she would be in a better place. But that's just it—now that she *is* safe and loved, her soul can quit pushing it all down. Before she is pursued and wanted, she fears that she cannot be herself or no man will want her. Now that she is loved, her heart comes forth and with it the sorrow of her life.

WHEN IT COMES TO AWAKENING, HEALING, MATURING THE LOVER IN A BOY and in a man, I am almost at a loss for words. Too much rushes from my heart and gets bottlenecked somewhere in my throat. (A condition common to the stage, actually, as any man knows who has tried to express his love to a woman, or write poetry or music.) Truth be told, each of these chapters deserves a whole book in its own right, but this—so close to the heart, so close to the heart of God—alas, there is so much to say that I am left nearly speechless. For we enter the realm of mystery when we enter the realm of the Lover, and our hope is in the Great Romancer, who pursues us. I will offer what I may, resting my heart in the fact that he comes, he comes, in ways deeper and greater and more timely than anything we might arrange for ourselves.

The story of the Lover in any man's life is the story of love and beauty, romance and sexuality. Hopefully in that order. Love, then Beauty, followed by Romance and Sexuality. If you'll think back over your own story, you might see how they got tangled, and in seeing that see also how they might now be disentangled.

Have love, beauty, romance, and sexuality gotten tangled in your story? What has been the order of progression in your relationships?

In my life as a young man, sexuality was the predecessor to beauty and romance. (Craig)

God wants to disentangle the wounding, confusion, and effect of the disorder of our younger years. Throughout this chapter God will be offering and inviting you into greater healing. Don't allow the "push" to get through the material keep you from pausing here and there and asking God for more healing, more life. You may want to do that now.

WHEN HE IS A BOY, THE GREATEST GIFT HE CAN BE GIVEN IS TO KNOW THAT his heart matters, matters very, very much. For one, it will encourage him to keep his heart as a living treasure, and not bury it so that forty years later he has to go on an archaeological dig to try to uncover it. Knowing his heart matters and matters deeply will also keep him from turning to the woman to know that he is beloved, a turn far too many of us have taken and from which many of us have not been able to find our way back. To live in a world of love when you are young enables you to love freely when you are grown.

Whatever the message about your heart was as a young boy/man, do you know your heart matters now?

Yes! Absolutely nothing matters more to God than my heart! My embrace of this is going deeper and deeper over time. I used to fear saying this or hearing it said, because in my thinking there are a zillion things that matter to God, and while "yes" there is a hierarchy and loving God with your whole heart is the most important, the other zillion are only an indistinguishable phi unit below . . . and we certainly don't want to encourage people to neglect the trillion for the one. (Craig)

Can you connect the dots between your turning to the Woman and never having heard from your God or father that you are the Beloved Son?

So, as God looks at you and your life, what matters most to him—your obedience, morality, knowledge, doctrine, success, or heart?

Is it difficult for you to pick "heart" over all the others? Why?

If you picked "heart," how does that make you feel about God?

What must you do to recover your heart fully?

As for Beauty, when does the aesthetic conversion come? That is hard to say. I suppose it need not come at all if the boy has been raised with a Lover's heart all his life, for in that case what conversion is needed? And yet . . . that is rare, if for no other reason than the stark reality that the love affair between man and God, and between man and woman, has an enemy, who ever seeks to ruin the Romance by shutting down the heart or trapping it in any way he can.

Can you recall a time when your heart was shut down? How were your relationships affected?

Where have you seen the enemy's ploys in your relationships? How has your relationship with God been assaulted? How about your relationship with your wife?

And so, with such an enemy you see why it's so important for a man to grow as a Warrior prior to becoming the Lover . . . for indeed you have an enemy.

ON THE OTHER HAND, WE HAVE UNDERTAKEN THIS JOURNEY BELIEVING THAT we have a kind, strong, and engaged Father, a Father wise enough to guide us in the Way, generous enough to provide for our journey, offering to walk with us every step. What that means for this stage is that our Lover has been wooing us all our lives.

The Romancer *has* been wooing us from when we were very young. There were things that pierced your heart as a boy—a special place, a book, a picture—and you might not have known it then, but that was God awakening the Lover in you. (Some of you might benefit greatly from returning to those things even now, as a way of recovering the heart that was lost.)

What rouses/pierces your heart now?

What as a young boy pierced your heart but has long since been lost, stolen, or forgotten?

What of those things, if returned to, might help you recover your heart?

Backpacking. After an exhausting hike, I'm above timberline in a tent I pitched just in time to shield me from a howling thunderstorm that will clear in an hour to a speechless sunset. Maybe surfing, too. (Craig)

YOUNG MEN

WHEN THE BOY BECOMES A TEEN, THE HEART OF THE LOVER MAY COME OUT in force, as an intense longing he knows not how to name, but nearly always attached to a Beauty. I remember something like this emerging in my heart during my last summer at the ranch. I would sit up on the hill in the evenings, looking out over the whole valley in which my grandfather's ranch lay, listening to the sound of a locomotive making its way up the far side of the valley. It filled my heart with longing and had I a spiritual mentor then and had he known the gift this longing is, I might have found God. Without that, I attached it to the beautiful cowgirl working the drive-up window at the burger stand in town.

Sometimes when the longing emerges in the young man he will take to music, or literature, either to enjoy them or as an artist himself. The young Lover David writes songs and poems to God during his nights out there in the wild, his heart so alive. A reminder that the young man had better also be a Cowboy, have lots of time out in the wild, feel caught up in epic adventures or the whole longing for Romance will be attached to a girl, for she will seem like the only adventure in his life.

Can you put words to the deepest desires and yearnings of your heart . . . those things, that to not have would seem like death and life wouldn't be worth living?

To not have an answer to this may indicate you are not yet living freely from your heart as God desires. That would be the direction you want to take now . . . *Lord, free my heart, restore it that I might live fully from it.*

How many of the longings you listed have you determined could be satisfied by a woman?

If those longings could not be satisfied by a woman, what would that change?

If God assured you that he could meet those deep yearnings, what would that change?

WHEN IT COMES TO GIRLS, THE GREATEST GIFT YOU CAN GIVE TO THE young man is to watch you love your wife.

Would your wife say you love her well? How would those who know the two of you describe your relationship . . . loving, romantic, respectful, dutiful, boring, platonic, cold, a disaster?

I hope so. I think others would comment on how we enjoy being together, that we're close, open, intimate. They'd comment that we laugh together, enjoy many things together, and always seem up for whatever's next when company leaves for the evening. (Craig)

We can settle for so little in marriage when it's God's desire for us to enjoy so much. Allow yourself to express your deep heart's desire for your relationship with your wife. What words or sentences would describe what you'd love it to be?

Are those descriptors any different from what you would picture God wanting for the two of you?

The greatest gift to an older man is for him to know how passionate God loves his wife (despite her wounds, sin, quirks).

TEACH HIM TO LOVE THE HEART, TO LOOK FOR THE HEART OF A GIRL. THIS can't start in adolescence. It begins earlier, as your family naturally talks about the heart, shares from the heart with one another. Point out the beauties in movies and stories (and in the neighborhood) who don't seem to have much going on inside, teaching the young man that "charm is deceptive, and [merely external] beauty is fleeting" (Prov. 31:30 NIV).

While women are forever a mystery, there is much we can learn about the feminine heart. How well do you know the heart of your woman . . . her story, wounds, fears, battles, and glory?

I've always thought I knew Lori's story pretty well. This year in our small group each person took an evening (about three hours) to share their story. After being married for thirty years, there were a number of events, seasons, and vulnerable moments Lori shared about her life that I never knew. Some of what she shared was huge for me to understand a bit more about why she is the way she is . . . her glories, interests, and passions, as well as fears and battles. So, I know Lori pretty well but realize there is still so much about her that remains a mystery to me. (Craig)

Is your posture one of emphasizing her physical or internal beauty or her heart?

Can God do whatever needs to be done in your heart and soul that would result in an authentic and passionate pursuit of your woman (regardless of whether or not she responds the way you'd like)?

THE MAN AS LOVER

AS I EXPLAINED EARLIER, THE LOVER EMERGES AROUND THE TIME OF THE Warrior, those stages overlapping, and let me add he continues right through to the end of a man's life, for the King must be a Lover as he must be a Warrior, and the Sage is a Lover long after he has handed the fighting of battles over to younger men. So what we are cultivating here is something that will grow all your life. We are opening a door that must never be shut. And again, before we talk of loving a woman, let us first turn to the romance with God.

How has God been wooing you? What has he stirred in your heart over the years?

Young man, it will take a lifetime to be the Lover God designed you to be. React to this statement.

Older man, are you still growing as a Lover?

Yes, you have to. Life changes after you have kids, then after twenty plus years they move away and you look at your wife and under your breath ask, "who are you?" Then bodies and hormones and all kinds of physical things change. Life, relationships, love isn't static. If you are not growing as a lover, you're probably not loving well. (Craig)

WE CANNOT CONTROL WHAT THE ROMANCER IS UP TO, BUT THERE IS A *posture* we can take. There is an openness to this stage that will enable us to recognize and receive the wooing.

So let me ask—are you willing to let go of your insistence to control, meaning, to allow for a life that exists beyond the realm of analysis, to let some portions of your life be impractical, to cease evaluating all things based on their utility and function?

Coming closer to the heart, are you willing to let passion rise in you, though undoubtedly it may unnerve you? To permit the healing of some of your deepest wounds? To let yourself be run through as with a rapier by Beauty itself? Are you willing, at some level, to be undone?

To enter into the Romance we must slow down, or we will miss the wooing. Turn off the news and put on some music. Take a walk. Take up painting or writing or reading poetry. Better still, what was it that stirred *your* heart over the years?

GO AND GET IT BACK. THIS IS HARD TO DO, ESPECIALLY FOR MEN WHO ARE out conquering the world. But remember—what the evil one does to a good Warrior if he cannot keep him in the battle is to bury him in battles. Wear him down with fight after fight. But life is *not* all about the battle. The Romance is always central.

What does this look like?

What will challenge this?

To be a Lover you must be a Warrior . . . You have to fight for it. If you haven't passed through a good bit of the Warrior stage, do you see how it will affect the Lover stage?

LISTEN AGAIN TO DAVID:

> Though an army besiege me,
> my heart will not fear;
> though war break out against me,
> even then will I be confident.
> One thing I ask of the LORD,
> this is what I seek:
> that I may dwell in the house of the LORD
> all the days of my life,
> to gaze upon the beauty of the LORD. (Ps. 27:3–4 NIV)

He knows battle, knows what it is to have God come through for him. He does not fear it; he is confidant as a seasoned warrior is confidant. But, he does not make it his heart's desire. What he *seeks* is not battle—what he seeks is the romance with God. "To gaze upon the beauty of the LORD."

What do you seek or desire most—the battle or the romance with God?

If it's still the battle that you seek/desire most, you probably haven't entered or gained all God intended in the Lover stage.

A VISTA JOURNEY

a view that enhances the journey

I've been enjoying some worship songs lately that help me make the shift—"Beauty of the Lord" by Jared Anderson, and "Beautiful One" by Tim Hughs. For we must remember: The battle is for the Romance. What we fight for is the freedom and healing that allow us to have the intimacy with God we were created to enjoy. To drink from his river of delights.

What worship helps you gaze upon the beauty of God?

Oh, how we must understand this, that there is a Beauty we long for calling to us *through* the beauty of the woman we are enchanted by. She is not the Beauty itself, only a messenger. If we never look beyond, we will try in vain to find it in her, causing both ourselves and the woman a great deal of pain. But to find it in God, to begin to experience in God what he sent Eve to foretell—now that is what David meant when he said, "Your love is better than life" (Ps. 63:3 NIV).

For some, we need God to open our eyes that we can see the Beauty beyond the beauty of the woman, for it is difficult to see beyond her.

What is it you long for that you need to look beyond the beauty, to God for?

Lord open my eyes, give me sight, show me, capture me, allure and entice me with your beauty. May I know that indeed, your love is better than the love of any woman, better than life itself.

HEALING THE LOVER'S HEART

THE PAST FIFTEEN YEARS HAVE BEEN A STORY OF HEALING, REPENTANCE, sanctifying, and strengthening the Lover heart in me. I wanted to be strong for Stasi, to initiate without fear, to have my whole heart to give to her. Yet I felt—how to describe it—uncertain with her, hesitant at times, even fearful at others. On an emotional level, I began to realize there were parts of my heart I had lost or left behind when girls I had loved broke up with me, and I needed to go get my heart back. Last spring I was on a ministry trip when it all surfaced again, and I felt so vulnerable to the beautiful women around me. Not for sex, mind you, but some broken place in my heart was crying out for medication.

God will do this. He will actually bring a woman across your path who speaks to your longings, and your wounds, your fears even, in order to raise the issue *so that he might heal*. This can't be done in the abstract. It must involve those very places in our hearts and souls that have been wounded, or surrendered. It feels dangerous, and it is, but the surgery is needed, and until a man gets that healed he will be more and more vulnerable to a fall. So God will do what he needs to do in order to bring our hearts to the surface. The woman at the hotel—looking just like a young girl I loved in high school—he'll do that, to get to the buried Lover.

What does God want to heal in you that he's used the woman to surface?

Can you put words to what God wants to do in your heart as a Lover?

NOW I KNOW—BEAUTY IS DANGEROUS STUFF. ESPECIALLY THE BEAUTY. BY now you've probably heard the quote from Dostoevsky: "Beauty is mysterious as well as terrible. God and the devil are fighting there, and the battlefield is the heart of man." He may have meant man*kind*, but you and I well know the battle over beauty is terrible in the heart of a *man*.

It goes without saying that there is something in the soul of a man that makes him profoundly vulnerable to The Beauty. Every man knows this, knows the breathtaking allure of a woman's form. I'll be flipping through some adventure magazine and whoa—there is a beauty and she stirs something in my heart. Vulnerable doesn't quite describe it. Powerless draws us a bit nearer the condition.

When do you feel the battle for your heart? When God is longing to be the Lover and Romancer of our heart and soul, while the enemy tempts us to worship and pursue the woman exclusively?

Failure here is so common, and it results in such shame, condemnation, and self-contempt. How have you handled this over the years?

OVER THE AGES MEN HAVE HANDLED THIS IN BASICALLY ONE OF TWO WAYS—surrender, or discipline. Surrender can be subtle, as when we let her in, when we allow ourselves to entertain the Beauty even though she is not ours. The lingering glance, the opening of our hearts to her. It can be blatant, as when we masturbate to a photo or a film, or give in to an affair. The damage is terrible, and many good men therefore choose discipline. Force yourself to look away, busy yourself with other things, fight it tooth and nail. Which is *certainly* better than surrender. Joseph ran for his life from Potiphar's wife, and it was the right decision. But discipline without healing doesn't work real well over time, and it can do great damage to our hearts, which begin to feel like the enemy so we'll do what we can to kill them in order to avert disaster.

Which of the two ways have you relied upon—surrender or discipline? Has it worked?

What's needed for victory/freedom here?

What needs healing here?

THERE IS ANOTHER WAY. THE WAY OF HOLINESS AND HEALING, AND IT involves what we do *in that very moment*, when our hearts are stirred by a Beauty. God and the devil were doing battle over my heart on that trip I just mentioned, and this is what I wrote in my journal:

> O merciful God, come to me in this place, this very place in my heart. I give this to you. I choose you over Eve. I choose your love and friendship and beauty. I give my aching and longing and vulnerable heart to you. Come, and heal me here. Sanctify me. Make me whole and holy in this very place.

I prayed it over and over, day and night. Whole, and holy. That is what we need.

When it comes to emotional entanglements, it might be good to ask yourself, "What girlfriends broke my heart?" And, "What have I done with that?" Have you let emotional ties remain with women you were in relationship with previously? Have you invited Christ into these old relational/sexual wounds?

AND THEN THERE ARE THE SEXUAL ISSUES, THE HOLINESS WE NEED DEEP IN our sexuality. I went back, one by one, and confessed to God my sins involving girls over the years—the ways I used them, the sexual intimacy that was not mine to have there. Sometimes we have to be very specific to find the cleansing and relief we long for, going back and renouncing specific events, inviting the blood of Christ to cleanse our every sin away, that our sexuality may be made holy. We bring the cross of Christ between us and every woman we've ever had an emotional or sexual relationship with (read Gal. 6:14). This would include affairs over the Internet, and with pornography, and every misuse of your sexuality. And, brothers, if you are in an emotional or physical relationship with a woman other than your wife even now, you must walk away. You must walk away. No stalling, no excuse-making. You will not find healing, holiness, and strength until you do.

Take the time now to be very specific in confessing your sexual sins to God. Go back and renounce specific events, inviting the blood of Christ to cleanse your every sin away that your sexuality may be made holy. Bring the cross of Christ between you and every woman you've ever had an emotional or sexual relationship with. Ask God for the cleansing and relief you long for.

And then there is the "live moment," when a beautiful woman crosses our path in person or in an image of some sort, and our hearts are stirred. How we handle that moment is critical. We do not surrender, we do not kill the longing. We give that very place over to Christ. That place in your heart, right there, right then, give to Jesus. Awakened by a beauty, we give that part of our hearts to God. This will take some time, and many repetitions. We've given it over to the woman so many times before, there is much recovering to be done. Again? Yes, again and again and again. That is how we are healed, made whole and holy and strong.

How do you react to the ongoing, repetitive reality of again and again going to Christ for more healing, wholeness, and strength?

It is reality, but oh, how I wish this could be over with quickly, cleanly and early in our lives. (Craig)

FINALLY, WE MUST OPEN OUR HEARTS TO ALL THE OTHER WAYS GOD IS bringing beauty into our lives. The beauty of a flower garden or moonlight on water, the beauty of music or a written word. Our souls crave Beauty, and if we do not find it we will be famished. We must take in Beauty, often, or we will be taken out by beauty.

How and where this week, prior to going through the next chapter, can you take in Beauty (but not via Eve)?

TOWARD A WOMAN

HOPEFULLY BY NOW—HAVING PASSED THROUGH SOME EXPERIENCE OF THE other stages, and this one, too—the heart of the man has been awakened, come alive.

Hopefully by now he is becoming a passionate man, a lover of beauty, haunted by the Great Romancer. Love, Beauty, Romance, Sexuality. It seems that when these are taking their place in a man's life, embraced, made whole and holy by God, then loving a woman comes quite naturally to a man.

Without them, it's like insisting a one-legged man take dance lessons. Eventually, a dancer of sorts may emerge, but it's not a pretty sight. A man detached from his heart might attempt to do the right things toward a woman—valentines, flowers, a night on the town—but it will lack essential passion, and she won't enjoy it. Principles do not a Lover make.

The similarities to our relationship with God are worth pointing out here. What does God want from us—our adherence to the laws and principles or the compassion of our heart?

What did God design us to *be* and women to *experience*—"nice" guys to do all the right things or passionate lovers pursuing the hearts of our spouses?

Read *Captivating*, which Stasi and I wrote to help unveil the beauty of a woman's heart, and to explain her wounds, and how God romances her. If you were traveling to a foreign country, you'd want to learn something about it before you ventured there, wouldn't you?

LOVING A WOMAN WILL PROVE TO BE YOUR GREATEST TEST AS A MAN, AND probably your greatest battle.

Have you found the statement above to be true in your life?

Is your internal response one of a confident expectation or a fear of failing?

What does this response tell you about your progress as a Warrior and a Lover?

I CAN'T THINK OF A YOUNG COUPLE WHOM I'VE EITHER MARRIED OR become acquainted with early in their marriage where the young man did not find himself suddenly and often deeply in a battle for his wife. And these are good people, quality young men and women who love God. The great surprise is that she is broken. Often her brokenness will remain hidden until she becomes engaged, or married, and then wham—it all comes out. Why is that? You'd think now that she is safe, now that she knows she's loved, she would be in a better place. But that's just it—now that she *is* safe and loved, her soul can quit pushing it all down. Before she is pursued and wanted, she fears that she cannot be herself or no man will want her. Now that she is loved, her heart comes forth and with it the sorrow of her life.

It presents an opportunity for healing, so long as the young man handles things well. Do not be freaked out by it. It is not the verdict on you. (Your life and validation are found in God—hang on to that!)

Married men, have you found yourself responding well to your wife's brokenness?

How have you fought for her and brought healing to her?

LEARN TO PRAY FOR HER, TENDERLY WHEN YOU ARE WITH HER, AND FIERCELY in your closet alone. You will need to fight the evil one for your wife, the historic demons that have assaulted her since her youth. She may need some counseling. She will certainly need some girlfriends, and learn to grow closer to God. Hang in there—it gets better. It really does.

Write out the prayer of your heart for your wife.

NOW TO ANOTHER ISSUE. THE MORE A MAN COMES ALIVE AS A MAN, THE more aware he becomes of what he wants in a woman. Yet he may now feel that the wife of his youth is not the kind of woman he would pursue now. Long ago he married her for safety, or out of their mutual brokenness, perhaps even out of guilt, and now he is coming alive and perhaps she is not yet and what is he to do?

Learn to love.

Isn't that the greatest call upon our lives—to learn to love? And let me say this as clearly as I can: There *is* the heart of a beautiful woman in there, and your strength can help to set it free. It will take time, during which you will be sorely tempted by women closer to your match, but this is the test of a man. What kind of man do you want to be? That is the question—not "Will this work, my rescue of her?" Not, "Will we have the romance of my dreams?" Those questions will undermine you at some point. The right question is, "What kind of man do I want to be?" What kind of man do you want to be? Remember what I said—what is the context God most often uses to make a man a man indeed?

So, what kind of a man do you want to be?

LOVING A WOMAN WHEN YOU ARE IN LOVE COMES EASILY. SURE, SOMETIMES awkwardly, in that there is much to be learned to be a Lover. But the motivation is fully in force when you are in love. Our development as men and Lovers comes in those times when things *don't* feel romantic at all. (And there will be plenty of such times, as you've discovered.)

You see, the Beauty is in there. She is in there. A real Lover makes love to the *soul* of a woman, not just her body. And her soul *is* lovely, whatever else might be going on. The beauty is there.

Is it your body, your intellect, your success that God loves, or is it the deeper, unseen realities of your soul, of your heart?

Is your love for your wife to be any different?

SO, LET ME SHARE A SIMPLE PIECE OF COUNSEL I HEARD FROM AN OLD SAGE when Stasi and I first married. I didn't hear much else of what he was trying to say, but I did get this: "Try to out-bless God in blessing her." Meaning, try to outdo the Great Romancer in finding ways to simply lavish upon your wife. The heart of a Lover simply wants to lavish her with their love, with no thought of return. It *does* return, as her heart is filled with gratitude. Not because something is owed, but because her heart matters to you and your heart matters to her more than just about anything in the world. This is love we're talking about.

What would your attempt to out-bless God in blessing her look like?

LEARNING TO BE LOVED, AND LEARNING TO LOVE, LEARNING TO BE romanced, and learning to romance—that is what this stage is all about. Not duty. Not merely discipline. But an awakening of our hearts to the Beauty and Love of God, and at the same time (we cannot wait until some later time), we offer our hearts as well—to God, to the women in our lives, to our sons and daughters, to others. This is a love story, after all. As William Blake said, "And we are put on earth a little space / To learn to bear the beams of love." Or, in Paul's words, "Be imitators of God . . . and live a life of love" (Eph. 5:1–2 NIV). He is a great Romancer, and you shall be also.

A PAUSE IN THE JOURNEY

an opportunity to reflect on the ground you've just covered

Has your understanding of the Lover changed or deepened a bit since you offered your definition in the beginning of the previous chapter? Before moving onto the next stage, pause and ask God if there's anything further he has to say or show you on the Lover at this point.

Are there any notes or reflections in this moment that you want to capture before you move back into all the others things facing you today? Capture them now.

12

KING

The highest heavens belong to the LORD,
but the earth he has given to man.
—PSALM 115:16 NIV

BEFORE STARTING

Without referring back to the book, from your recollection and in your own words, describe the King.

While the stages overlap, and there is some aspect of them in every phase of a man's life, there is also a time in a man's life when one of the stages is prominent. Is this stage, the King stage:

A stage you anticipate going through in the future? Read it knowing the time will come when God will guide you through this season . . . but until then, be patient in your current stage of the masculine journey. Give yourself the grace to learn, grow and take in all God has for you in *this* season of life without either jumping the gun or getting anxious about the next season.

The stage you think you're currently in? Obviously be alert. Read these next two chapters as a map for the journey you're currently on. With heart and eyes wide open, be keen to all God has for you. He will affirm, validate, convict, heal, and call you more deeply into all the lessons and growth he has for you in this stage of life. He will invite you into some difficult challenges and bless you with more intimacy with him. Another thought, don't prematurely assume you're ready to move on. God orders the seasons of a man's life, your graduation *will* come.

Or a stage you feel you have passed through? God will no doubt remind you of the people, events, hardships, and joys of this stage to affirm that indeed you have passed through this stage well. And while saying that, be willing to allow God to speak of the "more" he'd like to do in you as a King. You may find a number of things you missed in this stage. The good news is that it's never too late. Be expectant, there's more for you.

Before you begin this chapter, our suggestion would be that you scan the previous chapter in this manual, chapter 11. Skim over your notes, responses, and thoughts. What was the main point God seemed to emphasize in that chapter?

FIRST REACTIONS

What are your first reactions to this chapter? Does it stir up hope and longing for your development? What thoughts, feelings, and questions does this chapter raise for you?

KEY POINTS OF THE CHAPTER

- The goal of the masculine journey, the maturity for which God has been fathering the man since his first breath—is to be a King. To wield power, influence, and property in his name.
- Before a man is ready to handle power, his character must be forged. It might be said that all masculine initiation is designed to prepare a man to handle power.
- The great problem of the earth and the great aim of the masculine journey boil down to this: When can you trust a man with power? I remember Dallas Willard saying once that he believes the whole history of God and man recounted in the Bible is the story of God wanting to entrust men with his power, and men not being able to handle it.
- A good King uses all he has to make his kingdom like the kingdom of heaven for the sake of the people who live under his rule. That is why a man is given a kingdom. We are given power and resources and influence *for the benefit of others.*
- The true test of a King is this: *What is life like for the people under his authority?*
- A good King brings order to the realm.
- A good King also fights for the security of his kingdom, battling assault from without and sedition from within. That's why he must be a Warrior first.

Picture in your mind's eye an image of a great warrior, a renowned champion, returning home from far-off lands. His fame has long preceded him, and now the reports of his feats are confirmed by the scars he bears, the remembrance of wounds more noble than any tokens of honor. With dignity he moves up the main causeway of the city, lined with the faces of his people, the very people for whom he has fought bravely, whose freedom he has secured. The warrior has returned after years on the field of battle, returning only when triumph was achieved and not a moment before. This is his homecoming, and it is as a conquering hero he returns. Before him, at the head of the street, stands the king, who is his father. The scene is both a homecoming and a coronation. For the father-king will now hand the kingdom over to his son.

> Who is this coming from Edom, from Bozrah, with his garments stained crimson? Who is this, robed in splendor, striding forward in the greatness of his strength? "It is I, speaking in righteousness, mighty to save." (Isa. 63:1 NIV)

> After he had provided purification for sins, he sat down at the right hand of the Majesty in heaven . . . About the Son he says, "Your throne, O God, will last for ever and ever." (Heb. 1:3, 8 NIV)

It could be a passage from David's life, for he came to the throne after proving himself as a warrior. But I am referring to Jesus, of course, and while this is all quite true—biblically, historically—I'm afraid the power of it eludes us. Few of us have ever lived in a kingdom, under a king. Even fewer have ever met one. The scene of Aragorn's coronation from "The Return of the King" might help us imagine what a great King is like:

> And when the sun rose in the clear morning above the mountains in the East, upon which shadows lay no more, then all the bells rang, and all the banners broke and flowed in the wind . . . Now the Captains of the West led their host towards the City, and folk saw them advance in line upon line, flashing and glinting in the sunrise and rippling like silver . . . and upon either side of the Gate was a great press of fair people in raiment of many colors and garlands of flowers.
>
> So now there was a wide space before the walls of Minas Tirith, and it was hemmed in upon all sides by the knights and the soldiers of Gondor and of Rohan, and by the people of the City and of all parts of the land. A hush fell upon all as out from the host stepped the Dunedain in silver and grey; and before them came walking slow the Lord Aragorn. He was clad in black mail girt with silver, and he wore a long mantle of pure white clasped at the throat with a great jewel of green that shone from afar; but his head was bare save for a star upon his forehead bound by a slender fillet of silver.

. . . then Frodo came forward and took the crown from Faramir and bore it to Gandalf; and Aragorn knelt, and Gandalf set the White Crown upon his head, and said: "Now come the days of the King, and may they be blessed while the thrones of the Valar endure!"

But when Aragorn arose all that beheld him gazed in silence, for it seemed to them that he was revealed to them now for the first time. Tall as the sea-kings of old, he stood above all who were near; ancient of days he seemed and yet in the flower of manhood; and wisdom sat upon his brow, and strength and healing were in his hands, and a light was about him.

Jesus lived the days of his youth as the Beloved Son, secure in his father's love. He matured as a young man working in the carpenter's shop, and through his time in the wilderness. And then he went to war, and as the great Warrior he rescued his people from the kingdom of darkness, threw down the dark prince, set the captives free. As Lover, he wooed and won the hearts of his bride. And now, he reigns as King. Thus the progression of his life as a man, and thus ours.

A VISTA JOURNEY

a view that enhances the journey

To capture a picture of the coronation of a king and all its power, view the scene of Aragon's coronation that John refers to in the film *The Return of the King.* What does such a scene, with all the pageantry, the honor, the respect, and the crowd celebrating stir up in you?

BORN TO RULE

WE COME NOW TO THE GOAL, IN SOME SENSE, OF THE MASCULINE JOURNEY, the maturity for which God has been fathering the man since his first breath—to be a King. To wield power, influence, and property in his name. It is as great and noble an undertaking as it is difficult; history makes that very clear. The reason behind many of our miseries upon the earth in these days is that we have lost our Kings.

What do you think most Christian men would say is the goal of the masculine journey?

It so depends upon their context. I think some would say the goal is to be successful in your career and provide for your family, while others would frame it as being a "nice" guy. For me it would have been to be viewed by others as being very "biblical." Looking back, I took my cues for godly masculinity from popular conservative teachers who seemed to present the goal as being biblical, what I now understand to be sub-biblical, or superficial and ignoring the internal issues of a man's heart. The goal was merely to have a submissive wife, to witness, to be devoted to faithful study of the Word of God evidenced by a growing doctrinal-purity-swagger, to have no obvious sin (smoking, drinking, voting Democrat, being demonstrative in worship), to quote a lot of verses, and to attend the monthly men's breakfast. The goal was conformity to a set of behaviors. I now see the goal as being much deeper, more profound, more God-centered . . . more (truly) biblical! (Craig)

What have you understood the goal of your masculine journey to be?

YES, WE FIND MEN IN POWER, BUT THEY ARE NOT TRUE KINGS. IT IS NOT through initiation that they have come to the throne, nor do they have the heart of a King. And that is a dangerous situation indeed, when a man is made King who is unfit to be one, and it has brought the ruin of many kingdoms—homes, families, churches, ministries, businesses, nations.

Why are positions of power and influence so alluring to men?

Are such positions alluring to you?

Have you been under the rule of a King who was unfit?

> Yes. The impact upon me, my family, and the kingdom he ruled was atrocious. To make things worse, the elders, who could have fought for his redemption and the salvation of the church, were men without chests, unfit to rule themselves. Ahhh . . . where are the kings we need so? (Craig)

Have you ruled over others while not having the heart of a King? What was the impact upon those you ruled? Upon you? Is there any issue of forgiveness or repentance in how you've ruled?

A DAY IS COMING WHEN THE KINGDOM OF GOD WILL APPEAR IN ITS fullness, when we will be given kingdoms of our own. We will rule, just as we were always meant to. Meanwhile, God is training us to do what we're made to do. Every man is a King, for every man even now has a kingdom of sorts. There is some aspect of this world, however small, over which he has say. And as we grow in character and strength, in wisdom and humility, God tends to increase our kingdoms. He *wants* to entrust us with his kingdom.

What we will someday be fully, we are now partially, significantly. What at this stage of life is the kingdom you rule over?

And what kind of King are you in terms of heart, character, strength, wisdom, and humility?

THE HEART OF A KING

THE GREAT PROBLEM OF THE EARTH AND THE GREAT AIM OF THE MASCULINE journey boil down to this: When can you trust a man with power? I remember Dallas Willard saying once that he believes the whole history of God and man recounted in the Bible is the story of God wanting to entrust men with his power, and men not being able to handle it. That was certainly true of Adam, and has proved true for most of his sons. The annals of the kings are, for the most part, a very sad record. Moses, David, Charlemagne, Lincoln—men like that seem hard to come by. My sincere hope is that as we embrace the masculine journey, submit to its lessons, learn again how to initiate men, we shall make good Kings available once more.

As a young man, what were you given power over?

Were you ever given too much, or was it given prematurely?

I became a Christian at age twenty-one. My conversion was pretty dramatic. My zeal and passion for God blinded most from seeing my immaturity and cavernous need for healing and fathering. Within three months, I was on a pastoral staff as a teaching pastor. I was thrust into a leadership role way too soon. I think I would die if I heard some of those early sermons I preached now. (Craig)

When can you trust a man with power?

Can God entrust you with greater measures of his power at present? If so, to do what? If not, what must change before he can?

BEFORE A MAN IS READY TO HANDLE POWER, HIS CHARACTER MUST BE forged. It might be said that all masculine initiation is designed to prepare a man to handle power.

What, at this point of your journey, are the areas of character God would like to work on prior to enlarging your kingdom?

Is there anything about being a King that frightens or concerns you?

IT IS A MATTER OF THE *HEART*, MY BROTHERS. THERE ARE MANY *OFFICES* A man might fulfill as a King—father of a household, manager of a department, pastor of a church, coach of a team, prime minister of a nation—but the *heart* required is the same. "The king's heart is in the hand of the LORD; he directs it like a watercourse wherever he pleases" (Prov. 21:1 NIV). The passage is often used to explain the sovereignty of God, in that he can do with a man whatever he well pleases. Certainly, God is that sovereign. But I don't think that's the spirit of this passage. God rarely forces a man to do something against his will, because he would far and above prefer that he didn't have to, that the man *wills* to do the will of God. "Choose for yourselves this day whom you will serve" (Josh. 24:15 NIV). What God is after is a man so *yielded* to him, so completely surrendered, that his heart is easily moved by the Spirit of God to the purposes of God.

That kind of heart makes for a good King.

Describe what being "yielded to God," being "completely surrendered" to him, means or looks like for you.

What are the offices you fulfill as a King? List all of them.

Look at each of those offices and ask yourself, "Is my heart in the hand of the Lord in this office/role?"

Are you so yielded to him, so completely surrendered, that your heart is easily moved by the Spirit of God to the purposes of God?

What areas of your life have you yet to yield or surrender? Is it time to do so now?

John presents a couple of biblical examples of Moses, David and Jesus as kings/leaders who ruled out of a yielded and surrendered heart concluding: Regardless of age, position, or natural abilities, a man is ready to become a King only when his heart is in the right place. Meaning, *yielded to God in all things.* Starting each day in a posture of yieldedness is essential; otherwise we just live in the matrix of this world. We recommend referring back to The Daily Prayer in Chapter 9, page 161. But at this moment write out a prayer yielding yourself, all you have, to God.

ON BEHALF OF OTHERS

WHEN THE RIGHTEOUS THRIVE, THE PEOPLE REJOICE;
when the wicked rule, the people groan. (Prov. 29:2 NIV)

Let us return again to *The Kingdom of Heaven*, to Balian's initiation. Following his father's instructions, Balian arrives in Jerusalem and reports to King Baldwin, who in turn sends Balian to protect the Pilgrim Road leading to the Holy City. "All are welcome in Jerusalem—not only because it's expedient, but because it is right." Balian rides out with his men to what was his father's estate there—a small farm settlement centered around a castle, like many medieval hamlets, only this one is out in the middle of the desert, more dust than anything else. Balian sets about making the place a refuge of life. What is needed is water, so he has the men dig wells, build aqueducts. Sybilla stops in on a visit, and when she sees him out there in the fields with his workers, sleeves rolled up, she asks, "Would you make this like Jerusalem?"

Beautiful. Exactly. That is what a good King does—he uses all he has to make his kingdom like the kingdom of heaven for the sake of the people who live under his rule.

"And David knew that the LORD had established him as king over Israel and had exalted his kingdom for the sake of his people Israel" (2 Sam. 5:12 NIV). For the sake of his people. That is why a man is given a kingdom. We are given power and resources and influence *for the benefit of others.*

The motives that underlie our actions are often subtle and unknown without times of reflection. What are the motives behind your ruling/leadership? Is it the building up of others or the building up of your comfort, power, or control?

Man, this is the million dollar question. The enemy would have me believe that at all times and in every way my actions are solely self-serving expressions of a heart devoid of the Spirit of God. And while I can and at times do live according to the flesh, I hope by this stage of life I can move beyond comfort, power, and control governing me. However, I think diligence is still required of me here. (Craig)

Are you willing to ask God to expose the motives of your ruling?

THE TEST OF A KING

TOO MANY MEN, HAVING REACHED THIS POINT IN THEIR JOURNEY—OR rather, finding themselves Kings even though they have *not* taken the masculine journey—seize the opportunity to make life good . . . *for themselves.* The average man in his forties or fifties comes into a little power and influence, a little discretionary cash, and he spends it making himself comfortable. He works if he has to, but the purpose of his labors is only to build his savings so that he can lead a life of leisure. Is it not so?

The man has worked hard to get here, and something in him says, *Hey—I've paid my dues. Now it's my turn to have some fun.* "Take life easy; eat, drink and be merry" (Luke 12:19 NIV).

Jesus called them together and said, "You know that the rulers of the Gentiles lord it over them, and their high officials exercise authority over them. Not so with you. Instead, whoever wants to become great among you must be your servant, and whoever wants to be first must be your slave—just as the Son of Man did not come to be served, but to serve, and to give his life as a ransom for many" (Matt. 20:25–28 NIV).

Younger man, is seizing every opportunity to make life good for yourself the life you want to live in your fifties and sixties?

Older man, is a self-centered life of comfort, leisure, and fun the life you want to be living?

What posture do you want—people serving you or you serving others?

Does it seem possible for you . . . is this the man you want to be?

BUT THAT IS THE TRUE TEST OF A KING. SIMPLY PUT, THE TEST IS THIS: *What is life like for the people under his authority?* Really? It's that simple. What is life like for the people in his kingdom?

What is life like for the people under your authority?

I will ask them . . . (Craig)

What would your wife say? (Consider asking her.)

Is being your wife stressful, full of pressure and/or manipulation, fearful of your reactions?

Does she feel dismissed or overlooked?

What would your children say? (Consider asking them in an appropriate way.)

Do you spend most of your energy getting them to behave as you'd like versus understanding their hearts and looking for ways to bless them?

What would those you work with or supervise say?

Do they feel they are simply building your kingdom, or that you are serving them? Are they growing in their own talents and abilities, joyful because they are cared for, given a place in the kingdom?

If you are in church leadership, look at the congregation—are they enjoying the genuine freedom and life Christ promised? Or is the unspoken system of the church one of fear, guilt, and performance?

ORDER, PROTECTION, AND BLESSING

A GOOD KING BRINGS ORDER TO THE REALM. GOD BRINGS ORDER OUT OF chaos at the beginning of creation, and then he hands the project over to Adam to rule in the same way. Not as a tyrant or micromanager, but offering his strength to bring order to the realm. The reason we depict a king on his throne is to convey order, well-being. The King is on his throne and all is well in the world.

Where in the past have you brought order to chaos?

> I used to be the guy who was good at organizing, bringing order to things. It felt "kingly" to have the garage, and every room, closet, and drawer in the house (including my wife's "junk" drawer) cleaned, organized in a box or baggie, and labeled appropriately. That part of my world/kingdom was easy to rule. It was the internal world of feeling inadequate, overwhelmed, frightened . . . it was in the relational world of disappointments, hurts, and needs that I didn't do well as king. I think the internal and relational realms are actually now my strong suit. (Craig)

Where currently is there chaos or a need for well-being in your realm?

What's your plan?

When and where have you been either the tyrant or the micromanager?

A GOOD KING ALSO FIGHTS FOR THE SECURITY OF HIS KINGDOM, BATTLING assault from without and sedition from within. That's why he must be a Warrior first.

Think of Churchill, unyielding to the Nazis, and the pacifists in his own government who would not hold fast. Or Lincoln, and his unrelenting efforts to preserve the Union. A family with a good father feels protected. Spiritually, emotionally, financially, physically, he is the one to bring peace and covering to his family.

All this in order to bring blessing to his people. "From the fullness of his grace we have all received one blessing after another" (John 1:16 NIV).

What are the assaults against the security of your kingdom and the well-being of those within that need to be confronted and fought?

THE COST OF BECOMING A KING

AUGUSTINE WEPT WHEN HE WAS MADE BISHOP OF HIPPO IN NORTH AFRICA. Those of you who have been Kings will understand. There is a cost the King pays, unknown and unmatched by any other man.

I think unless there is this profound reluctance to take the throne, a man does not understand the cost of what is being asked of him. You will be tested. On every conceivable front.

You don't want to be a King. Trust me. It is not something to be coveted. Only the ignorant covet a throne. Augustine didn't want the job because he knew what it would cost him, and he felt a profound inadequacy to the task. He wanted a quiet, simple life. But he accepted the role on behalf of others. Becoming a King is something we accept only as an act of obedience. The posture of the heart in a mature man is reluctance to take the throne, but willing to do it on behalf of others.

Do you want to be a King? Why or why not?

If so, a couple of questions: Who's asking you to be one? Are you ready? What do you anticipate the cost being? Where will you be tested most?

If you don't want to be King, why not? Is it because you're not ready yet or is it asking too much of you?

Kings, on what fronts have you been tested? How's your heart doing in all this?

THE WOUNDING OF THE KING

The King is wounded early in a boy when he is never given a territory of his own, when his territory is violated, or when his territory is too big for him.

Were you wounded here?

What's been the message about your being a king that's come from this wound?

It's not true, right? Battling the message of your wound requires you be a true Warrior.

God your Father wants to heal your wound and dismantle the lies attached to it.

IF A BOY HAS A DOMINEERING MOTHER OR FATHER, IT CRUSHES THE YOUNG King in him. He never gets to develop his own willpower and determination. For the King is also wounded early in a boy when his boundaries are violated.

Sexual abuse would be among the worst violations, for the child is invaded and cannot make it stop. How then can he (or she) develop a sense of sovereignty over his life, a confidence that he can assert his will, protect his boundaries? The child becomes accustomed to being run over, demanded of, used.

Was either a dominating parent or the violation of your boundaries (the extreme case being sexual violation) a source of wounding in your life?

If so, what's been the message about your being a King that's come from this wound?

It's not true, right? Battling this message from your wound requires you be a true Warrior.

God your Father wants to heal your wound and dismantle the lies attached to it.

I SAID IN CHAPTER I THAT A BOY IS ALSO WOUNDED WHEN HE IS MADE A King too soon. We often make young men Kings too soon as well. The senior pastor leaves, and the church makes the youth pastor senior and he is twenty-five. Business schools give young men the impression that an MBA qualifies them to become a King, also in their twenties. The young man has barely learned to be a Warrior, may never have been a Cowboy.

Were you made a King too soon (corporately, in a business or church prematurely)?

Does this mean a young man cannot become a King?

NO. JOSIAH WAS TWENTY-SIX WHEN HE BEGAN HIS REFORMS, AND HE RULED well. But I would say that a young man should not be made King over too great a kingdom. He should be a manager before he becomes a vice president, and only after those stages should he become president. *If* he finds himself in the role of King as a younger man, he should *not* forsake the other stages of the journey, for he will need all they have to teach him and develop in him. It is not the *season* of the King for him, but of the Warrior and Lover, and it is at those stages he should live, looking to older men to help him fulfill the *office* of King.

Young King, what do you need to go back and develop in your life to be a better, more mature King in time?

YOUNG MEN ARE WOUNDED BY KINGS WHO BETRAY THEM, AND THE WOUND often causes them to resent all Kings and the role of King. Perhaps this is why so many young men today do not want to enter the stage of King, and think that they are more righteous for it.

Have you been betrayed by a King?

What was the message his betrayal sent you about your being a King?

It's not true, right? God your Father wants to heal your wound and dismantle the lies attached to it.

MANY OF MY READERS WILL BE OLDER MEN, FINDING THEMSELVES KINGS and realizing they never received the initiation they needed as Cowboys, Warriors, or Lovers. They feel a weakness inside, feel hard-pressed to rise up as King. That should alert them to go back and take the journey (more on this in the next chapter).

Older man, if the shoe fits, go back and pick up the journey where it got cut short. What do you need?

SOMETIMES A KING IS FORCED OUT OF HIS KINGDOM, AS DAVID WAS BY Saul, and later by Absalom. He might be forced into early retirement. In other cases a good man more than ready to become a King is passed over for a promotion, and the job is handed to a younger man. You can be assured that the enemy will do whatever he can to keep a man from rising up as King. He will tempt, dishearten, assault—as he did Adam, Moses, David, and Jesus.

Whatever has diminished your heart as a King, or toward the King, you must not let it win. It is as a King you were born, and it is as a King you must rise. There is great good to be done, and many people to rescue—all that we are missing are the Kings of the earth.

Father, it is with some hesitation that I ask this—but still, I ask that you come and take me into this stage, initiate me here, when the time is right for me. Show me how the King was wounded in me as a boy, as a young man, and in my adulthood as well. Show me where I've acted weakly, abdicating my authority. Show me where I've been a tyrant. Show me also where I have ruled well. Let me see what life is like for those under my rule, and, by your grace, let me become a great King on behalf of others. I give my life to you. Give me the heart and spirit of a man yielded to you. Father me.

A PAUSE IN THE JOURNEY

an opportunity to reflect on the ground you've just covered

So, having completed this chapter on the King, what notes must you record about your life, God, action items, desires, and dreams? So often, what impresses us in the moments we finish a chapter quickly gets lost as we get back into the distracting realities of our day-to-day. Capture them now.

13

Raising the King

Well done, good and faithful servant!
You have been faithful with a few things;
I will put you in charge of many things.
Come and share your master's happiness!

—Matthew 25:23 NIV

BEFORE STARTING

You have spent a good amount of time on the King in the previous chapter so don't hold back on this chapter. The hard work of reflection, thinking, pondering your life and listening to God we are asking of you is the very thing God may use to affirm or prepare you for this stage in your masculine journey. Don't get distracted.

While there is much in this chapter about *raising* or *fathering* a King that a dad will immediately relate to and benefit from, the exercises are written from the perspective that every man, whatever his age, still needs fathering as a King.

As a parent reading this chapter, ask yourself: What does my son need at this time? What is required of me as a father, or what kind of father do I want to be? What do I want to offer, protect, guard, and resist on behalf of my son?

FIRST REACTIONS

Once again react to what you've read and where you went with it, what God stirred up in you, what shook you, blessed you. How did God use your reading of this chapter to encourage you?

KEY POINTS OF THE CHAPTER

- We should seek the character before we seek the office. A man should be measured by the way he has lived, *prior* to coming to the throne. Though David was anointed by God and therefore the rightful heir to Saul's throne, he did not seize it. He lived like a King before he became one.
- A man cannot be a good King unless he has first lived through the other stages of the masculine journey.
- A man may have a noble and good heart.
- Many men fail as Kings through abdication, through some sort of passivity. They refuse to take the role, or they refuse to make the tough decisions, refuse to lead their people in battle. They look for a comfortable life.
- God most often teaches a man to fight by putting him in situation after situation where he must fight. The same idea holds true in the time of the King—our Father will put you in situations where you will need to act decisively, and strongly, on behalf of others. The King-heart in us is formed and strengthened in those moments—especially in those moments of sacrificial decision, where we do put others before us, and in those moments of unwavering decisiveness, where we take a difficult stand against great odds or opposition.
- My sincerest counsel to Kings is, *Don't isolate yourself, and don't let it happen to you.* Surround yourself with good counselors, and listen to them. Let your allies and colleagues make decisions that affect you. Seek out friendships with a few other men—Kings, if you can find them. Be intentional to fight the isolation.
- The one quality above all others to guide a man into, so that he might become a good King, is to acquire a friendship with God.

THE NOBLE HEART

As we set out to raise the King—in a boy, and in a man—we should begin with the heart of a King. Certainly this is the lesson of David's life, for when God sent the prophet Samuel to anoint one of the sons of Jesse as the new king of Israel, he counsels the old prophet, "Do not consider his appearance or his height . . . Man looks at the outward appearance, but the Lord looks at the heart" (1 Sam. 16:7 NIV). Having looked for himself, God chose the youngest in the family, an odd choice in the eyes of men, but he found a man he knew was after his own heart.

Far too many books have been written on leadership principles and strategies, and I am not going to try to add to that mass here. What we need is the heart of a King, and what better place to look than to our King:

> And I saw a mighty angel proclaiming in a loud voice, "Who is worthy to break the seals and open the scroll?" But no one in heaven or on earth or under the earth could open the scroll or even look inside it. I wept and wept because no one was found who was worthy to open the scroll or look inside . . .
>
> And they sang a new song: "You are worthy to take the scroll and to open its seals, because you were slain, and with your blood you purchased men for God from every tribe and language and people and nation. You have made them to be a kingdom and priests to serve our God, and they will reign on the earth." . . . "Worthy is the Lamb, who was slain, to receive power and wealth and wisdom and strength and honor and glory and praise!" (Rev. 5:2–4, 9–10, 12 NIV)

Worthy. That is different from, say, entitled, as the firstborn is entitled to the throne. Different also from gifted. Jesus is the Firstborn, and through him all things were created, but when he comes to the throne there is an overwhelming sense that he is worthy to be King.

Which would you prefer, to be *entitled to* or to be *worthy of* being a king? Why?

Worthy. I would know, because I'd proven myself to have what it takes, that I could rule well as a king. To become a king in any other way would simply breed self-doubt and insecurity in both me and those under my rule. (Craig)

FIRST, THAT WE SHOULD SEEK THE CHARACTER BEFORE WE SEEK THE OFFICE. A man should be measured by the way he has lived, *prior* to coming to the throne. Though David was anointed by God and therefore the rightful heir to Saul's throne, he did not seize it. He lived like a King before he became one. He walked in humility, fought for the people, and when he did finally come, the people rejoiced.

Are you ready to take the throne?

How have you lived? That is, have you lived like a King? Not just externally, but internally. Have you walked in humility, fought for people? Who will rejoice when you become a King?

What would you like God to work on to further your preparation to be King?

Jesus is worthy to take the throne because he has *earned* it. John presents a number of Christ's qualities that point to his worthiness on page 237 in *The Way of the Wild Heart.* How do you measure up in these categories?

(There are a umber of questions here . . . and they require reflection, a bit of time, and lot of honesty. Don't rush them and miss out on what God wants to say to you as an aspiring King.)

Do you have an incorruptible integrity?

How do you handle temptation?

How do you live on a business trip or in the times when you are all alone?

Can you be bought?

I don't know what the underlying issue is here, but this has always been one of my fears. That I know of, I haven't been bought, but so many of my nightmares are on the theme of some major compromise—that I will sell my integrity and lose everything. Yuck. May Christ protect me and guide me through life with my integrity intact. (Craig)

Are you immensely kind?

How do you relate to those less privileged, to the sick, injured, helpless?

Are you moved by the stories and plights of others?

I often find myself reading a person's story in their face, countenance, posture. If you hear a person's story, you understand their life. There are so many sad stories out there. (Craig)

Do you touch and speak personal words of encouragement to others?

How would a food server describe you?

Friendly, kind, personable, and a big tipper! (Craig)

Are you humble?

Jesus, Lord of Heaven and Earth, is born among the poor, takes time to feed the hungry, teaches unschooled people about the kingdom of God, eats with whores and dies among thieves. Never once do you see him exalt himself. He waits to be exalted by his Father. How about you?

> I would love to answer this in the affirmative, but, I really don't know the answer without asking those around me. Sometimes I get on a roll in a group setting and have been accused at times of "sucking all the air out of the room" . . . is that a hint that I'm exalting myself? I'm really not sure. I'll ask them. (Craig)

He is generous. Though he has suffered far more than we ever will, when he comes to his throne he chooses to share it with us. Are you generous?

He is just. Jesus knew what a King must know—that there is a difference between the letter of the law and the Spirit of the law (see 2 Cor. 3:6). The Pharisees were moral men; they kept the Law. But they were not noble men, not by a long shot. What I am describing is something richer, deeper, higher, greater. Jesus was far more than just a good man. The Pharisees were moral, to the point of being ruthless moralists. Jesus understands the heart of the matter. And you?

ALL THIS TO SAY, THERE IS A NOBILITY ABOUT JESUS, EVEN WHEN HE WALKS barefoot through the countryside with a bunch of fishermen. He lives like a King long before he is made a King. And his noble heart is revealed to all the world in that he gives himself to be killed in our place.

Again, describe the King you would want to be.

Despite what the church may have told you, a man may have a noble heart. Jesus says so himself:

> But the seed on good soil stands for those with a noble and good heart, who hear the word, retain it, and by persevering produce a crop. (Luke 8:15 NIV)

What kind of heart is represented by the seed that fell on good soil?

A NOBLE AND GOOD HEART. LET NO FALSE HUMILITY KEEP YOU FROM YOUR birthright. Let me say it again: A man may have a noble heart. Was this not true of David, of whom God said, "If you walk before me in integrity of heart . . . as David your father did" (1 Kin. 9:4 NIV)? And was it not also true of Josiah, "who turned to the LORD as he did—with all his heart and with all his soul and with all his strength" (2 Kin. 23:25)? It allows us to ask a new kind of question, when we are faced with any situation: "What is the noble thing to do?" It's a far better question than simply, "What is the expedient thing to do?" or, as I am apt to ask, "How can I get out of this quickly?" "What is the noble thing to do?" awakens the noble heart, arrests our attention, arouses our courage.

Which question most often guides you in a difficult situation: "What is the noble thing to do?" or, "What is the expedient thing to do?"

How can I get out of this quickly and painlessly? is probably more the question that has guided me all too many years of my life. I hate saying that, but it's been true. (Craig)

AND NOTICE—THE NOBLE HEART IS FOUND IN THE ONE WHO PERSEVERES, which brings us back to the Stages.

BUILT UPON THE OTHER STAGES

A MAN CANNOT BE A GOOD KING UNLESS HE HAS FIRST LIVED THROUGH THE other stages of the masculine journey. If he aches still to be the Beloved Son, he might buy himself all sorts of toys. And he will also use his influence to win the approval of others. He will avoid the hard decisions because he wants everyone to like him. (That will paralyze a King, by the way.) If he was never allowed the Cowboy Ranger stage, he spends too much time at the country club playing golf, skiing, going on adventure trips, or perhaps now is when he buys the sports car. If never a Warrior, he will now wield his power in anger, doing great damage to make himself feel powerful, chasing dragons, making mountains out of molehills, simply so he can go to war. Never having been a true Lover, he will go out and buy himself a trophy wife, or find a lover on the Internet.

Are you an Unfinished Man, an uninitiated man, trying to fill in the gaps of his soul when what he should be doing now is acting like a King?

AND SO MY GREATEST ADVICE WHEN IT COMES TO RAISING THE KING IS, simply, "Live the other stages." If a man has been the Beloved Son, he will not need to be the center of attention. If he has been the Cowboy, he will be brave and daring. Having been a Warrior, he will not flinch from battle—the number one problem of most Kings I know. He will be valiant, cunning, and resolute. He will also know how to "keep his head." This will be balanced by tenderness and compassion if he has also been a Lover. He will understand the heart, and how crucial this is, for now the hearts of many are in his hands. And so you see that it is after they have been all of these things that Moses, David, and Jesus come to the throne.

Do you need to be the center of attention?

Eegads . . . I don't think I need to be. My wit, humor, and fun-loving nature often put me there. This kinda goes back to the "sucking all the air out of the room" thing. I think that used to be a more significant theme in my story than it is now. For decades I looked to the applause of others for validation, less so now I hope. (Craig)

Do you use your influence/gifts and energy to win the approval of others?

Do you wield your power/authority in anger, doing great damage to make yourself feel powerful, chasing dragons, making mountains out of molehills, simply so you can go to war?

Do you flinch from battle?

Are you valiant, cunning and resolute, knowing how to keep your head?

Are you looking for, or have you bought yourself a trophy wife, or found a lover (real or imaginary) on the Internet?

Answering yes to any of these may indicate there are some stages you need to revisit.

To those men reading this who find themselves at the age when they should be a King, or in the office of a King, but have never lived through the stages of masculine initiation, I would say that you need to go back—with God as Father guiding you—

and get what you missed. I don't mean quit your job. But I said at the outset of the book that life will test you as a man, as a ship at sea is tested, and it will reveal the unhealed and unholy places within you. This is true to the tenth power when you become a King. So you cannot skip those stages. You will need all they have to offer your soul as a man.

There is no disgrace in intentionally pursuing that which is vital to your maturity and growth as a man. What is God inviting you to revisit?

AUTHORITY

ADAM WAS GIVEN THE EARTH TO RULE, BUT WHEN THE TEST CAME—HE folded. He didn't speak, didn't act on Eve's behalf. Satan was there, attacking his wife, threatening the whole kingdom, and Adam didn't do a thing. He fell through his *acquiescence*, through his silence and passivity. That was how Satan became "the prince of this earth," as Jesus called him. And why John said, "The whole world lies in the power of the evil one" (1 John 5:19 NASB). Might I point out that many men fail as Kings through abdication, through some sort of passivity? They refuse to take the role, or they refuse to make the tough decisions. Refuse to lead their people in battle. They look for a comfortable life.

In what area of the realm God has given you do you realize, having been passive, you now need to step up and rule well?

Around the house—in budget, finances, and paying bills. (Craig)

THE OTHER EXTREME, AFTER ADAM'S FALL, IS TYRANNY. KINGS LIKE PHARAOH and Saul and Herod. Men who use their power in order to control and manipulate. The pastor who won't share the pulpit with anyone. The CEO who won't take advice. The father who keeps his family cowed in fear. If a man would be a good King, he would do well to keep in mind these two extremes.

What will keep you from being either tyrannical or a controller/manipulator as King?

THE EARTH WAS GIVEN TO MAN, BUT SATAN USURPED THE THRONE, AS DID Absalom, who seized David's throne. Jesus came to win it back—to throw down the usurper, to break the claims of his rule, which were based entirely upon the sin of man. Through his absolute obedience to God and through his sacrificial death, he did indeed break every claim Satan might make to the kingdoms of this earth (see Col. 2:13–15). Now, "all authority in heaven and on earth has been given" to Jesus (Matt. 28:18 NIV).

And you, my brother, have been given that same authority. "And God raised us up with Christ and seated us with him in the heavenly realms" (Eph. 2:6 NIV). To be seated with Christ in the heavenlies means that we share in his authority. He makes it plain in Luke 10:19: "I have given you authority . . . to overcome all the power of the enemy" (NIV). Learning to live in this authority, to bring the kingdom of God to our little kingdoms on earth, that is what it means to become a true King.

Let me repeat, for this understanding about the kingdom of God is not broadly explained in the church just now. Adam (and all his sons, including you) was given the earth to rule. Born a King. He abdicated that authority to Satan through his sin and fall. But Jesus came and won it back, the Father giving all authority on earth to him. Jesus in turn shares that authority with us, gives us his authority, to rule in his name. For as he said, the Father is delighted to give us the kingdom (Luke 12:32). The course of a man's life is coming to the place where he can be made a King in his experience, where all that Christ has bestowed can be *realized* in the man's life.

As you've been working through this manual, what have you been discerning is the ploy of the enemy against your masculine journey? Take the authority of Christ and exercise it against the enemy of your maturity.

FATHERED INTO KINGSHIP

BACK IN THE CHAPTERS ON THE WARRIOR, I EXPLAINED THAT THE WAY GOD most often teaches a man to fight is to put him in situation after situation where he must fight. The same idea holds true in the time of the King—our Father will put you in situations where you will need to act decisively, and strongly, on behalf of others. The King-heart in us is formed and strengthened in those moments—especially in those moments of sacrificial decision, where we do put others before ourselves, and in those moments of unwavering decisiveness, where we take a difficult stand against great odds or opposition.

What are the situations you can look back on and wish you had acted more decisively, strongly, and on the behalf of others?

What situations have you been avoiding that God may intend to form and strengthen your King-heart? Is there something current you need to step into soon?

IF YOU ARE LIKE MOST MEN, YOU'LL FEEL LIKE YOU'RE IN WAY OVER YOUR head in moments like these. But this is how our initiation unfolds in our daily lives, how we come to discover that we do have the heart of a King, *can* act like a King. Not perfectly, not every time, but more and more as our initiation develops the King in us. I think we all know that such nobility and integrity can be formed in a man only by the Spirit of God. The question to us is, *Will we let him?*

PRIDE

WHEN HE NOTICED HOW THE GUESTS PICKED THE PLACES OF HONOR AT THE table, he told them this parable: "When someone invites you to a wedding feast, do not take the place of honor, for a person more distinguished than you may have been invited. If so, the host who invited both of you will come and say to you, 'Give this man your seat.' Then, humiliated, you will have to take the least important place. But when you are invited, take the lowest place, so that when your host comes, he will say to you, 'Friend, move up to a better place.' Then you will be honored in the presence of all your fellow guests. For everyone who exalts himself will be humbled, and he who humbles himself will be exalted" (Luke 14:7–11 NIV).

So many of Christ's teachings are brutal heart-checks, and the above Scripture passage is one of them. What are your reactions to Luke 14:7–11?

WE SHOULD *FEAR* BECOMING A LARGE CHURCH, CORPORATION, KINGDOM. We should be forced into it, by God. As Schaeffer said years ago, in a sermon entitled "The Lord's Work in the Lord's Way," "If we are going to do the Lord's work in the Lord's way, we must take Jesus' teaching seriously: He does not want us to press on to the greatest place unless He Himself makes it impossible to do otherwise."

What ambitions has God refined by fire? What ambitions *must* be refined for us to reign over others well?

HUMILITY IS ESSENTIAL TO THE OUTCOME OF WHETHER OR NOT A MAN will make a good King. It is one of the truest expressions of that yieldedness I described earlier.

Moses was one of the greatest leaders ever to walk the face of the earth. He was a great King. And this is what was said of him: "Now Moses was a very humble man, more humble than anyone else on the face of the earth" (Num. 12:3 NIV). That is the posture of the noble heart, choosing humility in the very situations we find it hard to do so. The truth is, either we choose it for ourselves, or our Father will arrange to have us humbled. For me, I'd prefer to forgo those moments if possible. I'd much rather *choose* the humble heart.

What are the situations in which you find it most difficult to be humble?

ISOLATION

PRIDE IS BLINDING, AND PRIDE HAS BROUGHT DOWN MANY A KING. BUT perhaps the greatest *occupational* hazard for the King is the profound, utter loneliness of it all. This is something that must be admitted, and understood, for the life of a King is a lonely life. We must see that with compassion or it will lead us to our demise. Yes, pride is a profound test. One that brought the fall of the greatest of all the angels. Something to be vigilant against. But I do not think that will be the greatest danger for a good King, not for a man who has taken the masculine journey. I think the greatest danger is isolation.

How have you handled loneliness in the past? Did you handle it well?

Run somewhere. Run to something that will distract me from my loneliness. The struggle comes with the accusations the enemy throws at me, *See, you're not a good leader . . . No one really cares/loves/likes/enjoys you . . . You are so failing, . . . You have no one. . . . Even God has left you.* (Craig)

There is isolation/loneliness we cannot control and then there's the isolation we either choose or create because of our immaturity. How does your immaturity contribute to your loneliness?

THINK OF THE MEN YOU KNOW IN POSITIONS OF POWER. HOW MANY OF them have close friendships with other men? Isolation is like a plague of office, and it is *not* good. The man becomes removed from companionship, from counsel, and from accountability. He begins to see himself as the only one who really understands, the only one with the right to rule, the only one whose opinion is valid. He will tend toward the tyrant at this point.

How will you prevent this from becoming your story?

MY SINCEREST COUNSEL TO KINGS IS, *DON'T ISOLATE YOURSELF*, AND *DON'T let it happen to you*. Surround yourself with good counselors, and listen to them. Let your allies and colleagues make decisions that affect you. Seek out friendships with a few other men—Kings, if you can find them. Be intentional to fight the isolation.

Who are the good counselors you listen to?

A couple of authors have counseled me well and I'm grateful. I have a few good friends that know my story and heart that I can turn to and interact with on any subject or issue. (Craig)

If you haven't found them, what must you now do?

YOU SEE, OUR JOURNEY OF MASCULINE INITIATION REQUIRES INTENTIONALITY on our part. We are not passive observers of the process. We must *engage*. Now, when we are boys, and young men, we need our earthly fathers and heavenly Father to provide most of the momentum for the journey. They initiate, and thus it is called initiation. By the time we have entered the stage of the King, the Father will treat us like men, leaving many decisions up to us, choices of whether or not we will continue to mature *as* men. The process of maturity is one of coming to make ever-more-meaningful decisions for ourselves.

What are some choices you've made or haven't made that would stimulate your maturity?

How would you describe your history of pursuing masculine maturity?

So what do you need to be intentional about now?

A FATHER TO YOUNG MEN

SPEAKING OF THE RELATIONSHIPS A KING NEEDS, BY THIS POINT IN YOUR life you ought to be a father to younger men. Jesus went everywhere with his disciples, young men he was training. David drew many warriors to himself, even before he was king, and he acted as their leader.

Who are the young unfinished men in your life?

Younger men, who are the older men in your life who can speak affirmation into your heart?

THE FRIEND OF GOD

HAVING SAID ALL THIS, IF I WERE TO CHOOSE ONE QUALITY ABOVE ALL others to guide a man into, so that he might become a good King, that secret would be friendship with God. For if he has this, it will compensate for whatever other deficiencies the man may have, and if he does *not* have this, no matter how gifted he might be, he will not become the King he could have been. One of the big lies of the King stage is the idea that now you ought to know enough to operate out of your own resources. Not true. You will be faced with new challenges, bigger challenges, and the stakes are *much* higher. Many lives hang in the balance when you are a King.

Describe your friendship with God.

How many Kings do you know who act as if they ***know*** God, in the manner that friends know one another?

Two, maybe three (Craig)

PRECIOUS FEW, WOULD BE MY EXPERIENCE. I'VE SAT IN HUNDREDS OF ministry meetings, board meetings, high-level gatherings of leaders; I have known a number of very successful businessmen, and very rarely have I met a King who acts like a friend of God. To give but one example—very rarely will a leader stop in the middle of a deliberation and say, "Let's ask God," then do it, right then and there, and listen, fully expecting to hear from him. (Have you?) But wouldn't that be one of the natural expressions of intimate friendship with God, that familiar turning to him in the hours of each day? If he *is* there, don't you want to know his thoughts on the matter at hand?

Allow me to make a distinction. I believe a man can be a good King over some aspect of this world—a home, a school, a church, a nation—without having to be an intimate friend of God.

In the middle of a meeting or a conversation, have you ever stopped and said, "Let's ask God," then done it, right then and there, listening and fully expecting to hear from him?

If you have, did he speak up?

If you haven't, why not?

Consider the story of the rich young ruler who came to Jesus (Matt. 19:16–22 NIV) and could not take the next step in his journey (part with his wealth) and at that point, his conversation with Jesus ends. George MacDonald gave me great light on this passage. It is a picture of initiation: "Having kept the commandments, the youth needed and was ready for a further lesson. The Lord would not leave him where he was; he had come to seek and save." So, he gives him the next lesson in his journey: The reason for our existence is to walk with God. And yet, the young man cannot take the step.

MacDonald writes,

> Was the Lord then premature in his demand on the youth? Was he not ready for it? Was it meant for a test, and not as an actual word of deliverance? Did he show the child a next step on the stair too high for him to set his foot upon? I do not believe it. He gave him the very next lesson in the divine education for which he was ready . . . And that the lesson was not lost, I see in this—that he went away sorrowful. Was such sorrow, in the mind of an earnest youth, likely to grow less or to grow more? (*Unspoken Sermons*)

How have you responded to the difficult requests God has made of you? Have you resisted God's timing, believing that his demands are either inappropriate or premature?

So according to MacDonald and John, what's the lesson of the Rich Young Ruler?

IT WOULD BE GOOD FOR US TO REMEMBER THAT IF WE WOULD BE KINGS IN the kingdom of God, help to bring about his rule here on this earth, then we must follow the Master. We must learn to walk with God. Perhaps the single greatest weakness common to good men now acting as Kings is that they do not walk with God. They have learned some principles of leadership, they have their market analyses, they have their opinions, and they try to govern by these alone. They are not bad men, per se. But they live by a practical agnosticism, even men who are leaders in the church. I promise you, you cannot master enough principles to address every situation you will meet.

Friendship with God is essential for a King for two reasons.

First, because a man in power is positioned to do great good or great damage, and he will not have the wisdom to address every situation. Humility demands he turn to God, and often.

What situations are you facing now that you need to turn to God with and ask him for direction, expecting to hear from him?

BUT THERE IS AN EVEN DEEPER REASON THAN EXPEDIENCE. THIS IS WHAT A man was made for. To be a King and not know God intimately is like a son who runs part of the family business, but never talks to his father. Yes, we are here to serve as Kings. But that service was never meant to take the place of our relationship with God.

How easy is it for you to run the "family business" but never talk to your father?

HOW IS THIS CULTIVATED? IF YOU WOULD BECOME THE FRIEND OF GOD, your orientation needs to be to walk with God through the day. It's a *posture*, where you are aware of God and asking, "What are you up to here, God?" And, "What is this about? How do you want me to handle this?"

This intimacy cannot begin in the King stage without having moved through the stages preceding it well. If this orientation is not currently your posture, it would indicate an invitation from God to go back through the stages, particularly the Beloved Son.

WITH THIS ORIENTATION, THIS POSTURE, I WOULD ADD AN OPEN HEART. THIS is also why most men don't know God in an intimate conversational way. Without a heart alive, awake, and somewhat free, you cannot know God.

Finally, and pardon the obvious, but you must actually want it. Because unless you really do, you will not be able to fight for the time required to cultivate friendship with God. I mean, something's gotta give. God doesn't offer his friendship to men who don't care enough to make room for it. I'm troubled to think how often I have shied away from time with God. I'm not quite sure why. But I have noticed this: There is in men an irritation at having our agendas tampered with. God is the ultimate disruption. A godly man just confessed to me, "I don't want to ask because I don't want to hear 'No.'" We don't want our agendas messed with.

But of course, all this you will have learned, or will learn, as you accept the orientation that is the premise of this book: Your life as a man is a process of initiation into masculinity, offered to you by your true Father. Through the course of that journey, in all the many events of the Beloved Son, the Cowboy, the Warrior, the Lover, whatever else you learn you will learn to walk with God, for he is walking with you.

Father, raise the King in me. Develop in me the heart of a King. Help me to rule well, in your name. Teach me to be a good King, like Jesus. Help me to rule well right where I am. But above all else, teach me to live as your friend. Open my heart to the ways you are speaking to me, and leading me. Show me how to cultivate an even deeper relationship with you. To be one with you, even as Jesus is one with you. In all things.

And show me the men you want me to father. Show me what stage they are truly at, whatever their age, and show me how to offer what they need. Teach me to initiate my sons as Kings.

A PAUSE IN THE JOURNEY

an opportunity to reflect on the ground you've just covered

Has your understanding of the King changed or deepened a bit since you offered your definition at the beginning of the previous chapter? Before moving on to the next stage, pause and ask God if there's anything further he has to say or show you about the King at this point. Then be still and listen.

Any notes or reflections in this moment that you want to capture before you move back into all the others things facing you today? Capture them now.

14

Sage

The glory of young men is their strength,
gray hair the splendor of the old.
—Proverbs 20:29 NIV

BEFORE STARTING

This stage, the Sage, is rarely enjoyed, offered, or experienced by most of us. Without referring back to the book, from your recollection and in your own words, describe the Sage.

For most of us, this is a stage we anticipate going through in the future. Read it, knowing the time will come when God will guide you through this season, but until then, be patient in your current stage of the masculine journey. Much is needed to prepare a man to be a sage. Give yourself the grace to learn, grow, and take in all God has for you in *this* season of life without either jumping the gun or getting anxious about the next season.

Read this with a genuine sense that it is this man God is making you to be. Many seasons of life, risk, intimacy, challenges, and hard work, as well as profound timeless experiences of gazing upon the beauty of the Lord, precede a man's becoming a Sage. This is the man you are becoming.

FIRST REACTIONS

What all did this chapter on the Sage stir up in you? Longing, disappointments, questions, hopes? Write out your first reaction.

KEY POINTS OF THE CHAPTER

- Too many men are far too willing to offer their thoughts on subjects in which they have no real personal experience—*especially* experiences of God—and their "wisdom" is not grounded in reality. It is theory, at best, more likely speculation, untested and unproven.
- The stage of the Sage begins in the waning years of the King, sometime between the ages of sixty and seventy.
- A Sage differs from an expert the way a Lover differs from an engineer. To begin with, expertise quite often has nothing to do with walking with God, may in fact lead us farther from him. For the expertise of the specialist gives us the settled assurance that he has matters under control, and that we will also, as soon as we put our trust in him. The psychology of expertise comes indistinguishably close to the psychology of the Tower of Babel. "We have matters under our control now. Expertise has given us power over our destinies." And we know how God feels about that.
- The Sage communes with God—an existence entirely different from and utterly superior to the life of the expert. Whatever counsel he offers, he draws you to God, not to self-reliance. Oh, yes, the Sage has wisdom, gleaned from years of experience, and that wisdom is one of his great offerings. But he has learned not to lean upon his wisdom, knowing that often God is asking things of us that seem counterintuitive, and thus his wisdom (and expertise) are fully submitted to his God. Humility might be one of the great dividing lines between the expert and the Sage, for the Sage doesn't think he is one. The experts impress. The Sage draws us to God. He offers a gift of presence, the richness of a soul that has lived long *with God.*
- The heart of a Sage goes *undeveloped* when a man has been a fool for most of his life, either in the form of a refusal to take the journey, or a refusal to take note of the journey he has taken.

I NEVER PLANNED ON BEING A WRITER—IT WAS SOMETHING I JUST SORT OF fell into. When I was still a Beloved Son, like most boys, I didn't think much about growing up at all, but when I did, my dream was to become Batman, then a cowboy like my grandfather, then a NASCAR driver. When first I became a Christian (around the age of nineteen), I thought I should go to seminary and become a pastor, because at the time I knew I wanted to give my life to God, wanted to change the world (as a young Warrior) and pastoring was the only category for Christian service I had. (Many, many young men have felt the same, and struggled with the fact because their gifts and desires lay in other places.) And, for too many years, I had no idea what I should do with my life.

The writing thing came up over coffee one day as I sat with Brent Curtis talking about a lecture series we were giving on The Sacred Romance. Brent said, "I think we should write a book about all this—I think there are some people out there who would like to hear what we're saying." "Oh, jeez, Brent," I said, "I don't have time for that." I was working forty-plus hours a week and going to grad school, giving what was left of me (which often wasn't much) to Stasi and the boys. There was a long pause, and then Brent said, "Well, okay. I think we should, but if you don't want to . . . why don't you think about it?" I rose and walked out of the coffeehouse. It's funny how our destinies turn on such simple moments. By the time I'd gotten my old '71 Wagoneer to start, I'd changed my mind.

In the nine years hence I have had no formal mentor in writing, no earthly father to father me in this beautiful, awful, lonely calling, fraught with dangers. But the Father has fathered me, in so many known and unknown ways, and he has sent a Sage or two along at just the right moment.

For this book, God put into my hands (rather serendipitously) a wonderful work by Norman Maclean, author of A River Runs Through It. Late in life—in fact right up to the moment of his death—Maclean wrote another book, Young Men and Fire, a sort of detective story/Western on the Mann Gulch fire in Montana in 1949, which claimed the lives of thirteen young smoke jumpers. It is masterful in many ways (the New York Times called it "a magnificent drama of writing"), and I drew so much from its style, pace, prose. The effect of Norman Maclean's words, his posture, his life poured out on those pages cannot be fully described.

Thus Maclean was my Sage in writing this book. I sat at his feet. (An important reminder that mentors and fathers need not be physically present, nor even still living.)

Who are the Sages (authors, lecturers, teachers, older men, etc.) that God has brought into your life?

Larry Crabb's writings and conferences radically shifted everything for me in the direction of God. For decades now, Dennis Prager, an ethical monotheist with a syndicated radio program based out of L.A., has modeled so many qualities I emulate. Pascal's book Penses and Kenneth Scott Latourette's The History of Christianity rooted me in something larger than the life I knew. An older man I regularly met with for a couple of seasons, Pat Trimm, gave me time, taught me to tie a Patrick (fly), and dismantled any fear of growing old. (Craig)

MACLEAN WAS IN HIS EIGHTIES WHEN HE WROTE *A RIVER RUNS THROUGH It* —the research for the book requiring years of inquiry—and yet he wants to make his life *harder? Fresher?* I am amazed. This is the point at which most men retire to Sun City, spend their days at bingo or in front of the History Channel. Maclean undertakes a very difficult book, hoping in part that it "might save me from feeding geese." This is the heart of the Sage—to make his greatest contribution with the last years of his life.

Why are there so few Sages in your community?

It requires so much of a man to become a Sage, few are the men who have taken that journey. (Craig)

What do you hope or picture yourself doing with the last years of your life?

What would you like your greatest contribution in the last years of your life to be?

Older men, how have your answers to the last two questions changed over the years?

THE STAGE

YOU'LL NOTICE I HAVE DEVOTED ONLY ONE CHAPTER TO THE SAGE. Humility demands I speak briefly here, for I have not lived this stage, and over the course of my life I've known only a few who have. Thus my remarks must be more observation than experience. Whenever this is the case, it should give us pause. I'm recalling something I read from Oxford Bishop Richard Harries:

> One of the most remarkable religious publications this century was the book of sermons by Harry Williams entitled *The True Wilderness*. This spoke to millions because, as he avowed, there came a point in his life when he was unwilling to preach anything that was not true to his own experience.

That is the secret of a truly powerful messenger, who carries weight, whom God will use mightily. Too many men are far too willing to offer their thoughts on subjects in which they have no real personal experience—*especially* experiences of God—and their "wisdom" is not grounded in reality. It is theory, at best, more likely speculation, untested and unproven. The Sage, on the other hand, knows of what he speaks, for he speaks from his experience, from a vast reservoir of self-discovery. Thus they said of Jesus, "The people were amazed at his teaching, because he taught them as one who had authority" (Mark 1:22 NIV).

What's it like to leave a conversation with a man who has a lot of knowledge, who knows truth but doesn't seem to have filtered it into and through his life? The words probably ring true, but they lack something that only personal experience and real life add to it.

Assuming this is a conversation with a good man versus the Pharisee, I'm usually impressed with his knowledge, but leave pretty untouched on the level of my heart. I typically will forget the conversation and time together quickly. Whereas a man with heart, insight, experience, years and wisdom will have me reflecting and pondering our conversation for days, making me want to spend more time with him. (Craig)

On what subject do you present yourself as a Sage but really lack the experience and seasoning a true Sage would have?

This question will take some time and reflection, so don't blow through it: When it comes to the things of God, what do you know with confidence that experience and time have confirmed to be true?

THUS, REGARDING THE SAGE, I WILL BE BRIEF. I WOULD PLACE THE STAGE OF the Sage as beginning in the waning years of the King, sometime between the ages of sixty and seventy.

There comes a time when the King must yield the throne. This does not mean failure. It means it's time to become a Sage, and let another man be King. It will appear that at this stage a man's "kingdom" may be shrinking, *but*, his *influence* should actually *increase*. For now the man is a mentor to the men who are shaping history.

Younger man, how does it make you feel that your greatest season of influence may be decades away? Why do you react that way?

Older man, how will you handle your kingdom shrinking? Do you see yourself being satisfied with increasing influence?

THE BIBLICAL ARCHETYPE WOULD OF COURSE BE SOLOMON, BUT MYSELF I often think of Paul, writing his letters from jail. Rembrandt gave us a wonderful painting of the old Sage, candle burning low, head resting in his hand propped up by an elbow on the table, writing—what? Ephesians? Philippians? Colossians? I love his letters to Timothy in particular, the tone of a loving father to son, a Sage to a young Warrior and King.

Knowing how hard it is to find a Sage, you might for the time being draw strength and inspiration from those we find in books and film. Yoda is a classic Sage: "Fear leads to anger, anger leads to hatred, hatred leads to suffering."

There is also the wonderful old priest in *The Count of Monte Christo.* "Here now is your final lesson: Do not commit the crime for which you now serve the sentence. God said, 'Vengeance is mine.'" "I don't believe in God," replies Dantes. "It doesn't matter. He believes in you."

The Sage who saves Seabiscuit is the wise horse trainer, Tom Smith, counselor to the old King Charles Howard and the young Warrior Red. "I just can't help feeling they got him so screwed up runnin' in circles he's forgotten what he was born to do. He just needs to learn to be a horse again."

Balian loses his father before he reaches Jerusalem, but he is not left alone. At this point enters a knight who is also a priest, by whose counsel Balian navigates the treacherous political and religious terrain of Jerusalem during the Crusades. Balian, unable to hear from God, says to him, "God does not speak to me. Not even on the hill where Christ died. I am outside of God's grace." To which the compassionate priest replies, "I have not heard that." "At any rate, it seems I have lost my religion." "I put no stock in religion. By the word religion I have heard the lunacy of fanatics of every denomination be called the will of God. Holiness consists in *right action.* And courage on the part of those who cannot defend themselves. And goodness. What God desires is here," he says, pointing to Balian's mind, "and here," pointing to his heart. "And what you decide to do every day, you will be a good man. Or not."

Finally, there is Gandalf, the hero behind all the other heroes in *The Lord of the Rings.* To him everyone looks—the young Cowboys, the Warriors, and the Kings. I believe he is the secret to the trilogy's success, for he embodies that mythic longing deep in all our hearts for a true Sage to walk the road with us. Certainly he completes the stages of the masculine journey as portrayed in this epic.

What movie or story that you love inspires you with a true Sage as a character?

The first couple that come to mind are The Legend of Bagger Vance, The Mask of Zorro, Lord of The Rings Trilogy. (Craig)

PROVERBS SAYS, "THE GLORY OF THE YOUNG IS THEIR STRENGTH; THE GRAY hair of experience is the splendor of the old" (20:29 NLT). How necessary is gray hair (or any hair at all, some might ask with hope)? Can a younger man be a Sage?

Certainly, to some extent. Solomon was King when he wrote Proverbs. But then again, he was given an extraordinary gift of wisdom from God. Jesus was a Sage, for there is no teaching that even comes close to his insight and compassion. And he was just into his thirties. So yes, a younger man can offer wisdom, advice, experience, counsel—that is what I've tried to do in this book.

And yet . . . there are some things we just cannot know or understand until we have passed through the years that gray hair signifies. Say you are going to war in the Middle East. Would you rather spend an hour with a young officer from West Point, valedictorian of his class, who wrote his dissertation on Middle East conflicts, or, would you want to spend that time with Norman Schwarzkopf?

It requires humility to accept that time and experience will teach you things books cannot. Do you accept that?

I do now, but I didn't as a younger man. The "older" generation was pretty much written off as out of touch with the contemporary issues I was passionate about. Furthermore, I simply believed God would instantly give me the wisdom most people had to wait years to gain. I was so arrogant. (Craig)

In what area of your life would you like to have a Norman Schwarzkopf?

AND WHAT IS IT THAT A SAGE OFFERS?

WE LIVE NOW IN A CULTURE OF EXPERTISE, SO COMPLETELY SECOND NATURE to us that we don't give it a second thought. In business circles experts are sometimes even called sages. They are worlds apart.

Are your aspirations to be an expert or a Sage?

Which would you prefer to be in the issue of prayer?

Which would you prefer to be in the issue of your teenage daughter's rebellious attitude?

Which would you prefer to be in whether or not to purchase this particular home?

Which would you want to be in your son's heart surgery?

A SAGE DIFFERS FROM AN EXPERT THE WAY A LOVER DIFFERS FROM AN engineer. To begin with, expertise quite often has nothing to do with walking with God, may in fact lead us farther from him. For the expertise of the specialist gives us the settled assurance that he has matters under control, and that we will also, as soon as we put our trust in him. The psychology of expertise comes indistinguishably close to the psychology of the Tower of Babel. "We have matters under our control now. Expertise has given us power over our destinies." And we know how God feels about that.

Has your use of "experts" affected your turning to God?

As a pastor it did. So much is riding on your decisions regarding vision, policy, personnel, finances, and programs. I found myself jumping from expert to expert, book to book, trend to trend, and spending very very little time turning to God. How many meetings on tough and profound issues did I just plow through once we dispensed with the token "opening prayer"? (Craig)

How strong is your desire to have matters under your control?

The beauty of my personality has been that I have generally been viewed as a laid-back type person while the truth is, on the inside I've been a control addict in some areas and issues. On a scale of 1 – 10, with 10 being the ultimate control freak, I used to be, in some areas (but not all . . . for some reason it's important for me to qualify this) an 8 – 9. Now I'm probably, on average a 4 – 5. A 2 – 3 is on the horizon (if I squint). (Craig)

Do you see how ungodly this desire *can* be?

THERE IS NOTHING WRONG WITH EXPERTISE—PER SE. I'D BE THE FIRST ONE to find the best heart surgeon in the country should my son need heart surgery. And yet, why is it that we seem to have so few Sages in our midst?

Is it that they don't exist, or might it be that our near-worship of expertise has pushed the Sage to the sidelines?

Given mankind's inexplicable reluctance to rely on God, and nearly limitless ability to rely on anything else, can you see how the culture of expertise actually plays right into our godlessness, despite all our protestations to the contrary?

THE SAGE, ON THE OTHER HAND, COMMUNES WITH GOD—AN EXISTENCE entirely different from and utterly superior to the life of the expert. Whatever counsel he offers, he draws you to God, not to self-reliance. Oh, yes, the Sage has wisdom, gleaned from years of experience, and that wisdom is one of his great offerings. But he has learned not to lean upon his wisdom, knowing that often God is asking things of us that seem counterintuitive, and thus his wisdom (and expertise) are fully submitted to his God. Humility might be one of the great dividing lines between the expert and the Sage, for the Sage doesn't think he is one.

The experts impress. The Sage draws us to God. He offers a gift of presence, the richness of a soul that has lived long *with God*.

Does a desire for self-reliance and wisdom keep you following a God who may be counterintuitive to your instincts and goals?

Is there someone you have spent time with or you do spend time with who leaves you with a hunger for more of God? Explain.

I remember attending a seminar put on by Dan Allender and Larry Crabb in 1983. I went expecting to be trained as a counselor. I don't think I took any notes, but the entire five days was a deep and personal encounter with God that left me not only a more skilled counselor but a man hungering and thirsting for God. Ever since, that's been my standard for a good retreat/conference and book: Do I leave/finish wanting more of God or feeling more competent? (Craig)

Do you offer wisdom, advice, and compassion to those you relate to or do you point them to deeper reliance/dependence upon God?

As the ministry we started in 2000 began to take off like a wild horse, I found myself in desperate need of counsel. I sought out a well-known pastor, whose humility I will respect by leaving him unnamed. We sat in a café while I riddled him with questions about the growth of his own ministry and how he handled it. He said, "Of course, it is my joy to do this. But God has asked me to do certain things I did not want to do, and yet I did them because the kingdom needed it." That was the threshold I was about to step over—to accept the burden of becoming a King, a burden I did not want but felt God was asking me to bear. And while this old saint's counsel was immensely helpful to me, there was something more given during our two hours that even still I find hard to describe. To sit with a man who has walked with God some seventy-plus years, to be in the presence of a father, to have the eyes of a wise and gracious man fixed upon you, to have his heart willingly offer you affirmation and counsel—that is a sort of food the soul of a man craves. All my years of loneliness and fatherlessness came into stark contrast. I could have wept.

What would it mean to you to have regular time with a man like this?

It would be a cold rushing stream to a parched soul. (Craig)

How would he be an encouragement to you?

What would it mean to you to be this kind of man?

Who will benefit from your being a Sage?

I HOPE YOU HAVE HAD THE OPPORTUNITY TO SIT IN THE PRESENCE OF A genuine Sage, for then you will know that there is an indescribable something that a seasoned man brings with his presence. It's more than just wisdom, much more than expertise. It is the weight of many winters.

I come back to Maclean's resolution to live his life to the full, to the end. "There are still new things to love, especially if compassion is a form of love." Compassion. That is a beautiful word. As I think on the Sages I have known and loved, I conclude, *Yes, that's it—that's what seems to undergird the counsel of a Sage. It is their compassion.* There is something a man who has lived a full life carries with him that cannot be learned from a younger source, however smart that source might be. The wealth of their experience is part of it, an essential part. But I think you'll notice that true Sages offer the wisdom they've gained through experience with a sort of humility and tenderness, a graciousness I believe is best described as compassion.

When you offer advice, opinion, and counsel (to spouse, kids, friends, etc.), is it with humility, tenderness, a graciousness and compassion?

IT IS A MATTER OF PRESENCE. A SAGE DOES NOT HAVE TO BE HEARD, AS A Warrior might, does not have to rule, as a King might. There is room in his presence for who you are and where you are. There is understanding. He has no agenda, and nothing now to lose. What he offers, he offers with kindness, and discretion, knowing by instinct those who have ears to hear, and those who don't. Thus his words are offered in the right measure, at the right time, to the right person. He will not trouble you with things you do not need to know, nor burden you with things that are not yet yours to bear, nor embarrass you with exposure for shortcomings you are not ready yet to overcome, even though he sees all of that. For he is wise, and compassionate.

Is your presence becoming more and more like that of a Sage?

I'm a ways off. But I hope Christ is building into me that which will, in a couple of decades, make me a Sage. (Craig)

Would those close to you (friends, spouse, children) agree? Where might they say you need to grow?

UNDEVELOPED AND WOUNDED

THE HEART OF A SAGE GOES *UNDEVELOPED* WHEN A MAN HAS BEEN A FOOL for most of his life, either in the form of a refusal to take the journey, or a refusal to take note of the journey he has taken. That man made something other than maturity his aim—success, usually meaning pleasure; or safety, meaning the path of least resistance.

Are you on the journey God has for you?

If not, how will you feel when, in your final seasons, you may have accomplished many things in your life, but are either a fool or an undeveloped Sage?

If so, are you taking note (learning, journaling, applying) of all God is teaching you?

THE FOOL MAY HAVE SEEN MANY WINTERS, BUT THEY DO NOT SEEM TO HAVE had any other effect on him beyond fatigue, or perhaps cynicism. Scripture describes a fool as a man who will not submit to wisdom, a man who refuses to be taught by all that life has to teach him. Gray hair does not a Sage make. No doubt you have experienced that by now.

The heart of the Sage is *wounded* when he is dismissed as a has-been, too old to have anything to offer.

How do you feel at *this* stage being dismissed when you offer your thoughts, insight, or wisdom and experience?

YOUNG WARRIORS WILL SOMETIMES DISMISS THE OLDER MEN IN THEIR lives because those men no longer yearn for battle, or simply because they don't come from "my generation." Thus the sixties adage, "Never trust anyone over thirty."

As a young Warrior have you, in arrogance, dismissed older men simply because they don't come from your generation?

Is repentance for arrogance in order?

INSECURE KINGS OFTEN DISMISS THE OLDER MEN AROUND THEM, SEND them into early retirement, threatened because the older men know more than they do. Thus the heart of the Sage is wounded when he is dismissed, or sent into exile. No one seems to want what he has to offer, and he comes to believe after a time that it is because he has nothing to offer.

Kings, have you, out of your insecurities and woundedness, felt threatened by Sages and dismissed them, isolated or buffered yourself from them? Is repentance in order?

RAISING THE SAGE

THE GREATEST GIFT YOU CAN GIVE TO A SAGE IS TO SIT AT HIS FEET AND ASK questions.

It's important that we ask because often in humility the Sage will not offer until he is invited to do so. It's also important that we ask because quite often the Sage himself is not aware of all that he knows. It is the questions that stir his soul, and memory, as a smoldering fire leaps to life again when stirred. In this way we can help to raise the Sage.

What are the questions or issues you'd love to bring to a Sage and simply sit at his feet to listen and converse?

Older man, are you available, accessible, and intentional in inviting young men to bring their questions or issues to you?

YOUNGER MEN, DON'T WORRY MUCH ABOUT THIS STAGE, FOR IT WILL COME in due time. When you are young, commit yourself to take as few shortcuts as possible. Learn your lessons. Take note of all that God is teaching you. Submit to the journey. Be a student of the Scriptures. Hang out with the wise, living or dead, for that is how we, too, become wise.

You fathers of sons—the best you can do to prepare a boy for this stage is to begin the lessons of wisdom. In the woodshop and in the field, in the use of language and even in prayer, show him that *there is a way things work*. Your initiation will show him that the way of a fool is a fruitless way to live.

As for you older men, if the Sage has gone undeveloped in you because you didn't take the journey or take note of the journey you have taken, well, you'd better get busy, 'cause time's a-wastin'. At this point you haven't years to go back and gather through many experiences all that you need; you had best walk closely with God, let him focus you on what he'd have you learn now. Some of you just need to be a Beloved Son. Or perhaps a Lover. The wisest thing to do is to seek the communion with God that age and large amounts of time on your hands now allow for. The boy knows God as Father, the Cowboy knows God as the One who initiates, the Warrior knows God as the King he serves, the Lover knows God as his intimate One, and the King knows God as his trusted Friend. The Sage has a deep *communion* with God.

Those of you older men who have been wounded, or dismissed—have you made a vow never to offer again?

Seek the comfort and healing Christ offers. Let your heart be restored, for you *are* needed. Despite your wounds, I urge you to offer. We need you to offer.

THIS IS ALSO THE STORY OF GEORGE MACDONALD, A PROPHET FOR THE MOST part unwelcomed and unhonored in his time. His church ran him out because he unsettled them with his heart-centered theology and true holiness. His books did not sell all that well. His health suffered also. One of his best books (in my opinion) is *Diary of an Old Soul*, which begins,

> Lord, what I once had done with youthful might,
> Had I been from the first true to the truth,
> Grant me, now old, to do—with better sight,
> And humbler heart, if not the brain of youth;
> So wilt thou, in thy gentleness and truth,
> Lead back thy old soul, by the path of pain,
> Round to his best—young eyes and heart and brain.

I am not alone in being profoundly grateful that he did. Much of what we have received from C. S. Lewis is a result of MacDonald's choice, for he became Lewis's mentor of sorts, through his writings.

In the spirit of MacDonald's prayer, what would you ask God now for the strength to do? What is on your heart?

Remember, "The problem of self-identity is not just a problem for the young." Consider yourself a Sage, and ask yourself, "What would I love to now be my greatest contribution?"

What we need is your heart, and the life you've lived. Please—do not fade away.

READ *TUESDAYS WITH MORRIE*—THE STORY OF A YOUNG MAN AND A SAGE, and then ask yourself, "How can I offer this?" There are many fatherless young men out there—find a way to draw them in. Teach a class. Take them through this book (provided that they've first read *Wild at Heart*—in fact, start there). Start a poker night, and invite four men to join you. Take some guys fishing, or to a cabin in the mountains. Call the younger men in your family who live out of state, and pursue relationships with them. Make yourself *available*—the questions will arise in time. Offer yourself to a King you know—your pastor, or youth pastor, a missionary serving overseas with whom you can correspond, or a young businessman. Serve on the board of your church, or the local board of education. Take up pen and paper. Tell your story. This is not the time to be feeding geese.

Think of what they said of Gandalf: "This shall be his great task, and maybe the end of his labors."

Father, I need you now, need you to the end of my days. I ask you to raise the Sage in me. Help me to become a man of genuine wisdom and compassion. [For you younger men:] Show me the Sages you have for me, both living and dead. Help me find them, and sit at their feet. [For you older men:] Show me the men and women who need my counsel, and show me how to pursue them. Speak to me, Father; stir the fire in my heart. Show me what my contribution is now to be, and father me in making it with all my heart.

A PAUSE IN THE JOURNEY

an opportunity to reflect on the ground you've just covered

So, having completed this chapter, has your understanding of the Sage changed or deepened a bit since you offered your definition at the beginning of the chapter? Before moving on to the next stage, pause and ask God, and listen to hear, if there's anything further he has to say or show you on the Sage at this point.

Any notes or reflections in this moment that you want to capture before you move back into all the others things facing you today? Capture them now.

15

Let Us Be Intentional

You have made known to me the path of life.

—Psalm 16:11 NIV

BEFORE STARTING

In chapter 7, John told the story of his eldest son Sam's Vision Quest year, and in this chapter, John shares the story of his middle son Blaine's Vision Quest year. Over the course of Blaine's year, John found himself at many points realizing that he was the one being initiated, and he thought that in telling his story and Blaine's, you might find something that tells you about yourself too.

Though this is the last chapter in the manual, there's still more for you and your journey. Read this with your ears open to all God may have to say to you about your being initiated by the Father.

FIRST REACTIONS

What did this story of Blaine's year stir up in you? What are your reactions, thoughts, impressions, or questions?

KEY POINTS OF THE CHAPTER

- The enemy is a thief, and you must understand—if you have not already noticed this—his greatest target is simply *your joy.*
- Jesus enjoyed a relationship with his Father that we *crave.* They were close, those two, so close that they were One. We were made for the very same thing, and our lives just aren't right until we have it.

THE SNOW BEGAN FALLING AROUND 4:00 P.M., AND CONTINUED TO FALL through the night—big, soft, chicken-feather snow, falling so gently, slowly, it seemed like the ashes of a great fire drifting down, or like a hundred thousand tiny parachutes swaying to earth. Heaven-sent, not merely for the beauty of it all, and the beauty with which it adorned the trees, but because maybe now I wouldn't kill myself. Blaine and I had come to the mountains in January, for his thirteenth birthday, to learn how to snowboard. I had no fears for him, gifted athlete that he is. I knew he'd pick it up in a couple of hours. It was me I was worried about, worried that in trying to teach this old dog a very new trick he'd do serious damage, either to himself or to someone else. I watched the snow falling heavily from our window before we went to bed, looking like someone was emptying a down pillow from the roof above us, making the mountainside soft for what I knew would be my many falls. And I smiled, some of my apprehension fading away.

Blaine's vision quest began on the same theme that Samuel's did—a special trip, just with Dad, no formal test or challenge yet, simply, You are prized. You are my delight. Blaine had been wanting to learn to snowboard for a couple of years, most of his friends having abandoned skiing for the much cooler culture of snowboarding. Okay. Snowboarding. We'll learn together. I booked three nights at a resort here in Colorado—condo, lessons, rentals, the whole shebang—for the weekend just after New Year's. Blaine's birthday is January 1, and his mom and I gave him the trip as a present. And thus his quest began.

In the course of going through this manual, have you heard again, or perhaps in new ways from God, that you are prized, that you are his delight? Write out all you heard about being the delight of God.

In our attempts to understand how our Father truly feels about us, Jesus gave us as the starting point of our own posture as a reference: "Which of you, if his son asks for bread, will give him a stone?" (Matt. 7:9 NIV). If we have some natural inclination of generosity toward our own sons, "how much more" is the Father's heart toward us?

I wanted to give Blaine a trip he would never forget. It makes me wonder—why don't I expect even more from my Father?

What have you learned, thought about, or pondered when it comes to the generosity of God's heart for you?

When you feel desolate, or abandoned, or simply feel that the weight of the world is once again on your shoulders, is it then you tend to doubt God's heart toward you?

If so, it's at those points you should return to the truth: You *are* the Beloved Son. It all starts there.

The enemy is a thief, and you must understand—if you have not already noticed this—his greatest target is simply *your joy*. What I've come to see is that the joy and life God wants to bring us are the things most fiercely opposed. But of course, now that I think about it—isn't that just what Jesus said? He links them in the same verse: "The thief comes only to steal and kill and destroy; I have come that they may have life, and have it to the full" (John 10:10 NIV).

As you have gone through this manual, have you identified the assaults the enemy has set against you and your joy? What are they?

THIS IS THE FLIP SIDE OF FORGETTING WE ARE BELOVED SONS, THIS PLOY OF the enemy to steal the Father's gifts from us and so bring us back to the belief we are fundamentally fatherless. You'll want to keep this in mind as you pursue your own masculine quest, your healing and strength, and the journey of your sons or the men you will guide.

When things turn sour, or become suddenly difficult, do you give up—surrendering the trip, or the relationship, or the dream? Let the Warrior rise in you. It's worth fighting for.

DURING THE CEREMONY WE HELD FOR BLAINE AT THE END OF THE YEAR one theme that several men spoke to was Blaine's big heart. His compassion is rare for a boy his age, and while I love that about Blaine, he sure doesn't. In the rough world of adolescent boys, where verbal jujitsu is the relational style of choice—and often a matter of survival—Blaine's tender heart has felt to him like a liability. Adolescent boys turn on any apparent weakness like a pack of hyenas, hoping in their insecurity to feel better about themselves, secure their place in the pack by bringing someone else down. (Many men, still adolescent inside, do the same.) We talked about that as we drifted above the treetops. "Sometimes the tears come pretty easily, don't they?" Blaine just nodded, looking away. "I love that about you, Blaine. I absolutely love that." He turned back, a look of bewilderment in his eyes—and a touch of hope. "It doesn't feel like a good thing at all." "Oh, but Blaine, it was. Look at David—he was a great Warrior, but he had a tender heart. Look how emotional he is. And then there is Jesus. He was pretty free with his tears."

As we ascended the mountain, and talked, something in Blaine loosened. A tension left his body. "Thanks, Dad. That's really good to hear."

What is it about you that you wish were different or you (perhaps others as well) view as a negative that God wants to address by saying, "*I love that about you. I absolutely love that*!"?

JESUS ENJOYED A RELATIONSHIP WITH HIS FATHER THAT WE *CRAVE*. NOT A stained-glass churchy sort of thing, but masculine oneness. They were close, those two, so close that they were One. We were made for the very same thing, and our lives just aren't right until we have it.

So Jesus prays for us, just before he leaves, "that all of them may be one, Father, just as you are in me and I am in you. May they also be in us . . . one as we are one; I in them and you in me" (John 17:21–23 NIV). Jesus wants us to enjoy oneness *with the Father*: "just as you are in me and I am in you." We need oneness with the Father. "I in them and you in me. Then they'll be mature in this oneness" (John 17:23 *The Message*). *This* is the healing of the masculine soul. This is masculine maturity—"mature in this oneness." To be fathered by the Father, loved by the Father as he loved Jesus, to in fact become one in heart and mind with him and with his Son. Until then, we are fatherless, and lost.

How has your desire for and understanding of "oneness" or intimacy with God developed or changed as you've gone through this manual?

Describe what "oneness with the Father" would look like for you.

As we've said a number of times, don't rush past the whispered invitation of God to commune, to pray, to listen. Is this one of those moments?

DRIVING

I GAVE BLAINE A CHANCE TO DRIVE ON ONE OF THE BACK ROADS DURING our Moab trip. During the course of our desert adventures, every time we turned off down some isolated dirt road, he'd say, "Hey, Dad, how 'bout a turn at the wheel?" Being entrusted with that is a big deal. *I believe in you. You can handle this.* Everybody else jumps out and gets on the running boards, and off we go.

It makes me wonder what God is wanting to entrust me with, what joys he has in store.

What does God want to entrust you with? What joys does he have in store for you?

JESUS' GOOD NEWS ABOUT THE KINGDOM CAN BE AN EFFECTIVE GUIDE FOR our lives only if we share his view of the world in which we live . . . It is a world in which God is continually at play and over which he constantly rejoices. (Dallas Willard)

God at play? Have you viewed God as a stodgy old guy who doesn't delight in our joy and laughter? What is he delighting over you about today?

BOW HUNTING

AS DID SAMUEL TWO YEARS BEFORE, BLAINE JOINED THE MEN ON OUR annual elk hunt the year before his quest, when he turned twelve, enduring the demands of high-country hunting like a champ. The privilege of entering into the fellowship of men cannot be overstated. As Harrington discovered,

> Over the years I've read an awful lot about hunting, and one of the recurring themes is that hunting is for men a social ritual that imbues their lives with meaningful tradition in

> an era when tradition is hard to come by . . . the men don't think of their breakfasts at the C&J, or The Hunters Breakfasts, or cleaning rabbits behind Bobby's barn as ritual. That's the beauty of it. The men don't try to create ritual in the same way, that, say, Martha Stewart goes about teaching America to remember how to trim a Christmas tree in the old-fashioned way, as if doing so could somehow rekindle the old-fashioned values we've lost. That's when ritual becomes sentiment, a desperate shadow of ritual. The men don't plan the memorable moments in their lives; the moments happen. (*The Everlasting Stream*)

The moments happen as men live together in adventures and hard work they've been sharing for years. That's the main reason I hunt—to create over time that social ritual where men can be men, together. Hunting is merely a *context*. There are many. It might be basketball down at the Y. It might be fixing cars in somebody's garage. Make sure you develop them, if only for your own sake, and make sure you protect them. Life will present a hundred reasons to forsake this, as you'll notice when you look at the lonely, bored men around you. Fight for experiences that over time become their own rituals of masculine camaraderie.

If you currently have a fellowship of men you gather with, what can you do to change, develop, or more intentionally encourage one another in your masculine journey?

If you do not have a fellowship of men, who are the men you can begin to gather with?

WHEN IT CAME TIME FOR HIS YEAR, BLAINE WAS GOING TO GET TO HUNT himself, and he wanted to learn to bow hunt. I took it up as a way to be with Blaine in the woods. It's become a love.

There is something sloppy about the way I live most of my life in town, in the day-to-day, something unconsidered and unintentional. But I get away with it largely due to a knack for winging things. You can't do that bow hunting. You have to be keenly aware—of every subtle shift in the wind, of every sound, of signs like a small aspen whose bark has been rubbed off by a buck raking his antlers on the tree. It requires incredible presence, being utterly present to the moment.

Blaine and I spent many September evenings up in the woods behind our house, decked out in camo, stalking deer. One evening we jumped a huge black bear, who, thankfully, ran straight up the mountain to get away. Blaine had a shot, only once, at a doe, right at dusk. We came upon several feeding in the mahogany just down the ridge from us. We eased up on them without flushing them, but Blaine missed the shot and when the season came to an end Blaine did not get a deer. And that was very good. We need to remember something essential to the masculine journey—life does not come easily. Not the real thing, anyway.

How has your view of the place and value of hardship, tests, and challenges in your masculine journey been challenged, changed, or confirmed?

THERE IS FAR TOO MUCH AT OUR FINGERTIPS IN THE ARTIFICIAL WORLD MADE for our comfort and ease. Cable television and air-conditioning and hiring someone else to fix the sink or do your shirts. The masculine soul atrophies under those conditions. And God would have us become men. If life always came easily to us, we wouldn't benefit from it. The things we value are the things we've paid for. The victories we treasure are from the hardest battles.

When life is hard or disappointing, we have a new framework for understanding that, a new orientation. We haven't been forsaken. We are not on our own. This isn't just the way it goes. God is treating us with respect, treating us like men. He has something for us in the difficulty. We need to find out what that is, be shaped and strengthened by it.

What have you discovered that God has for you in the disappointing situations you didn't see previously?

Have you sensed his respect of you as a man by the challenges he's brought your way?

MASCULINE SPIRITUALITY

ALL MASCULINE INITIATION IS ULTIMATELY SPIRITUAL. THE TESTS AND challenges, the joys and adventures are all designed to awaken a man's soul, draw him into contact with the masculine in himself, in other men, in the world, and in God, as Father. I make no distinction between taking a boy or a man on an adventure and, say, teaching that man to pray. The adventure—rightly framed—can be a powerful experience of God. And prayer or Bible study—rightly framed—is meant to be the same. Most boys and men share the perception that God is found in church, and that the rest of life is . . . just the rest of life. The tragedy of this is that the rest of life seems far more attractive to them than church, and thus God seems removed and even opposed to the things that make them come alive.

Most of the stories of men encountering God in the Bible do not take place in church (!). Moses is met in the desert, in a burning bush. Jacob wrestles with God in the wilderness also, in the dead of night. David wrote most of his psalms out under the stars. Paul is met on the desolate dirt road *between* Jerusalem and Damascus.

We have got to recover the wildness of spirituality—especially masculine spirituality.

What have you discovered about the role of adventure and the outdoors in your development as a godly man?

What adventure do you hope to live in this next season?

YES, AS WITH SAMUEL, I LED BLAINE THROUGH A NUMBER OF BIBLE STUDIES in his year, studies about identity in Christ, and the New Name, and the epic story which is the gospel. We also watched movies together, and talked about what God was saying to us through them. And so much discipleship took place in the field, in experiences, as it did for the men who followed Jesus from town to town. Everything I've described in these pages *is* discipleship.

What needs to be added to your discipleship regimen to stimulate your heart for God and your development as a man?

SOME FRIENDS INVITED US TO COME WITH THEM TO SEE THE WORK OF Compassion (a child sponsorship ministry) among the poorest of the poor in Guatemala. I want to say as clearly as I can that the goal of masculine initiation is to endow a man with a strength he *knows* he has, and knows it is *for others*. Men need to know that life really *is* found in God. They also need to know that life at its highest is found when we give ours away on behalf of someone else. You want to present a Cowboy with the question "What good can I do? How can I help someone?" It's a good question for a Warrior as well, and by the time he is a King, hopefully it is what his life is all about. Power held on behalf of others.

As a Cowboy, Warrior, Lover, or King, what can you do for others? How can you help someone?

As you've gone through this material, do you now see your life as being in the service of others?

AND THEN IT WAS INTO THE WOODS AGAIN, FOR A DAY OF PRAYER AND fasting, seeking God. The ritual is found in nearly every culture that has taken initiation seriously down through the ages, and you see it practiced in the Scriptures. Blaine's year was coming to an end, so we grabbed the first warm December day and rode our horses out into the woods. Blaine and I talked about the day, and I counseled him as best I could. "Don't try too hard to experience God, Blaine. That never works for me. Just be available to him. Be quiet, and listen. Notice the direction your heart goes. God will speak to us in lots of ways—in a memory, in a Scripture (he took his Bible), in our desire, and in that still, small voice within. Journal about what you are sensing, what you are feeling. Take your questions to him."

I rode off, leaving Blaine to be with God. Much to his delight—and a little to his surprise—he did hear from God, heard some wonderful things, things his heart very much needed to hear. When he rode back to the stable hours later, he had this big smile on his face. My heart sighed. *Thank you, Father—thank you for meeting with my son.*

You see, we must put ourselves into situations that will thrust us forward in our journeys. So much of our daily lives is simply routine, and routine by its very nature is *numbing*. Get out of it. Break away. I didn't get my time in the mountains with God this year, and not only did I miss it, but I can tell. My heart is not in the same place it would be in if I had; something is missing. The tank is half full. The connection is somewhat frayed.

What is needed to thrust you forward in your journey?

How will you prevent your routine from numbing your heart and soul this year?

GOD HONORS OUR INTENTIONALITY AS MEN, AND WHILE HE WILL ARRANGE for much of the journey, he asks us to take part as well, to *engage*. Ask, seek, knock, as the Scriptures urge. I took Blaine into many things, because he is young and learning. But I don't wait for someone to take me there. Though you may still feel very young inside, and at times our Father will be tender with those places, you are still a man and he will treat you like one. Be *intentional* about your own initiation into masculine maturity, as intentional as you would want to be toward your own sons, as intentional as you hope God is toward you. This is not a spectator sport.

THE BIG CLIMB

JOHN SHARES THE STORY OF HE AND BLAINE CLIMBING THE PROW ON KIT Carson Peak in the Sangre de Christo mountains in Colorado. The Prow is made of a kind of rock called conglomerate, a sort of hodgepodge of large and small stones held together by ancient clay. Wonderful for handholds, terrible for placing protection because there are no cracks. As one guidebook says, "The nature of this climb is abundantly clear at this point. Escape and protection are difficult," meaning, there is no way off but up, and as you go up, finding places to use the gear you brought proves elusive. "There is tremendous exposure in every direction, and the commitment increases with every pitch."

Blaine was marvelous, through all of it. Both he and Nick kept their spirits up, faced each pitch with courage, never let themselves give way to fear or uncertainty. We made the summit at 6:00 p.m., the time at which we'd planned on having been back in camp for hours and now making dinner.

Climbing is wonderful practice for living. If you will choose to take the risk, it will be beautiful, exhilarating, and dangerous. Yes, at times it seems insurmountable. That is true for all of us. Blaine later told me that when he started up after me on the first pitch, he had to keep telling himself, *I've done this before. I've done this before. The only difference is the exposure.* Thankfully, climbing, like life, comes to us one piece at a time. You cannot take on the whole mountain at once, just as you cannot create a marriage at once. You make the next move, committed that your only plan is to do it. Much of it is unpredictable.

Looking at the masculine journey as a whole can be overwhelming . . . it can seem insurmountable. Thankfully it comes to us one piece at a time. You cannot take on the whole journey at once. What is your next move?

CLIMBING TAKES YOU BEYOND YOUR PHYSICAL AND EMOTIONAL LIMITS, AS life will do. How else will we discover that there *is* more to us, that indeed God is our strength and our life? And, it doesn't always go well. I have been turned back from many summits because of weather or safety. My best friend was killed in a climbing accident. Do we let these things stop us?

This journey will take you beyond your physical and emotional limits, but God is your guide, and his intention is for you to discover that there is more to you than you realize. What has caused you to stop "climbing" in the past?

Whatever is the enemy of your journey, how will you counter that enemy?

FINALLY, AT SOME POINT IN YOUR JOURNEY, YOU WILL BE REQUIRED TO TAKE the lead, even though you don't feel up to it. You can choose to do this yourself, or, God can force it upon you. It seems that just when we feel we've begun to get the hang of a certain stage, he calls us on to the next.

Have you gotten the "advanced" words from God about where he wants you to take the lead, where he wants you to step into something new and risky?

Take the time now to ask God if, when, and where he is calling you on to the next challenge in your journey.

BEFORE WE PART, A WORD UPON THE GRAVER TEACHING OF THE MOUNTAINS. See yonder height! 'Tis far away—unbidden comes the word, "Impossible!" "Not so," says the mountaineer. "The way is long, I know; it's difficult—it may be dangerous. It's possible, I'm sure. I'll seek the way, take counsel of my brother mountaineers, and find out how they have gained similar heights . . . we know that each height, each step, must be gained by patient, laborious toil, and that wishing cannot take the place of working . . . and we come back to our daily occupations better fitted to fight the battle of life and to overcome the impediments which obstruct our paths, strengthened and cheered by the recollection of past labors and by the memories of victories gained in other fields. (Edward Whymper, *Scrambles Amongst the Alps*)

God has no doubt reminded you of challenges, tests, wounds, victories, hardships, and more that he's taken you through and through which you lived well. What are your "recollections of past labors and memories of victories gained in other fields" that would strengthen and cheer you on?

RECOGNITION AND INVITATION

WHEN WE CAME DOWN OFF THE MOUNTAIN, OUR FAMILIES GATHERED TO hear the stories. I told them that during the trip we often referred to Blaine and Nick as "the boys," as in, "Where have the boys gone?" and "Tell the boys to gather some more firewood." "But I cannot call them that now, not after what they've just done. They are young men." I shared that again the night of Blaine's fourteenth birthday, when we held his ceremony. Stasi prepared a montage of photos from Blaine's life. Blaine stood before the fellowship to tell us the epic story of the gospel. Stasi spoke some beautiful and affirming words to Blaine, and then she let him go, to enter the fellowship of men. One by one men who have known Blaine and walked with him spoke into his life—words of validation, words of invitation. We gave him a shotgun.

I found a beautiful and deadly Celtic sword, called an Irish Hand-and-a-Half. That fit Blaine perfectly. A Celtic Warrior. We also give each other swords as men, in our fellowship. For none of us received anything like this from our fathers. And we speak words to one another. It is a form of recognition, and a calling out. This is so vital, and so rare. But you've got to have those defining moments in your own masculine journey. They may come in a fellowship; they may come alone, in the wilderness. Even the bravest Warrior and the noblest King need to hear words of validation, words of recognition along the way. Not just once, but again and again. Is this not the heart of our Father?

> And a voice from heaven said, "This is my Son, whom I love; with him I am well pleased." (Matt. 3:17 NIV)

And so the formal year of Blaine's quest ended. But the informal initiation continues in many, many ways—just as our quests continue in many, many ways. For our life *is* a quest, my brothers, arranged by our Father, for our initiation. There are gifts along the way to remind us that we are his Beloved Sons. Adventures to call forth the Cowboy Ranger, and battles to train the Warrior. There is Beauty to awaken the Lover, and power on behalf of others to prepare the King. A lifetime of experience from which the Sage will speak. This is the masculine journey. This is our orientation. It all comes down to this:

> I will not leave you as orphans; I will come to you . . . My Father will love him, and we will come to him and make our home with him. (John 14:18, 23 NIV)

> Because we are the sons of God, we must become the sons of God. (George MacDonald)

A PAUSE IN THE JOURNEY

an opportunity to rest/reflect on the ground you've just covered

You did it! What a journey you've completed reading the book and working through the manual. It is a journey indeed. You probably experienced a bit of everything a journey involves:

Hard work . . . perhaps even exhausting at times with the subtle suggestion to "*give up, quit, this is too hard*" looming close at hand. Well done!

Clarity and confusion over the next step. As in any journey, there were probably times you asked, "*Where do I go, what direction do you have for me . . . help!*" And God came through, directing, speaking, guiding. And while some of your questions may remain, our hope is that you have a settled confidence that because his heart is so for you he will guide, speak, prod, poke, and encourage at the right time.

Hunger and thirst. Don't you find yourself ending this manual with an insatiable hunger for more of what God has for you? It is a good thing to hunger and thirst for righteousness.

You finished! Not the whole journey of course, but a significant portion. Rest, take it all in . . . don't start another book or study just yet. It would be good to take a Sabbath and perhaps skim through your notes again and recapture anything more God has for you.

Well done, sojourner . . .

APPENDIX: SUPPLEMENTAL FILM INFORMATION

THE KINGDOM OF HEAVEN

Our core assumptions about the world boil down to this: We are on our own to make our lives work. We are not watched over. We are not cared for. Whatever our fathers might have provided, we are not much different now from Balian at the start of his story. When we are hit with a problem, we have to figure it out ourselves, or just take the hit. If anything good is going to come our way, we're the ones who are going to have to arrange for it. Many of us have called upon God as Father, but, frankly, he doesn't seem to have heard. We're not sure why. Maybe we didn't do it right. Maybe he's about more important matters. Whatever the reason, our experience of this world has framed our approach to life. We believe we are fatherless.

Balian had many lessons to learn, much catching up to do from his years of fatherlessness. He was about to get a sort of crash course in the way of the Cowboy, and the Warrior, and not long after that the Lover, so that he might become a King. But first, he had to take the risk, accept the fact that his father had come for him.

Evil typically doesn't yield its hold willingly. It must be forced to surrender, or be destroyed. Balian is trained to be a Warrior by his father, and his first act upon reaching the Holy Land is to lead a charge of cavalry against the enemy.

I'm thinking of the scene in *The Kingdom of Heaven* where Godfrey and Balian have taken to the road, and we find them at camp in the woods. Godfrey begins to train his son in the way of the Warrior. He throws a sword on the ground next to Balian—"Pick it up. Let's see what you're made of." Balian tries to defend himself as best he knows how as Godfrey suddenly comes upon him. "Never use the low guard. You fight well. Come over here. Let's work on your skills." The academy in the woods has officially opened. "Take a high guard, like this." Godfrey raises his sword overhead, with a two-handed grip. "The Italians call it 'la costa de falcone.' The guard of the hawk. Strike from high. Like this. Do it." Balian attempts to imitate his father's skill. "Blade straighter. Leg back. Bend your knees. Sword straighter. Defend yourself." The Warrior is being called out, trained for battle.

There is another scene where, through ancient ceremony and ritual, Balian is given the oath and office of a knight. As he kneels, Balian's father gives him his oath: "Be without fear in the face of your enemies. Be brave and upright, that God may love thee. Speak the truth, always—even if it leads to your death. Safeguard the helpless and do no wrong. That is your oath." And a noble oath it is. My boys love scenes like this. I love scenes like this. There is something in a noble oath, a code, a cause, that stirs the heart of a man. To learn, for example, that *samurai* means "to serve." To be dangerous and powerful in order to serve. As with the samurai, nearly every warrior society down through the ages had a code of some sort. After all, we aren't raising reckless warriors; we are raising men who fight *for a cause.*

Following his father's instructions, Balian arrives in Jerusalem and reports to King Baldwin, who in turn sends Balian to protect the Pilgrim Road leading to the Holy City, saying, "All are welcome in Jerusalem—not only because it's expedient, but because it is right." Balian rides out with his men to what was his father's estate there—a small farm settlement centered around a castle, like many medieval hamlets, only this one out in the middle of the desert, more dust than anything else. Balian sets about making the place a refuge of life. What is needed is water, so he has the men dig wells, build aqueducts. The king's sister, Sybilla, stops in on a visit, and when she sees him out there in the fields with his workers, sleeves rolled up, she asks, "Would you make this like Jerusalem?"

Beautiful. Exactly. That is what a good King does—he uses all he has to make his kingdom like the kingdom of heaven for the sake of the people who live under his rule.

Late in the story, the king of Jerusalem is dying, and he knows that upon his death the throne will go to his sister, Sybilla, whose arrogant husband, Gi, lusts for power and for war. King Baldwin and his adviser, Tiberius, offer Balian Sybilla's hand in marriage, and thus the throne when Baldwin is gone. The arrangement has one little catch—Gi will have to be eliminated (echoes of the story where David, having taken Bathsheba to himself, arranges for the death of her husband, Uriah). Balian refuses. Earlier, he compromised his integrity by sleeping with Sybilla. Now, he repents, and does what he can to take his integrity back. As he leaves the palace, Tiberius follows him. "For the salvation of this kingdom, would it be so hard to marry Sybilla? Jerusalem has no need of a perfect knight." "No," Balian replies. "It is a kingdom of conscience. Or nothing."

Balian is given the oath and sword of a knight, his father also confers upon him his authority. Godfrey, baron of Ibelin, is about to die. His final act is to remove a ring from his finger and give it to Balian, a symbol of his authority passing now to his son. He is literally giving his kingdom to his son. "Rise a knight," his father's aide says to Balian, "and baron of Ibelin."

This, my brother, is what has happened to you through the work of Christ.

Balian loses his father before he reaches Jerusalem, but he is not left alone. At this point enters a knight who is also a priest, by whose counsel Balian navigates the treacherous political and religious terrain of Jerusalem during the Crusades. Balian, unable to hear from God, says to him, "God does not speak to me. Not even on the hill where Christ died. I am outside of God's grace." To which the compassionate priest replies, "I have not heard that."

Balian continues, "At any rate, it seems I have lost my religion." "I put no stock in religion. By the word religion I have heard the lunacy of fanatics of every denomination be called the will of God. Holiness consists in *right action.* And courage on the part of those who cannot defend themselves. And goodness. What God desires is here," the priest says, pointing to Balian's mind, "and here," pointing to his heart. "And what you decide to do every day, you will be a good man. Or not."

ANTWONE FISHER

The movie *Antwone Fisher*—based on his true story—is the story of a wounded and angry young man who becomes the Beloved Son. Antwone is in his twenties when we meet him in the film. He is a in the navy—barely. Barely because something is wrong inside Antwone, and it drives him to fight anyone and anything that provokes him, who threatens to step on his angry and frail sense of self. Not a good temperament for success in the armed services. After yet another brawl, Antwone is sent to the base psychologist, and thus his journey to redemption begins.

As we listen to Antwone's story, we find a young boy whose father dies before he is born, given up for adoption by his mother and raised by a black minister and his wife—a cruel woman who beats Antwone and his brother mercilessly for petty and even imaginary offenses, beats them unconscious. Needless to say, Antwone has no sense of being the Beloved Son. The distance between Beloved Son and what he experienced as a boy is about the same distance as between heaven and hell, and that yawning chasm creates a great, yawning chasm in his soul. It is this deep and primary wound that makes him the angry man he is. For when a young man like Antwone is tested (and every young man will be tested, especially in a place like the navy), he feels that test or challenge to be a rejection of him as a person. The young boy inside feels every challenge as a threat, a further pronouncement that *you are not the Beloved Son.* Never will be. So the young man is fighting mad.

Antwone has a recurring dream that makes this all clear. He is a young boy in his dreams, perhaps seven years old, and he is standing alone in a field. (The orphaned boy always feels alone. Men with unhealed souls feel alone even in the company of friends.) In his dream Antwone then pictures himself, still the young orphaned boy, coming into a large and happy family at a family reunion of sorts, a great feast spread on the table before him. The symbol of belonging, of coming home. Antwone is given the place of honor at the table, and a heaping platter of pancakes is set before him, butter melting down the sides, maple syrup cascading down with it. A symbol that he is being celebrated, that he is prized, that he is, beyond any shadow of doubt, the Beloved Son.

This is the past Antwone never had, the one lesson he must learn before his life can continue. The boy within needs to be raised from the depths of the soul where he has hidden or been banished so that the man can "get on with his life." The boy inside must be raised, and raised to the status of Beloved Son.

This is what happens for Antwone, over the course of his story. The psychologist he meets with comes to be a sort of father to him, and his delight in Antwone, his loving concern, his counsel, and simply his kind presence become major sources of healing and pronouncement. *You are the Beloved Son.* Antwone eventually goes to find his lost family, and through his aunts and uncles, cousins and grandmother, he experiences a kind of homecoming.

From a Christian perspective, I see all of these things Antwone experienced—the loving presence of another man, a recurring dream, an experience of homecoming—as illustrations of the many means God uses to reach our hearts with the healing message.

CPSIA information can be obtained
at www.ICGtesting.com
Printed in the USA
LVHW061505250922
729170LV00004B/8